WINTON LIBRARY

2/6

BOURNEMOUTH LIBRARIES

300021607

Peter Purves

Peter Purves

THE AUTOBIOGRAPHY

Here's one I wrote earlier...

Bournemouth Libraries	
WI	
300021607	
Askews	2009
B PUR	£18.99

This edition first published in the UK in 2009
By Green Umbrella Publishing

© Green Umbrella Publishing 2009

www.gupublishing.co.uk

Publishers Jules Gammond and Vanessa Gardner

Creative Director: Kevin Gardner

Picture Credits: Getty Images, Mirrorpix, PA Photos, Ferris Photographics and Peter Purves

The right of Peter Purves to be identified as Author of this book has been asserted by him in accordance with the Copyright, Designs and Patents Act 1988.

All rights reserved. No part of this work may be reproduced or utilised in any form or by any means, electronic or mechanical, including photocopying, recording or by any information storage and retrieval system, without prior written permission of the publisher.

Printed and bound by J. H. Haynes & Co. Ltd., Sparkford

ISBN: 978-1-906635-34-3

The views in this book are those of the author but they are general views only and readers are urged to consult the relevant and qualified specialist for individual advice in particular situations.

Green Umbrella Publishing hereby exclude all liability to the extent permitted by law of any errors or omissions in this book and for any loss, damage or expense (whether direct or indirect) suffered by a third party relying on any information contained in this book.

All our best endeavours have been made to secure copyright clearance for every photograph used but in the event of any copyright owner being overlooked please address correspondence to Green Umbrella Publishing, The Old Bakehouse, 21 The Street, Lydiard Millicent, Swindon, Wiltshire SN5 3LU

Although this book is totally from my memory, I am not really a nostalgic man. Tomorrow has always seemed so much more important to me than yesterday and consequently I have kept very little that reflects my life and work. Hunting for photographs has been very difficult, I realise that I have nothing at all from the days of shows like *Stopwatch*, or *Kickstart*, and the BBC who have hundreds of pictures of me are not very generous in coming forward with pictures on request. My son Matthew, and my wife Kathryn have been very supportive in reading the copy and I appreciate their feedback. There will be omissions naturally as I followed my memory wherever it took me, and I hope that you get as much pleasure reading the book, as I have had writing it.

Peter Purves December 2008

Peter Purves

Contents

Here's one I wrote earlier...

Peter Purves

Prologue

"Which way?" I asked John.

"I don't know", he replied, panic rising in his voice.

"That way!!"

The stentorian tones of Sergeant Major Tom Hutton boomed out as if from nowhere. We turned to see him sitting astride a camel, aggressively pointing along the path, the veins in his forehead standing out with the intensity of his shout. The signpost behind him indicated the direction of Egypt. We were at Burnham Beeches near Windsor!

This surreal scene came from an extraordinary film we made for *Blue Peter* in 1969, and it remains in my mind as one of the high spots of my career, certainly one of the high spots of my time in the most successful children's TV programme in the world.

The film was called *The Waiters' Orienteering Race* and the concept came from one of our assistant producers on the programme, Tim Byford. Earlier we had made an orienteering film with the aforementioned Tom Hutton and the members of the junior parachute regiment, and had also made films with John waiting at table to me and Valerie Singleton, both at the London Hilton and on a British Rail Express bound north out of King's Cross station in London. So, quite naturally, *The Waiters' Orienteering Race* was born.

It involved five teams of two waiters – one pair from an Italian restaurant, one pair from the London Hilton, a pair of Bunny Girls from the Playboy Club, a pair from the Army catering corps, and, of course, John Noakes and I making up the numbers. Sergeant Major Hutton was in charge, and the race involved us navigating round various locations and at each checkpoint performing some odd catering task. To be honest it was quite insane – we had to serve a fillet steak at a table in a clearing, and soup to an eccentric couple (one knitting her spaghetti, whilst her companion played the flute) at a table sited on the edge of the lake at Virginia Water. We got lost a number of times, but Tom was always on hand to both terrify and chivvy us along. On one occasion he appeared out of an old hollow tree, and another time hurtled through the woods on a bicycle, like the wicked witch on her broomstick, before crashing headlong into the lake itself.

Don't ask me what the point was, or who won. All I can say is that it was hilarious to make, and when it was transmitted, I got home that evening to find a household in hysterics. My children and some friends had been watching with my wife, and they all thought it was wonderful. The best reaction I ever received from friends and family for a film made on the programme.

It was also an absolute watershed, because it was when John and I seriously fell out.

But a lot of water had flown under the bridge before that sad moment was reached, and a lot had still to flow after it, so I'd better begin at the beginning.

Here's one I wrote earlier…

Chapter One

Earliest memories; The move to Blackpool;

First school days; First acting attempts;

Holiday in London

I was fortunate enough to have had an unfashionably happy childhood – no tales of abuse and drunkenness, no beatings and fears. Both my mother and father were what I would call the world's nicest people. My father's family came from Preston, and my mother's from Newcastle-upon-Tyne. I have some early memories that have stayed with me of my very young life. I can remember the kitchen of my grandparents' house in New Longton, near Preston, and sitting on my grandfather's lap in a rocking chair in front of the old kitchen range, and listening to the ticking of his fob watch that he kept in the pocket of his waistcoat. It is my earliest memory, and must predate my first birthday, since my grandfather, John Purves, died when I was 11 months old. I have a number of other memories of that house, The Shieling, playing in the garden on several occasions, and some wartime memories of bombing raids on both Preston and Liverpool. Actually my clearest memory of that time was when staying at my Uncle Alan's house in Houghton, where Alan was the police sergeant, watching the fires over Preston when the docks were bombed, before being bundled under the stairs for safety.

I can remember the trains at the crossing in the village, and the Monkey Puzzle tree outside the small parade of shops near the station. I also remember happy playtimes with two or three of the village children – my dad had created a good size sand-pit to the side of the house, bordering the field that I also recall being reaped by a big red tractor in what seems to me now like an ever sunny summer. This would have been 1941 or 1942, and I had been born in the February of 1939.

I know that my mother struggled during the first three years of the war. My father, Kenneth, was a military tailor, working in Preston. As a diabetic since the age of 11, and one of the first to survive any length of time following the introduction of insulin, he had not gone to fight in the 1939-45 war, but was a member of Dad's Army, the Home Guard. Florence, my mother made do on his none too great income, but she managed well enough. She also took in some refugee children from London, but they didn't stay long, and I gathered later in life, that it had not been a happy experience, and mum was most relieved at their departure.

Things changed for all of us in 1942, when my dad went into a partnership with a musician friend of his called Arthur Sharples, and between them they bought a hotel in Blackpool. Dad's mother, my grandmother Elizabeth, now a widow, came to stay – permanently it transpired. Again I remember clearly my first sight of that wonderful seaside town. We drove over the railway bridge at Squires Gate, and there was not only the sea, but also the trams, the fabulous Blackpool trams in their cream and green paint. I was three and a half. The image is as clear today as it was when I first saw them.

I have to say that I have a real soft spot for Blackpool. I know that in many ways it is a catchpenny town, but it has an honesty about it, that says, "If you come here and pay your money you'll have a really good time." But that sort of good time was a long way off in those austere days of the war.

In 1942, The New Mayfair Hotel was the next to last hotel on the South Shore. After that there was some open land, and then you were at Squires Gate, and the RAF base that became Pontin's Holiday Camp after the war. All of South Shore has been built up now, but then there was a lot of open space. In front of the hotel was a crescent shaped road, there were ornamental gardens laid to grass, then the main road, the tram tracks, and the south promenade itself, before the concrete sea wall with its steps down to the golden sands. I loved the sea at Blackpool, even though I now know it was absolutely filthy. But somehow that didn't matter. The tide came in twice a day, just like magic and then went out again leaving the great expanse of beaches that extend for miles to both Fleetwood in the north and to the mouth of the Ribble Estuary in the south. The best playground in the world.

But it was wartime. We all rushed out one day to the sea wall to watch as a German bomber ditched in the sea, and the Lifeboat, launched from its station by Central Pier, went out to rescue the crew, who could be seen clambering out of the cockpit onto the fuselage to await their fate. Our hotel was commandeered as a convalescent home for Polish airmen who had been injured during the fighting. I remember one chap in particular, whose upper body was almost totally encased in plaster. He was known as tin ribs, and he was quite happy to have me play wooden spoons on his chest, like a xylophone. I don't think he spoke a word of English, and we spoke no Polish.

The Black Market in food and provisions flourished in the town, and there was one memorable occasion when the revenue officers came round to check up on the hotels. Word got out in advance, and hoteliers all along the south shore could be seen carrying black market purchases across the promenade and dumping them over the wall into the sea. Apparently it wouldn't have done for anyone to be caught with an illicit side of pork in the fridge. Sacrilege though.

I started junior school just before the end of the war. Arnold School was reputedly the best school in the area, and it had both a junior and a senior school. So I began in the preparatory class at the age of five and a half. My first teacher was Miss Lamb – funnily enough I had a letter from her in 2006, the first contact since I left school. Miss Lamb was very important in my early school life, in fact right the way through junior school, because she was also the Cub mistress, Akela. Junior school was a real pleasure, the headmaster, Mr Beech, was a delightful man, and I remember him very well. Certainly as I got older, he was instrumental in my liking to read. He would read stories to us in the English class, Joseph Conrad, and Robert Louis Stevenson. He always made the stories exciting – choosing different voices and accents for the various characters and situations. Consequently I wanted to read the books for myself. I must say that I found Joseph Conrad pretty hard going by myself but in Mr Beech's rendering he was the most exciting writer of all.

As the war finished and things started to get back to a semblance of normality we were able to travel a bit more. My dad was still running his tailoring business in Preston and would leave early for work and get home late, so I saw little of him. The partnership in the hotel was not going too well and I gather there were some fairly acrimonious arguments, although I wasn't involved and didn't suffer from them. But mostly life was fun and there was always music. Arthur played the piano very well. In fact I believe he was a composer of some note at the time. My dad sang well, as did my grandmother, he a bass, she a contralto, and on occasion my Uncle Doug, on leave from the Army where he was a captain, was a fine tenor. Together they made wonderful live music and excellent impromptu concerts were given for the hotel guests and for the Polish airmen.

My mother's family was a large one. She had been the daughter of a former miner in the North East, who gave up going down the pit to become an insurance salesman, and moved to a nice part of Newcastle, Jesmond. Floss, as she was known to one and all, was the fifth child of the family that ultimately was eight strong. My Uncle Will was her eldest brother, and lived near Tewkesbury in Gloucestershire. I only ever met him once. Jenny was next eldest and she became a teacher in Whitley Bay. Then came Belle who married the headteacher of a primary school in Pegswood. Her next brother

Lionel died of cancer aged only 21. Floss was next, and then came the three boys, Charlie, Les and Don.

When Floss was 16, both her parents died, and she left school to look after the rest of the family. Will had moved away, so Jenny and Belle went out to earn the money, and the three boys had yet to grow up and get through school. So my mum became pretty good at looking after the others. Eventually, when the boys had grown up, she married a much older and very successful bookmaker, Will Gilhespie, who sadly died after only a short marriage in 1936. Will Gilhespie's sister, Elizabeth, was married to my grandfather John Purves, and so Floss, through marriage, was my dad's aunt. After a happy courtship Ken and Floss were married in 1938.

My mum loved the cinema, my dad liked music and they both liked theatre. Actually, my dad had been a wonderful boy soprano. Three times he won best boy soloist at the Blackpool Music Festival, one of the prime singing competitions in the country in the 1920's. He would also have won it a fourth time, but was convinced that his voice would have broken and he declined to enter. But his voice didn't break, and he was singing even better than ever. The previous year he had been snapped up by a record label, not EMI because they had already signed a boy soprano called Ernest Lough, whose recording of *Oh for the Wings of a Dove* is still reckoned by many to be the yardstick by which other boy sopranos are measured. My family were convinced that the oft-played recording was by my dad. They were wrong, but his voice was exceptionally good. Woolworths owned dad's record label, and his recording of *Oh for the Wings of a Dove* sold 350,000 copies. He was given a gramophone, no money!!! He regularly broadcast on the BBC during 1927-28 on a teatime show. Sadly his diabetes prevented him from taking to the stage as a full-time career after his voice did break to a fine bass. A musicologist Stephen Beet has recently compiled a book and remastered recordings onto CDs called *The Better Land – a search for the Lost Boy Sopranos* for which I wrote the foreword and in which my dad is featured.

Blackpool in the summer was the Mecca for all variety of shows, second only to London in the number of shows and talented performers working there. There were theatres everywhere; two on the South Pier and one on both the Central and North Piers. The Opera House, the Winter Gardens, the Hippodrome, the Palace, the Grand, Redmans, numerous others and lots of movie houses. Not forgetting what was reckoned to be the best circus in Europe at the Tower. With all these outlets, it wasn't surprising that I would want to explore as much as I could. I saw all the variety acts of the time, the circus every season, several plays, ice shows and children's spectaculars. Life was such fun. And so far as I could remember, it never rained.

We had a sort of handyman who worked for us at the hotel, called Bill Plant. He also worked for The Tower Company where he had a job putting up posters around the town for lots of the movie houses and theatres. That meant that he had a smelly old van – it was smelly because of the glue or whatever the paste was that was used for putting up the posters. And he always had lots of them around. He also changed the publicity pictures in the foyers of some of the cinemas. He gave me many sets of these pictures, but sadly I never kept any of them. I didn't collect anything as a child, but I really wish I'd kept a collection of old publicity stills and movie posters from the 40's. They would have been worth a fortune today. I remember Bill very fondly – he would drive me to school a couple of days a week and I always liked that – no one else turned up at school in such a high profile vehicle. It had three frames on each side with posters in them and one big frame that had the poster for the show that week at the Grand Theatre. He also cooked a mean breakfast.

I mustn't forget the happy times I had away from Blackpool in those summers of the 1940's. I would regularly travel by train up to Northumberland to stay with one or other of my aunts and uncles. There were three places I stayed most. One was Pegswood, near Morpeth where I stayed with my

Auntie Belle and Uncle Dodds in the School House. My cousin Angela was less than a year older than I so we had good times together, walking in Bothel Woods, and wondering if we would meet the hermit who reputedly lived there. Dodds was a fabulous gardener, and looked after the school garden, so there was always good fresh food and fruit that I would pick with him. We would take lovely picnics to the beaches at Whitley Bay, or Cullercoats, or up the coast towards Blyth and Seaton Sluice. After the war, these weren't just ordinary picnics, but feasts in wicker baskets – homemade pies, boiled eggs, tomatoes, fruit, jellies and blancmanges, and proper china plates and cutlery. Then I would stay with lovely Auntie Jenny in Shiremoor, a stone's throw from Whitley Bay. The Spanish City at Whitley Bay was a great amusement park, mind you after the Pleasure Beach at Blackpool everything is second rate, but Jenny would take me there and indulge me with multiple rides on the Helter Skelter and the Dodgems. Jenny, who never married, became the family traveller, going abroad every year at a time when not many people did that. And occasionally I would go north to Scremerston, just south of Berwick upon Tweed, where my Uncle Les and Auntie Sadie lived. There were three cousins there, Fraser, who is my age, Dorothy a couple of years younger, and the baby, Donald. Naturally I spent most of my time with Fraser, whom I considered very sophisticated – he could change an electric plug! We would cycle down to the coast where there were great rock pools, and we'd swim, but the water was absolutely freezing, even on the hottest day. We would get back to the house almost blue from the cold on some occasions, to be warmed up by one of my Auntie Sadie's super meals. It was great fun and I guess I took after my mum a little, in that she had always swum in the sea, on that northeast coast every day of the year, at places like Seaton Sluice, even having to break the ice on the shoreline. And when seawater freezes, you know it is cold.

They were lovely years. Trips to the open air baths in St Annes, journeys on the trams up to Fleetwood and across the little ferry to Knot End and back.

Peter Purves

Again, I can't remember the rain, only glorious sunshine day after day. Once, when Jenny came to stay she took me over to the Isle of Man on the *Tynwald* out of Fleetwood. That was the first time I had seen seawater that wasn't full of muddy silt – you could actually see to the bottom, even in Douglas Harbour. The delightful little horse-drawn trams plied up and down the promenade, and I gather still do today. I was eight.

Sometimes my mum and dad would take me up to the Lake District from Blackpool, where we would meet up with Dodds, Belle and Angela at places like Tarn Hows and Grasmere for another stupendous picnic. And on one fabulous summer's day we met up with them at Ulpha Bridge on the Duddon Valley, where there is a deep pool and lots of stepping-stones. After swimming in the icy waters of the river, nothing tasted quite so good as my mother's picnic of bacon and egg pie, washed down with lemonade. I truly loved all of those aunts and uncles and cousins who made my childhood so completely happy and it is sad that, apart from the cousins, none remain.

There was one presence unforgettable throughout all of these early years – my grandmother. I can't recall times when my mum and dad were able to be alone; in fact many years later when she was dying, my mother said it was the biggest regret of her life that Elizabeth had come to stay. My dad, the youngest of the Purves family took her on board and clothed and fed her for the rest of her life, with no support from his two brothers and one sister. They just let him get on with it, and so my poor mother shared her life with her mother-in-law. I understand that she lent my dad £1000 to buy the Blackpool hotel, and I guess he felt obliged to her. I can't remember a complaint, but there must have been some. But as good, caring parents, they shielded me from it and I must admit that my grandmother was always very kind and loving towards me. As I grew up, she would take an interest in my singing and helped me to develop what became a good soprano voice, though not, I hasten to add, in the same class as my dad's voice. She played the piano well and tutored me in that too.

But, she was always there, until long after I had left home and I know she made my mother very unhappy.

I suspect that my mother always wanted a girl. At Christmas in the hotel in the first two years after the war, when I was seven and eight, my mum and my dad would organise a dinner dance and I was to wait at the tables – as a waitress! My mum dressed me up in a black satin frock, make-up was applied, a white apron and hat added, and I was unveiled as the star attraction. God knows what the guests thought, but my mum was very proud of me and I was very happy as the new waitress. There were two other girls who worked at the hotel as waitresses and chambermaids, Joyce Maughan and her friend, Jean, who both came from Spennymoor in County Durham. They were always kind to me, and at the time can only have been teenagers themselves. Joyce still keeps in touch to this day – she lives near Colchester and visits me once a year. Until my mum and dad died, she was always keen to have whatever news of them I could give. Now it is all about reminiscence, and I have never been a great one for nostalgia. Writing this book is the first time I have really addressed my past, and it is extraordinary how memories and events and people come crowding back from whichever corners of the mind they have been resting.

Although I saw little of my dad, I remember him always at Christmas times. When he couldn't buy toys, he would make them, rather well. When I was four he had made me a big engine on wheels in which I could sit. It was the envy of the two or three local children with whom I played. Goodness knows how he found the time to make it. On occasion I would go to Preston with him to his shop. It was on the first floor of a building in Guildhall Street, and I found plenty with which to amuse myself. When I was very small I would get great pleasure from playing with the boxes of buttons, and watching the comings and goings of the green delivery vans to the DCL depot across the street. Funnily enough the Distiller's Company Limited was where my cousin

David, Uncle Alan's son, was to become the head of the legal department in later years, defending the indefensible, Thalidomide!

By 1948, the hotel partnership was falling apart, and I never discovered quite why. At the same time, the first of the multiple chain bespoke tailors, The 50 Shilling Tailors (later to become Burtons) was appearing on the northern high streets. My dad realised that he was not going to be able to compete. I think this was when he made his first major mistake. I think he ought to have gone to that chain of shops and offered himself in a managerial capacity. He was an excellent tailor, and my clothes, and my mother's, were always beautifully made. His cutters and finishers were amongst the best, and I believe he would have risen fast in a big organisation. But dad was always his own boss and wasn't prepared to become an employee.

Dad sold the hotel in 1948 and we moved into a dark rented flat not far from Squires Gate. He was still commuting to Preston, but he had correctly seen that the writing was on the wall for the small, bespoke tailor and he began to look for some other work. It took him some time to find the right place and in the meantime we moved to an airy flat on the first floor of a large house on Lytham Road, within walking distance of Arnold Junior School.

That autumn term was when I discovered acting. When I was nine and a half Mr Beech and Miss Lamb organised the junior school play. It was *The Pied Piper of Hamelin* and I was cast as the Pied Piper. Let's face it, the title role can't be bad. I took to it like a duck to water. In fact I had always had a bent for performing – since I was five I had done radio plays for my granny from behind the sofa and had made up plays that I performed on an old toy theatre that had been my dad's. It had always been fascinating to me, so doing the school play was the natural progression. It was a great success. I loved it. Whilst still at the junior school I had two more leading roles to play, *Robin Hood* the following year, and in my last year, Alan Breck in *Kidnapped*. I'd got the bug.

Here's one I wrote earlier...

I was coming up to 10 years old when we had a wonderful Christmas to remember. We went to the Windermere Hydro Hotel. It was four days of absolute joy. There were lots of families staying there, and that meant lots of children. The hotel organised wonderful parties every day; there were treasure hunts and brilliant games of hide and seek. I think I appreciated good food and good living from that one short holiday. There were dinner dances for the adults and fancy dress competitions for everyone. I won the major competition as Bonnie Prince Charlie – we had gone to a theatrical costumier in Cleveleys before leaving home, and I can remember posturing around the place in a fabulous Stuart dress tartan, complete with an ornamental dirk in my sock. Mum and dad had gone to the party as Gypsies, and they won as well – a triumph for the Purves clan.

It is amazing what one forgets. I had a friend at junior school called Alec Monroe. His dad was a professional footballer – he played full-back for Blackpool in the Cup final they lost to Manchester United in 1948. I remember listening to the match with Joyce in the hotel kitchen and her weeping when the final whistle went and we had lost. I liked football and would play sometimes in the ornamental gardens with some friends and a lovely man who owned a hotel about seven along from ours. His hotel was The Romford, and he was quite a good player I believe – Stanley Matthews was his name! Unfortunately none of his magic rubbed off on me. One more footballer I must mention is George Eastham – he was two years older than me but we played occasionally, we'd walk to school together and often listen to *Dick Barton* on the radio. Like *Blue Peter* for later generations, that was a show not to be missed. A few years later George made history by driving a coach and horses through the FA's retain and transfer system that was blocking him from moving from Newcastle United to Arsenal.

Also when I was nine, mum, dad and I (and grandmother too) went to London. Amongst other things I was taken to see *Oklahoma* on stage, and *The*

Crazy Gang at the Victoria Palace. These shows just reinforced my love of the theatre, but even more spectacular was the fact that my Uncle Douglas, whom we visited in Croydon, had a producer friend at the BBC who had been the producer of the now defunct *Dick Barton* but was now producing its replacement show, *Adventure Unlimited*. Actually the show wasn't as good as its predecessor, but I was taken to the BBC in Portland Place and allowed to watch a recording of an episode. It was magical. Afterwards we all adjourned to The George, then, as now, the favoured watering hole of the BBC. I had to sit in a back room – children weren't allowed in the public rooms, of course, and I was asked what I would like to drink. "Dandelion and Burdock" I said, which produced guffaws from everyone. It wasn't a drink they'd heard of in't south! I can remember my disappointment that mum and dad joined in with the amusement and didn't stick up for me. But the substitute lemonade went down well.

London also had Hamleys toyshop, which at that time had a model railway layout running around a central circular staircase. It was without doubt the best thing I'd ever seen. And that love of model railways has always stayed with me, though I haven't had a model layout for almost 30 years now.

Arnold School gave out fortnightly reports on its pupils, which we had to take home for our parents' signature. The report commented on our prowess in Arithmetic, English, French, Geography, History, Reading and Spelling. We were given marks and a position in the form. My reports always said I could do much better, and invariably I was bottom of the class. I can remember my dad saying to me that the report was terrible and that if I became top of the class he would buy me an electric train set. He must have thought he was onto a pretty safe bet. But, the following fortnight I was top of the class, a position I continued to hold until I moved up into the senior school. The train set was a Trix Twin Railway, which was the first electric train set that allowed you to run two trains independently on the same track. It was the envy of all my friends. Now, I hear you ask, how did it happen that one fortnight I could be a duffer and the next a genius? Easy. Until then I couldn't see the point in schoolwork. But the incentive of the train set, bribery if you like, was enough to start me working.

But all good things come to an end, though I didn't realise it at the time. Dad had found his next project. He decided to buy a country pub in Derbyshire, and I went to boarding school.

Chapter Two

Boarding school and disillusion;

Holidays in the Peak District and North Wales;

Blackpool Illuminations restored;

I start to get cynical

I had always wanted to be a boarder. The boys in my year who boarded were the most interesting and I wanted to join them. So when it was decided that mum and dad were to move, I was delighted. What fun. Away at school. How good is that? Well it was a damn sight better in prospect than in execution, but at first there was a honeymoon period, and I was excited by it.

"Westover" was the senior school headmaster's house, and there were 12 junior boarders living there. It was spartan compared with home, linoleum floors and threadbare bedside rugs. I shared a small dormitory with two other boys my age, Michael Andrew and David Harbottle. They had been friends since they first came to the school two years earlier and I found it difficult to be friends with them. They had an air of independence about them that I was going to have to learn to absorb myself – at nine I was probably a bit of a mummy's boy, and to be accepted by them meant I had to toughen up quite a lot. I don't know how tough I was, but I certainly soon learned to keep my emotions to myself and to try not to show any weakness and a sort of friendship blossomed between the three of us. Michael was the son of a Bury mill owner, and his brother was in the senior school. David's family came from Poulton-le-Fylde, then a small village just to the northeast of Blackpool. I could never work out why he boarded, as it would have been comparatively easy for him to travel to and from school as a dayboy. I also made friends with a lad called Michael Outhwaite, who was eight months or so younger than I, and a year behind in school. He became a good friend for the next five or six years. His parents were abroad in Bahrain and he saw them very rarely. His contact with the outside world was with two aunts who lived in Anglesey. To me, Bahrain was no further away than Derbyshire!

The hardest thing about boarding school is that there is no escape. You live with the people who either rewarded or spoilt your days. By that I mean both staff and pupils. In those days school was strictly regimented – the boarders had to walk in crocodile back from school to Westover under the supervision of a teacher. Once back there was a large room in which we could play until teatime. As at all mealtimes we were reprimanded for not sitting up straight, for putting our elbows on the table, for not holding our knives and forks properly, for chewing with our mouths open and so on. Not that I was reprimanded too often as my parents had already instilled my table manners from a young age. But the threat of disciplinary action was always there. Oh yes, and we weren't allowed to talk until permission was given, usually after the grace had been said. If we got too noisy, then we were "put on silence" and we soon learned to chat moderately at mealtimes.

Arnold School had wonderful playing fields, and after tea, if it was dry, we were allowed to go to the nearest field and play football or cricket. Again a teacher would always be present, Miss Lamb or Miss Butterworth, and they were as kind to us all as they could be, bearing in mind their responsibility for our safety. They were now our substitute parents for two thirds of the year.

By the time we were 10, we had to do homework (prep it was called), and so after half an hour or so on the playing fields we would troop back to the house, and sit at the dining room tables and do our work – supervised again by the same teachers. Once a week we had to write a letter home and that was done after the homework session. There was no opportunity to say what one really felt, because the letters had to be taken up to the teacher to read and pass before it could be sent. A minimum of four sides of the school notepaper had to be completed, and anything controversial would have to be rewritten. Hiding your emotions was the only way you could survive boarding school. I kept things to myself, and later, whilst still in the junior school, all I would want to write was "Please can I come home". But that never got written, we each, in our own way made the best of it and mostly it wasn't too bad. Normally we would sleep well, but after lights-out we weren't allowed to speak. There was lots of whispering, but if the duty teacher heard you then you got "the slipper". At least it wasn't the cane, but it still hurt through your pyjamas. Actually it depended on who was in charge – we were all terrified of the headmaster, Mr Holgate, and once a week he would do the rounds. The one person you did not want to get caught talking by was the boss. He beat me once when I was 10. I failed to see the point of it all then, and today it would just be considered child abuse. It wasn't the last beating I had at school. But we now live in a different age.

Food was another thing. I guess we had adequate rations, but I can remember almost always feeling hungry and there was rarely any of what I would have called "nice" food. Lumpy porridge at breakfast, horrible school dinners that were brought in from outside and tea was bread, margarine, and a not very sweet jam. Sugar, of course, was still rationed in the years immediately after the war. Even at weekends there was no escape. We were allowed to go out for the weekend with parents, and many of the children did, but Derbyshire was a long way away, and my parents only saw me at half-term and during the holidays. Often there would only be me and Michael in school for the weekend. At least in the summer we could play cricket together. He was better than I, even though he was younger. Later, in senior school he developed a good talent as a batsman, and even had a trial after he left school for Lancashire but he didn't like it. Actually I'd lost touch with him by then, but years later in the 80's I met him again in Rugby, where he was secretary of the rugby club. I played golf a few times with him, and he was still better than I. He was unchanged from the boy I'd known, and I was sad to hear of his death, at a youngish age, from cancer in the 90's.

As boarders we did have the advantage of having lots of playmates so we played lots of games and I was quite good at most of them. We would play British Bulldog in the school playground, where the aim is for one person to stop another in the mob from crossing from one side to the other. Having caught one, the two would then try to stop another one or more. Gradually the group in the middle gets bigger, until the entire class is trying to stop the one remaining boy from crossing. I was horrified recently to hear that games like that are now banned in schools. For goodness sake what a lot of cissies we are breeding. I liked the idea of football, but my execution was hopeless. I didn't kick a ball all that well, but I was quite brave as a goalkeeper. As I was tall for my age it was the ideal position for me, and eventually I was selected for the junior school team. I certainly wasn't the best! My mother told me years later that she came to watch a soccer match we were playing, and I was the team captain. The headmaster's wife, Mrs Holgate, was watching also. "There he is, your boy," she said. "The bossy one." And I probably was!

The first summer holiday after I started boarding I went home for the first time, and found that I had a dog. Rusty was an all black Cocker Spaniel, with a rust coloured muzzle. I absolutely loved him and we spent hours together in the hills and woods. I had no idea at the time that dogs would play such a big part in my life in later years. The Yorkshire Bridge Inn was in one of the most beautiful parts of the country, in the north of the Peak District and close to the trio of enormous reservoirs in the Derwent Valley. Two of the reservoirs, Derwent and Howden had been used for the Dam Busters' training during the war just ended, and the third and largest, Ladybower had only recently been finished. The pub stood half a mile from the dam wall, and on the hillside below were four terraces of houses built for the workers who had built this most spectacular feat of engineering. It was a famous place also because for the valley to be flooded it had meant the sacrifice of two villages, Derwent and Ladybower. In the height of summer, when near drought conditions occurred, it was possible to see the ruins of the villages, and if the mud baked hard, you could walk out to them, which on a couple of occasions out with Rusty I did. Earlier the Derwent village church spire had to be demolished because people tried to get out to it, and it was considered dangerous. It was a great place to grow up. There were lots of children my age in the workers' houses, and I soon made friends with them and we would play great games on the near hillsides, which had super woodland and a small waterfall. But the most exciting place was the river, which carried the overflow and controlled discharge from the reservoir. About a quarter of a mile from the huge banked wall there was a weigh point. This consisted of a small concrete island in the middle of the river, with stainless steel plates fitted between there and the banks, which also had precise concrete sections. The water was channelled over these two plates and its rate of flow was measured by the plates and recorded somewhere or other. Naturally the water flow was quite fast, and our favourite game in the summer was to jump the stream across to the island. If you didn't make it, you would slip into the fast water and be carried downstream towards the waterfall, but you never reached that because the flow became much less fierce when you were back in the natural river. Mostly we made it, but on a hot day, we just let ourselves splash in the water anyway. That first summer made me realise how much I didn't want to go back to school. There was everything at home, safe bike riding, lots of fun to be had, and occasionally my mum would take me over to Sheffield on the bus that used our pub car park as its Bamford terminus. It was only a 12 mile trip but it was a lovely journey over the hills.

It also meant that I got to go to the News Theatre – these were picture houses that ran an hour-long programme of short films, newsreels, cartoons and an adventure serial. It was there that I first saw *Superman* and *Captain Marvel* – each episode was about 10 minutes long and always ended with a cliffhanger so you had to go the next week to see what happened. Brilliant stuff in an age when TV had only just started and hardly anyone had a set. Actually my Uncle Douglas had the first I ever saw – it was a 12 inch screen that had a large magnifying glass in front of it. The picture was terrible but it was new technology, and I was reliably informed that it was the way things were going! That was 1949, and I was 10.

That same summer holiday, we went on holiday as a family, and I was asked if I'd like to take a friend with us. My granny had gone to stay for two weeks with her daughter, my Auntie Doff, in London, so I think my mum and dad wanted to take advantage of that freedom. The pub was left in the hands of our barman, Bob Gracy and his wife, and off we went in dad's latest car, a 1938 Morris 10. I took Michael Outhwaite with us – his parents weren't back in the country – and we went to North Wales, first stop Rhyl, where we stayed at the, supposedly, best hotel in town. Now I can remember that it poured down, and Rhyl on a stormy wet day is not Blackpool. There seemed to be very little to do, and the first two days were rotten. The only highlight was on the second morning at breakfast. My mum had ordered bacon and eggs (still a luxury after the war) and when it arrived and the waitress took off the cover, she just burst out laughing. The bacon was the smallest, most shrivelled up bit of meat you can imagine. I remember it so well, because the laughter soon turned hysterical, and she just couldn't stop, tears were pouring down her cheeks. I was initially embarrassed because people were taking notice, but in the end all of us were laughing fit to burst. The headwaiter sheepishly approached and asked if he could help, then saw the plate of food and quickly picked it up and raced off to the kitchen. Mum had only just stopped laughing when a fresh plate, this time with a nice neat portion of bacon and eggs on it, was brought back to her with quietly whispered apologies.

Dad decided we should check out and find somewhere else. As we left Rhyl the clouds lifted, and we found a small hostelry in a village called Tal-y-Cafn, where we stayed for the remainder of our holiday and the summer weather was glorious. There was a railway station near the hotel, and I found that fascinating because it was a single track railway. The drivers had to collect a baton, signifying there was no other train on the track before they could proceed. We also went over to Anglesey, and stopped at a small bay with golden sands. Michael and I waded out more than half a mile in search of deep enough water in which to swim but it stayed shallow and I suspect we could almost have walked to Ireland! We went to Caernarfon Castle, Snowdon, Llandudno, Conway and Colwyn Bay. It was an unforgettable holiday.

Holidays end, terms begin, and I was packed off back to Blackpool. Actually I was driven to Manchester and then put on the train with several other boys who were returning to school, and supervised by a returning teacher. The train journey was always quite fun – I do have quite a passion for trains, which I was able to enjoy to the full during my years with *Blue Peter* in the 60's and 70's. The trains were sometimes pulled by engines in the lovely maroon livery of the LMS; this was just before the nationalisation of the railways when everything turned to an uninteresting black. The carriages were maroon as well, and I always thought they looked so smart. The interiors were less than luxurious, however, and if my memory serves me right, there was no corridor. The more senior boys had a separate compartment, and no teacher, and where, I later discovered, they would smoke!! Blackpool South station was only about four tram stops along Lytham Road from school, and all too soon we were back in our prison – a reasonably liberal one, but a prison nonetheless.

One thing I really enjoyed at that time was being in the cubs. I had joined when I was nine; before I first became a boarder and by the time I got to 11 one of the arms of my cub jersey was full of badges with a couple on the other. They meant I could lay a fire, tidy a room, tie knots, do some gym, play games and so on. There was great rivalry between Michael Andrew, whose badges annoyingly covered both arms, David Harbottle and I. We were all sixers, which meant that we were the leaders of six other younger cubs, and we took great pride in winning various games and competitions. School was competitive and boarding school more so. The school had a house system – Romans, Greeks, Celts etc., and a few years later when we were getting on in senior school, the house system changed so that one house was for boarders only – School House. The other houses were based on where one lived in the wards of Blackpool. Needless to say, School House rapidly developed a passion all its own, the boarders bonded, and won almost every inter-house competition. But that was some years away.

One of the most interesting things I remember whilst still at junior school was the first time that the Blackpool Illuminations were re-instated. They had obviously been suspended during the war and it was only in 1950 that they started again. The school arranged for three charabancs to take the entire boarding school round the exhibits. Blackpool became a one-way street for the length of the promenade from Squires Gate to Cleveleys and we all marvelled at the display as we travelled along at a sedate 10mph. The Big Dipper at the Pleasure Beach had lights all over it, (though I must admit it looked even more impressive from our dormitory window as it burned down a couple of years later) and the tower was lit from the flagpole at its tip all the way to the ground. The piers looked wonderful and, as no doubt the council hoped, the crowds came in their thousands. We had never seen such lights before – on reflection they were dreadfully gaudy, and had little artistic merit, but we were enthralled. In fact the illuminations meant that the holiday season in Blackpool was extended by several weeks, giving the town the edge over its rivals. At this time the mill towns of Lancashire were still flourishing and the Wakes Weeks, as their annual holidays were called, made Blackpool the biggest and best resort in the country. Not only the Mill towns, but Glasgow and Liverpool also had their Wakes, when thousands from those cities would flock to the seaside. This was long before people could holiday abroad on package deals, and Blackpool was to remain at the forefront of the holiday industry for another 15 years or so.

The school had few facilities other than its extensive playing fields, but it arranged for weekly swimming lessons. We'd board a coach outside the gates and be driven to the great Derby Baths, sadly only a memory these days. This was an Olympic size indoor pool, with additional learning pools under the same roof. Being able to swim was one of the few treats we had, even though the visits were short. The main pool was flanked with theatre-style seating, and must have accommodated several thousand spectators. Naturally enough they occasionally held "water shows" and I was lucky enough to see the great Johnny Weissmuller perform there. He, of course, was the original Tarzan in the movies, and had been an Olympian for the USA. If anything, seeing him was my inspiration to be a better swimmer.

Although, as juniors, we had little to do with him, except acknowledging that he was "the boss", Mr Holgate was always a looming presence. The ultimate disciplinarian from the old school he was quite an awesome figure. Tall, with a military style moustache and thinning hair, he would sweep around the place during the day with his black gown flying bat like behind him, and often, when not teaching, with his black Labrador dog, Nigger (how times change), at heel beside him. We all made ourselves as insignificant as possible when he was near.

Arnold School had an excellent Cadet Corps. It was called a Combined Cadet Force, though in fact it was solely for Army Cadets, affiliated to The Loyal Regiment. In the senior school from the age of 13 it was compulsory to be a member, but as juniors, the cubs took part in the Corps' annual parade to the cenotaph on the nearest Sunday to November 11th. A baton twirling drum major and the cadet bugle band led the parade. The Corps followed in several platoons, all drilled to near perfection, and I can remember proudly leading my six in the long march up to the cenotaph, three or four miles away beside the North Pier. We were a very smart group indeed. I like to think we marched with precision, but I suspect the truth was that we were just a cute shambling addition bringing up the rear.

It was around this time that I began to realise that one's destiny is in one's own hands and that you shouldn't simply trust what people say to you. I rarely got out of school during term, mum and dad lived too far away to come over and take me out at weekends. One week Michael Andrew asked if I'd like to go out with his parents one weekend. Of course I said yes I'd love to. But in the ensuing couple of weeks, I could feel that something was being engineered, and it ended with us falling out on the Friday afternoon, and the offer of the weekend out was withdrawn. I have no recollection of what went wrong, but I've always felt it was a deliberate act on Michael's part. It may be the reason why I have always found it difficult to make friends – trust has to be earned over a long period of time. Having said that, I do take a lot of what is said to me at face value, and consequently am often disillusioned. But I would, even then, describe myself as a cup-half-full sort of person and the close friends I have kept to this day I would trust with my life. I was growing up.

Peter Purves

Chapter Three

Senior school; A bleak existence;

Sexual awakenings;

Some sporting prowess and success;

The Cadet Corps; Summer camps

At the age of 11 I won a scholarship to the senior school, and phase three of my life had begun. Suddenly we weren't the little kids any more, but we were the little ones in the new big pond. There were some 65 boarders at that time, and for the first time most of the disciplinary roles were taken by prefects and monitors. These were made up from the most senior boys, and there was a head boarder, who may even have been the school head boy. We youngsters were in awe of these seniors who we knew were the school representatives on the various sports teams, and we gave them a lot of respect. Arnold did not operate a "fagging" system that seems to have been the norm in most public schools, and senior prefects had been stopped from administering corporal punishment to juniors (usually in the form of a slippering) the year before I went to the senior establishment.

The school itself was housed in an original Victorian mansion that may or may not have been built as a school, and with numerous extensions that were added from the 1920's onwards. It was a red brick affair with big bay windows at the front, and during my time there, a whole new extension was built to the rear housing new science laboratories and other classrooms. Again, for the boarders, it was spartan. There was a lounge for us to use with an old radiogram (for the uninitiated that was a radio and gramophone combined), a long upholstered (in leatherette) window seat that spanned the huge bay window overlooking the tramway on Lytham Road, and two other lightly and uncomfortably upholstered bench seats. Two long tables could serve as desks and were used primarily by the prefects for doing their prep and other private study work. There was a half-size billiard table, which could be turned over to provide an ordinary table, and, basically, that was it. Every morning we were required to assemble in this room for inspection after breakfast and before going to school. This entailed a teacher examining our hands and nails, and shoes, and our school uniform. This was a green blazer with the school badge on the breast pocket, grey shorts or full-length flannel trousers, black shoes and grey socks, and a grey shirt and school tie. It was all very formal, and punishable with detentions or lines for being under the standard.

In addition, the school uniform included a cap that had to be worn at all times when off the school premises, and even the dayboys had to wear it on the way to and from school. Should a member of staff, or a parent known to you, be seen you had to raise your cap, and you would be reported to the school for failing to do so. Suitable punishments would be applied to those who were caught. The ramifications of this were that the boys were known locally as the Arnold Snobs. No other school in the close vicinity had a uniform and so we always stood out. I think the intention was that Arnold would always be the smartest school in the area, and to a degree, I think it succeeded in that aim. This applied even to the most senior boys; monitors wearing a cap that had a silver ring round it, and the prefects had an even more elaborately designed affair that looked rather like a large Maltese Cross on its top. That was something to aspire to. In fact everything seemed to be designed to make us want to achieve something. For example, much praise would be given at the morning assembly, to boys who excelled in a sporting event – scored 50 for the 1ˢᵗ cricket XI, or scored a hat-trick for the hockey team, or whatever. Competition was what the school had and would thrive at.

The school assembly hall was actually a very large classroom that had a dividing partition with another classroom making it an L-shaped room. This room was where most of us would spend our time. It had old-fashioned desks that sat two and some bench seats along its walls. It also had a raised stage on which was sited an old, foot-pump organ, at one end, and a row of chairs across the back, with a special large chair in the centre, behind a highly polished table. A lectern stood in the corner nearest to the organ, and a small set of steps led up from the body of the hall. I spent half an hour every morning for seven years in that hall as Mr Holgate solemnly led morning assembly. I think I was already at 11 beginning to feel the seeds of atheism creeping into my head. I found the whole process false and unbelievable. Add this to the fact that we went to a compulsory church service at the nearest church every Sunday morning (walking there in a supervised crocodile of course) and you can see that I felt religion was being pushed down my throat. It took years for me to fully understand those feelings, but eventually I became a confirmed atheist. Actually I had been brought up as a Methodist, insofar as my family were all Methodists. In fact only my grandmother actively went to chapel, where surprisingly the Arnold School RE teacher was the minister. Joe Brice was a lovely man, and I enjoyed watching him in church before I became a boarder, when I was really small, and he was a good teacher. He was a freethinker, and he didn't force the issue at all. He read us the bible and we discussed things with him, and many years later when my mother died from stomach cancer, he was a man with whom I had a considerable amount of correspondence. He had retired to Wells-Next-The-Sea in Norfolk, and he understood my rejection of his beliefs. I liked the man immensely, one of only three teachers with whom I had a genuine rapport.

The others were Sidney Law, who taught Chemistry and was the swimming teacher, and Sonny Liston who taught Maths and supervised hockey. Both were really nice men, with whom one could have been friends had they not been, in Sidney's case, at least four generations older. They had no involvement with the boarding side of things, but as a keen swimmer, and a competent hockey player in my later years at the school, I had a great deal of contact with them. More of that later.

The dormitories in the senior school were bleak. The walls were painted brown and cream, and the floor was covered in dull brown linoleum. The beds were the metal kind you might have found, if you were unlucky, in hospital. The mattresses were sparse but at least they stopped you from lying directly on the springs! We had an upright bedside chair, and when we got older a bedside cabinet too. What luxury. Threadbare mats were the only other covering. Yet somehow we didn't seem to mind that much. Nothing could be hung on the walls so there was no personalisation of any part of our home. The bedding was the minimum one would require, and we were encouraged to bring to school with us a travelling rug that could provide a little extra warmth in the winter months. Funnily enough, I don't ever remember the cold, but the bleakness of it all is firmly etched into my head. I had an early portable radio and after lights out we would listen to Radio Luxembourg – ever fearful of being caught. But at least we were able to keep up with the dayboys' knowledge of the hit parade! It usually meant that on a Monday morning we were all pretty bleary-eyed when the reveille bell woke us from our slumbers and the duty prefect would burst into the dorm and count us out of bed – "You've got five to be out of this room, One, Two....!"

The bathrooms, one on each of the two floors, were large affairs with half a dozen sinks at each end of a marble floored room, which also contained six baths. The baths themselves would be highly prized today, cast-iron with Victorian feet, standing in old-fashioned white brick-tiled cubicles. No doors, of course, and two toilets, which did have half doors. I said earlier that the thing about boarding school was that you had no escape. It also meant that you had no privacy at any time. I have to say it makes me laugh to watch people in changing rooms these days being so shy and inhibited about their bodies. You can spot the boarding school people a mile off!

School was school, so what can one say? The days, weeks and years merge into one and somewhere in the midst of it all were some true highlights that I will try to relate. I was 11 when I discovered sex. Well, not really, but the first time I understood about procreation. People of my generation were not given sex education as such; we found it out through our friends relating older siblings' experience and so on, and from books. This was the first time we had studied biology, and we had one lesson a week. The school textbooks were handed out, and mostly they were old and somewhat decrepit. But almost without exception they fell open at page 137 where there was the diagram of male and female productive organs with their proper names (giggle-giggle) and a couple of paragraphs. I'll never forget the one that began "the man places his penis inside the woman's vagina. An understanding wife will guide the penis into position". I can remember thinking at the time, "My God, I hope I get an understanding wife!"

Of course, boarding school is a hotbed of repressed male sexuality. Because the regime was so draconian, you had 60 or so young males with no outlet for the relief of their sexual energy. Your body tells you when it is ready, and so at that time masturbation becomes the principal occupation of most young heterosexual males, and I daresay homosexuals too. Though at that time homosexuality was still an illegal practice. The boss knew this well enough, and would occasionally, perhaps once a term, give a gruff and very ambiguous lecture from the stage. We didn't know exactly what he was talking about, but guessed he was telling us that mutual masturbation was prohibited. He also took a firm stance against the Sunday newspapers, banning the *Empire News* and the *News of the World*, as they would certainly lead us astray. We were all happy at one time or another to be led astray!

Smoking was also banned, but from a fairly young age many of us smoked. It was a mistake, I am the first to admit, and I wish that I had never started. But it was not a frowned upon activity. My mother never smoked, but my father always made a point of filling his gold lined silver cigarette case before going out for the evening, and at about the age of 13 he offered me my first cigarette. How grown up can you get? But at school it was disallowed and all sorts of sanctions could be applied, from being gated (no exit from the school grounds at all for a fortnight or so), to being caned (six of the best) or in my case much later, being banned from bringing my bicycle to school for a whole term. Mind you it was my third time of being caught and I had exhausted the other sanctions. Actually that was a nasty sanction, because at the age of 16 the bike was the means of getting some freedom from the regime. On Sundays one could ride out all over the Fylde, nice flat countryside, and a 20 mile ride on a Sunday afternoon was a joy.

The senior school was a little more liberal than the juniors – we were allowed to go out of the school between the end of lessons at 4pm and tea at 5pm. So it was an opportunity to go to the shops and spend a few pennies at the sweetshop or on Saturdays get a copy of the Green'un, the *Blackpool Gazette* football extra. In case you are wondering, my weekly pocket money at the age of 11 to 13 was one shilling and sixpence.

In the first year we were asked to choose between rugby and soccer as the principal sport in the winter term. Rugby won that vote hands down, and continued for many years after I left. So we were tutored in that very healthy and enjoyable, if violent sport. I was quite big, compared with others of my age, and so I was a second-row forward. I didn't enjoy it particularly, but that was the way it had to be. I was annoyed that I couldn't be a winger or centre where I could run. I was a good runner, and had always won the sprint races in junior school. I was about third fastest in my year, but I was big. So the second-row claimed me. There were some 60 boys in the first year, and I made the Under 13's team, which made me very proud. Later I was in the Under 15's, the Colts, the Second 15, and ultimately in the First. Arnold had a good rugby reputation. Three years older than I was Jimmy Armfield, who played full-back in the First 15, when I was in the Colts. Malcolm Phillips was an excellent centre in that same team, and he went on to play for Fylde and England, becoming an England selector for a while. Jimmy went on to become an England full-back and captain in the round ball game, and is still a brilliant commentator on the game for BBC Radio. Our trainer was Wilbur Howarth, a superb club rugby player with Fylde, and I believe he was an England reserve. Guy Watts was a Fylde forward, and a Maths teacher, and the two of them gradually knocked us into shape. Wilbur didn't like me, and it was reciprocated. Often in training he would give me a right thumping, and it almost put me off the game, but I realised you needed to be tough to succeed. The sad thing was that the animosity between us stopped me from studying Geography with him, and it has always been a regret. I took Physics and Chemistry instead and never quite made the grade. But History and Geography are what I like and I may have made more of an academic success for myself, had I pursued those subjects. Anyway I eventually made the First 15, and had a Lancashire schoolboy trial but didn't get into the team.

My swimming prospered. I became the youngest ever to swim for the school, and was in the school swimming team for three years being captain in the last. The big event every year was the inter-school swimming gala, in which eight local schools competed at the Derby Baths. I wish I could report that I won the events in which I competed but a second place in the 50m backstroke was the best I achieved.

Like the rest of my life, I was a bit dilettante in sports. I enjoyed them all, something my wife, even now, finds hard to understand. Whatever I was playing I thought it was the best. And consequently I played rugby in the winter term, hockey in the spring, cricket and athletics in the summer and swimming all year round. It was with great pride that I saw my name up on the team boards, a permanent record of my presence on every school first team – I think I was the only one in my year to do this. But it was only in swimming and hockey that I was rewarded with my colours tie. This was one of the three special ties we could wear at school, other than the official school tie. The others were for monitors and prefects. The colours tie was the one everyone envied, and was another real source of pride. I won my hockey colours as a result of scoring a hat-trick and three other goals in the Blackpool hockey festival in my penultimate year at school.

I had a number of friends who progressed through school with me. Ian Robinson was the one boy with whom I had a very healthy rivalry throughout the seven years we spent together. He was a tough lad from Bolton, short and stocky, and hard as nails. At the age of 12 he was nicknamed "Bull", because he charged round everywhere like a "bull in a china shop". He was a flank-forward at rugby, and was the driving force behind our successful junior teams. In fact he made the First 15 whilst I was still in the Second 15. He also gave me a good run for my money at swimming, and was a pretty good wicketkeeper at cricket. The rivalry was always there, and sometimes we'd fight, luckily it was never very serious, and there was a mutual respect for our individual abilities. I know he was unhappy on returning to school for our last year in the upper sixth to discover that I was appointed head boarder and deputy head boy of the school. We were the only two of the original boarders in our year to stay on into the sixth form. As a rule the boarders were not considered the brightest, and most left after taking their GCE Ordinary Level exams, often with no passes.

The rivalry between Ian and I continued when we had to have an election for the captain of School House. We each had our supporters, but I won the election, and that year School House won every inter-house competition.

Pride was at stake and the boarders bonded together as a unit. As captain I organised the evening training sessions, and was able to use all of the sporting facilities of the school, so I guess we had an advantage over the dayboys who were spread out throughout the different wards of the town.

Michael Outhwaite remained a friend – I was the only boy to call him Michael, everyone else used his nickname, "Pongo", given for no reason other than he was a big lad and a bit overweight. Actually I met Ian Robinson by accident in the High Street in Rugby, Warwickshire, in 1988 or '89. It was he who told me that "Pongo" was secretary of the rugby club. Amazing that he still used the nickname 30 years after we left school!

"Jaffy" Barker was another close friend, and he is the only boy from school with whom I still have contact. He was called "Jaffy" (Giraffe) because of his long neck, but his name was actually Philip. He was a strange boy in many ways, enjoyed life and was brave in a slightly dangerous way. He played goalkeeper in the school hockey team, and he was the one boy you didn't look forward to challenging for the ball. He cost us a few matches by charging out of his area, seriously upending the advancing forward. I think he just shut his eyes and hoped for the best. After leaving school he disappeared off the radar for a while before resurfacing as a retired Marine officer, who was taking part in a charity walk from John O'Groats to Land's End. He made many of the cinema newsreels at the time, and I remember being jealous that he had achieved an element of fame before me. But secretly I was pleased for him. When we were still 12 or 13 we had made one of those childhood pacts that we would both succeed in films and would have big houses next to each other. Kids' fantasies.

We were all compulsorily enrolled at 13 in the Cadet Corps and Philip and I were the only two not to get any form of promotion at all. Not surprising really, in that the senior officer was the aforementioned Wilbur Howarth. It was an incongruous situation – all week I was the second most senior prefect in the school, until on a Friday afternoon when we all donned our scratchy khaki uniforms, and I was just a cadet. Ian Robinson was the most successful of the group and eventually made sergeant.

We drilled and marched and learned about rifles and how to strip a Bren gun, and went shooting on the range. I got my marksman's badge, and I learned how we attacked as a section, and as a platoon, and we pretended to be soldiers. I would be lying if I said I thought it was a waste of time, but after a while I knew it wasn't what I wanted to do. My commitment wasn't there and promotion didn't follow. Every lunchtime the drum and bugle band would practice in the road outside school, and to this day I hate the sound of such bands. Still every Friday afternoon the boots were polished to a high shine, the creases in our trousers were pressed sharp, our cap badges and brasses were shone, and the webbing was all blanco'd. Once a year, the corps would have a general inspection, when a senior regular Army officer would inspect us and we'd do an official march past. The spit and polish leading up to that was a sight to witness.

Also, every year there was an official cadet camp that took place for a fortnight after the end of the summer term. I went to the first two when I was 14 and 15 – the first in Cheshire and the second at Comrie, near Crieff in Scotland. In each case we were under canvas, and lived like the Army. There were cadets from other corps' around the country, a large contingent from Armagh in Northern Ireland, and several more from the north of England and Scotland. We played war games, did mock night exercises, fired lots of blanks, we dug latrines, and got very damp and smelly. Keeping our kit moderately dry became the real challenge of the camp, that, and the food, which was awful. One day at breakfast in the huge canteen tent the catering corps officer asked us if everything was all right, and I said that the porridge wasn't very tasty. He replied "Well, you see, some people like it with salt and some like it with sugar, so we don't put either in!"

By the time I was 16, I'd had enough, and didn't go to the next two camps. Besides, I'd been regimented in school all term, and wanted to go home for a break. It was different for the non-boarders – camp was the opportunity to get away from home for a fortnight. Wilbur Howarth took me aside before the end of my last summer term and said it was a ridiculous situation that a senior prefect like me should not have at least a lance-corporal's stripe. If I would agree to go to camp that year, then he would promote me to full corporal. I declined. I was 18 and I have never camped under canvas since.

During those school years we entertained ourselves as well as we could. There was no television; in fact until 1953 hardly anyone had a TV. But in 1953 came the Coronation of Queen Elizabeth, and also the famous Stanley Matthews' Cup final between Blackpool and Bolton. Dad got a television especially for that, and as sod's law would have it, I wasn't at home. Philip and I were the only two boys in school that weekend and we listened to the match on the radio. What a joy. The commentary kept us on the edge of our seats, even though at 3-1 to Bolton we'd virtually given up hope. Then came the magnificent last three goals, engineered by Matthews. At last, Blackpool had won the cup, and Stan had the glory. That always has seemed a little unfair to me, because Stan Mortensen, the centre-forward had scored a hat-trick, and Frank Perry the South African winger had scored the winner. But it was dubbed and will always remain the Matthews' final. We went down to the promenade to watch the team parade the cup on the Sunday in an open topped tram, and cheered with the thousands who lined the route, in a glow of tangerine and white.

I didn't see many of Blackpool's home matches, much as I loved the game. At 15 I would have been allowed to go to Bloomfield Road on a Saturday afternoon had it not been for the fact that we had Saturday morning school and in the afternoon we would be playing for one of the school teams.

Actually the team fixture lists were very full, and I was representing the school at my age level every Wednesday and Saturday throughout the term. That was fun. We played all the local schools, and every now and again we'd play further afield, such as Preston, Southport and Morecambe. Competition was everything, and that competitive streak has remained with me. I don't like to lose, but learned to do it with good grace. I reckon over the years the teams in which I played had a slightly better win to loss record, but on occasion we were seriously stuffed! At rugby, Rossall School always beat us, and eventually refused to play their first team against us. St Bees was another side we couldn't beat. But, in spite of my continuing smoking, I remained pretty fit and played my hardest.

As a youngster I had singing lessons from my granny, and on Sundays at school, I had a private lesson with a teacher in the town. I'd also learned the piano up to about grade three. The singing paid off and at the age of 13 I was chosen to be the soloist at the school carol service, and the speech day. It was a nerve-wracking experience to sing in front of the congregation of seven or eight hundred at Holy Trinity Church, and a full Palace Theatre at the annual speech day. With training my voice may have been very good indeed, but I was losing enthusiasm for it and for the lessons. I gave up both singing and piano lessons that same year. I have no regrets about the singing, but deep regrets about the piano.

Academically, at school I had found my level fairly well. I started in a B-stream and was top of the form so I was moved up into the A-stream where I was bottom. I seesawed between these streams for the next four years. Eventually I took my GCE and passed all seven subjects with very good grades. But at 16 I stopped working.

One lesson we had each week from the age of 14 was elocution, where the long-suffering Mr Jack Priestley had the job of ironing out those flat Blackpool vowels. Some of us did quite well, and we often acted little playlets – on

Peter Purves

one occasion I played Peter Quince, and Ian Robinson played Bottom in the mechanicals' scenes from A *Midsummer Night's Dream*. We performed it at that year's speech day. In a later lesson we were asked what we wanted to be when we left school. We had been told that this particular classroom had been the one where a celebrated old boy who had created Jaguar Cars, Bill Lyons, had sat, and so we were supposed to be inspired. Most hadn't a clue; some wanted to be engineers, or scientists and I said I wanted to be an actor. Priestley laughed out loud and made me feel very small. "Don't be ridiculous, boy" were his exact words. I held my tongue, but deep down I thought, "I'll show you – one day they'll say I sat in this classroom".

Chapter Four

I am no longer an only child; Moving house again;

Being in Barrow; I break my leg – playing cricket!

I change school; My first professional acting work;

Teachers college and the Dramatic Society;

I find some soul mates, a band, and a girlfriend

I had just passed my 15th birthday when I was summoned from class to the headmaster's study. I couldn't for the life of me recall what I may have done wrong, but went along expecting the worst. In fact it was a happy surprise. My dad was on the phone to tell me that I had a baby sister, Judith.

It was an extraordinary moment. I had no idea a baby was even in the pipeline, as it were. Nor, for that matter did my mother. She had discovered she was pregnant only a few weeks before the birth. When I was three, she had been pregnant and unfortunately caught Mumps and lost the baby. She and my father had both understood that she would be sterile, and so when she became pregnant at the age of 45, she thought she was going through the menopause.

It was a birth that delighted everyone, and mum had the girl she probably had always wanted. I would be less than truthful if I said I had much of an involvement with my sister's early life. For a start I was away at school and there isn't much in common between a teenage boy and a baby girl, but I was very proud of her. I am happy to say that today we are very good friends indeed – very different, but quite close.

It meant a big change for my parents. My mum had been the cook at the pub, which provided meals and sandwiches, and my dad ran the bar and did all the administration of the place. Now it meant that they had to move again to something a little bit easier for them both. Dad looked at businesses up and down the country, from Hampshire to Northumberland. He sold the pub, and my Uncle Dodds and Auntie Belle, now living in Throckley, Newcastle-upon-Tyne gave them a roof until they got themselves sorted. It took time. For the only time I can remember, granny Elizabeth went to stay with her other three children, on a sort of rota system.

In the summer holiday from school I travelled down to some rural spot near Maidstone in Kent, with my dad, for an abortive viewing of a greengrocer's village store, with a summer trade boosted by the hop-pickers, who came down from London. Luckily he didn't buy it, because, we later realised, the writing was on the wall for the summer pickers, and the trade would have died. On the way back up to Newcastle, we just caught the Tyne Tees Pullman, but the only seats were in a non-smoking compartment. Dad couldn't cope with that so we went along to the bar and spent the journey there. Uncle Dodds was a temperance man, and when we had bought the pub, he and Belle refused to visit. Mum and dad could visit them, but they wouldn't set foot in a pub. So you can imagine we desperately had to try to cover up the fact that we'd been drinking and smoking on the train when he met us at Newcastle station. I suspect it was very obvious, but nothing was said, at least, not in my hearing.

A business was eventually found, almost a year after leaving the pub – it was a newsagents and corner shop in a nice part of Barrow-in-Furness. Barrow was, is and I guess will always remain out on a limb. At the end of the Furness Peninsula it is a town that no one passes through. You go to Barrow, and leave by the same route. So it was with some trepidation that I went home there for the first time from Blackpool in 1955. I was 16. To say it was a tedious journey is the understatement of the century. There is a well-told tale of a chap on the train from Barrow, which stopped at Carnforth station some 30 odd miles along the line.

There was a soldier sitting in the corner of the compartment, who just sighed and said, "Well that's the worst part of the journey over."

"Why, where are you going?" asked the man.

"Hong Kong," replied the soldier.

I have to admit I was happily surprised. The house was on a wide corner in an airy suburb of the town. Opposite was the Furness cricket ground, and the houses were all typical 1930's built semis. The shop was bright and airy, and adjoined the house. There were two good size bedrooms, one above the shop, plus a single room and a box room. Granny came back and took the best bedroom, mum and dad had the one above the shop, I had the single and Judy the box room. The shop was busy, and sold a lot of newspapers. Dad was up at the crack of dawn to go down to the town to collect the papers from the several wholesalers. I helped him during the holidays. Being out on a limb, the papers came to Barrow on the mail train. It was often late, and we would ring up each morning to find out what time it would arrive. If it was late, then first port of call was the station to help unload the train. This would be at about a quarter to six in the morning. We would get back to the shop by about 7am, and then the paper rounds would get prepared. Mum would be up by then, and the two of them would mark up the deliveries. An easier time than the pub? I'm not so sure.

I joined the cricket club, and in my first match fell and broke my left ankle. Annoying really because I had scored a very rapid 20 runs, and was running a quick four, when I had to jump over the returned ball. On landing, my ankle turned over, and swelled up stopping me from carrying on at the crease. The St John's man said it was a sprain, so I didn't go to hospital until three days later when it was hurting like mad. The x-rays showed a clean break and my leg was encased in plaster. When I returned to school I was on crutches for the first part of the winter term, and you wouldn't believe the speed that one could get up to when one tried.

Although Barrow was a heavy industrial town, it was tantalisingly close to the wonderful Lake District. Newby Bridge was a mere 20 miles away, and from there the most beautiful countryside in Britain was waiting to be explored. Coniston, Keswick, Bowness, Ambleside, Grasmere, and Ullswater were the places I got to know so well. As I reached 17, my dad started giving me driving lessons in his Morris Minor estate car. I took to it very well, drove all over the area, up and down some very difficult roads and as soon as I could I put in for my driving test. It never occurred to me for an instant that I could fail – but I did. The examiner said I left too much room on my nearside at traffic lights. "A bicycle could get in there," he said disparagingly as he handed me my fail certificate.

I was devastated. But then came the Suez Crisis, and petrol became rationed. Extraordinarily, the government decreed that anyone with a provisional licence could drive unaccompanied for the duration of the crisis. This was as good as having passed the test, and dad was happy for me to use the car on Saturday nights when I would go with three friends to a dance in Bowness. George was a mechanic at the garage from which we bought petrol, and the other two guys worked at the shipyard. I was the youngest by about three years. We always went for a couple of pints before attacking the dancehall and trying to get off with the girls, many of whom were visiting tourists, so there was always a steady flow of new talent. We got to know some of the local girls too, and I spent many a happy Saturday building up my confidence with girls – very necessary for a boarding school lad. And when driving tests were reinstated, I was an experienced driver, and sailed through it easily.

Here's one I wrote earlier...

Going back to school in Blackpool was still something to be endured. I learned to be very punctual. On one occasion I had caught the train from Barrow to Preston, and on changing there I asked a porter (do you remember them?) where I could get the Blackpool train. He directed me, and I boarded, only to discover that it went to Blackpool North rather than South, and it got me into Blackpool late. There was a deadline for arrival back at school after holidays of 7pm. I got back to school at a quarter to eight, and was gated by the headmaster for a whole month. I resented it then, and still do. I was told that I shouldn't have relied on the porter's directions. It was my responsibility to be back at school on time. It's a lesson that was reinforced five years later when I failed to get to a filming call on time, and I have always been early rather than late ever since.

Not being allowed out of the school grounds was pretty annoying, but once lights were out at night, who knew where we went! Several nights I went out over the school back wall. Actually that sounds easier than it was. There were two options. You could either bold it out and walk down two main flights of stairs, and then go out through the front door. Not the best option, as there were too many opportunities to get caught. Or climb out of the dorm window, and slide down a pitched roof and get into the main school building via a previously unfastened window, then creep through the school to the back door to the playground, keeping in the shadows of the walls and hedges, to get to the back wall of the school. Using a tree as a ladder one could slip out over the wall and move quickly away. Using the back streets I could then get onto Lytham Road and get a tram up town, or walk down to the beach.

One night, several of us, Philip, Michael Andrew, David Harbottle and a couple of others, all went out to the Pleasure Beach. It was out of season and the place was all closed up. But in we went and had a wander round some of the area, before going to the now defunct Fun House. This was a big building at the north end of the funfair, and housed big slides, and wobbly boards and mazes and rollers. All sorts. We had all been there when it was open, and the way in was a series of bendy corridors that eventually opened out into an area with several simple booby traps – a wobbly walk, a wind machine that blew girls' skirts up over their heads when they were not expecting it, and so on. There were even rows of seats from which the perverts could watch. Such fun. Anyway we decided we would try to get in, so we climbed over the turnstiles and set off along the bendy corridors. It was pitch black, and we had no torches, and one of the boys said he could make one, whereupon he lit a folded newspaper. It went up like an inferno in the confined space and he dropped it. Panic ensued and we fled back the way we'd come though Philip and I did stay long enough to stamp it out. I suspect that if we hadn't the whole place could have gone up in smoke. When, many years later the building did burn down, I wondered if it had been caused by someone doing exactly what we had done.

On a couple of occasions there were girls to meet for a cuddle in a tram shelter, and once I went up to the Winter Gardens to a dance when Ted Heath and his band were playing there. Fabulous stuff, but I had to leave early, when I was thoroughly enjoying a close smooch with some girl from Bolton, and over her shoulder saw a couple of teachers on the dance floor. I don't think they saw me, but it was a close call. I hotfooted it back to school and retraced my steps to the pitch black of the dormitory and no one was any the wiser. Or so I thought. I had been out a couple more times, when I received the summons to the boss' study again.

He confronted me straight away that a neighbour at the back of the school had reported my comings and goings on three occasions. What did I have to say about it? I just took a deep breath and said it wasn't true. It must have been someone else, and I brazened it out. I don't think I was believed, but I could have expected to be expelled for it, and decided I didn't want that on my record. And that was the last I heard of it. It didn't seem to block my various promotions, and shortly afterwards in my last year there I was made head boarder.

School was coming to an end, and my academic prowess really let me down. The sports kept me too occupied to have the energy for too much escapology, that and the responsibility. My friend Philip had left in the lower sixth, Michael Outhwaite likewise, and all the others with whom I spent time left after Ordinary Level exams. So maybe I should have worked a little harder. My Maths teacher, Sonny Liston, who had nurtured my hockey playing, tried very hard with me, and he made the subject interesting, but I was developing a selective memory. If I wanted to learn something I could – if not, I couldn't. Maths, Physics and Chemistry fell into the latter category. I'd studied Chemistry because of the aforementioned Sidney Law. This man was a pleasure to be with, and as he also was the swimming coach I spent much of the last two years at school in his company. But even this charismatic man failed to inspire me to chemical success.

I had been advised that I should go to Manchester University and study Fuel Technology, so I applied accordingly. I would have needed good passes in all three subjects. Three F's didn't quite cut it.

Now I had a dilemma. As a rebel in the Cadet Corps, and National Service beckoning, I wondered what to do. I certainly was not going to stay as a boarder at Arnold School, so I enrolled for a year at Barrow Grammar School in an attempt to gain success in my Advanced Level exams, and which meant that I could live at home for the first time in almost 10 years. I don't remember much of my year at BGS, but I remember thoroughly enjoying the freedom and the social life. I helped my dad with the papers; even after a heavy Saturday night I would get up and help him on Sunday mornings. Sometimes I would get up and do the paper collection for him before going to school, and if a delivery boy or girl failed to turn up, I would go and deliver for him. It provided some pocket money, and at that age, somehow one didn't get tired.

Peter Purves

And then there were girls that one could openly meet and talk to without the threat of damnation, or at best expulsion. Life was really very good. Then I broke my arm in a training exercise with the school rugby 15. The best thing about that was that I could cry off taking part in the compulsory school cross country run. I've never really been good at building up stamina. I was a fast sprinter, and a fast sprint swimmer, but more than a quarter mile race was the pits as far as I was concerned. And with a broken arm, even more so.

I had, during the summer holidays, written to the local repertory company at Her Majesty's Theatre in Barrow. I had no idea how these things worked, but I thought I might as well see if I was any good. The artistic director, Donald Sartain, contacted me and he asked if I would audition for him. This was 1957 and I was 18. Oh, the arrogance of youth – I learned the prologue from Shaw's *Caesar and Cleopatra*, and Hamlet's *Soliloquy*, and in due course I saw Donald and he was very nice to me. I stood on the stage of the lovely little Victorian theatre, and gave the pieces everything I could. I really don't know how good I was, and I suspect it was all very raw, but something must have been OK, because a few weeks later he offered me the part of the sheriff in *The Rainmaker*, which had been a film starring Burt Lancaster. It was only a small part, the character could have been at least 50, and I was still a teenager. Donald directed and played Starbuck, the rainmaker, and we started rehearsing on a Tuesday morning, and the show opened to a full house the following Monday. This was weekly rep, and it was my first experience of it.

I loved it, and did the best I could. I was paid £5.10s. It was my first professional play and obeying Oscar Wilde's dictum, I did get the words right, and didn't fall over the furniture. Coupled with the fact that the broken arm I had suffered had got some complications and I had just spent three days in hospital to have the tendons to my thumb repaired, meant it was a memorable time in every way. My hand was heavily bandaged, and I had to keep it mostly hidden when I was on stage. I am sure the audience are still puzzling over the significance of the injury! I played another part in a detective thriller during the next holiday period, so I felt I was nearly a pro!

And so I came to the end of my time at BGS, and I managed to pass Advanced Level Maths, but failed the other two subjects. Again, insufficient academic success for a University course, and with National Service still pending, I tried to get my parents to support me if I went to drama school. They wouldn't hear of it, and I suspect they thought it was just a pipe dream, and that without job security behind me, they couldn't support me. My dad, although not rich, was earning too much money for me to get a grant, and so I had to try to do something a little less frivolous. I applied to go to a Teacher's Training College, and was accepted by Alsager College, near Stoke-on-Trent. That September I was away from home again.

I suppose by this time I was pretty experienced at being independent. Most of the students I met at college were away from home for the first time, though there were one or two mature students, and a few who had already completed their National Service in the RAF or Army. The college was very much like a barracks, in so far as it had been a military camp during the war years. The accommodation was in H-blocks, and we were placed in these alphabetically. I ended up in Keats House (they were all named after poets) and I guess there were about 30 of us per block. A tutors' flat was at the front, and we each had individual rooms – slightly larger than a cupboard, with room for a single bed, a desk, a sink and a wardrobe. The cross piece of the H contained the toilets and bathrooms, and there was a sort of lounge – we called it the brew club – at the rear. There were approximately 10 blocks for men and the same for women.

The main college block housed the admin and the main hall and restaurant, and to be honest I was a little disappointed in that we were still treated not so very much differently from what I had experienced at school. Obviously we had a lot of free time, and we were expected to study on our own and unsupervised, but there was an air of boarding school about it all. I enrolled in Maths and English as my special subjects, and everyone had to take the Education course.

I soon found my feet there. Very early on, all sorts of groups and societies seemed to set up. The Dramatic Society immediately caught my attention, and for the first term, I spent as much time as possible at the weekly gatherings. There were a couple of very good amateur actors in the society, and a smattering of other talents, so it boded well for the future. I put my name down for the first show, which was the student pantomime. I was cast as the Pres. (sort of a Prince Charming) but actually a send up of the president of the local Students' Union. In the meantime, I got involved with the production and stage-management for a couple of touring professional companies that visited the college, performing works in which schools may have been interested. One was a first venture into theatre in the round, when a trio of talents, choreographer Geraldine Stephenson, and director, actor and musician John Dalby, and a singer whose name I've forgotten, performed for us. I organised their lighting and others in the Dramatic Society looked after sound and front of house seating. These were professionals and I wanted to be one. It never occurred to me that they were seriously scratching around for a living, though both went on to much more important things. A touring group also performed a primary school show for the college, and the big problem for us was in keeping a straight face with the double-entendres and innuendo's that those shows always contained. The principal actress straining to reach an important key saying "all I need is a few inches more" had us all in hysterics. The company arrived in a beat up van and after performing for us in the afternoon had to move on round the county for another show that evening somewhere. And then more the following day and so on. So seedy in many ways, but to me, the epitome of what I wanted to do.

So my time was taken up with the dramatics and with my girlfriend, Janet, whom I had met on the second day at college. She and I became an "on and off" couple for the duration of my time at Alsager. I found her company more interesting than that of many of my male colleagues, who liked nothing better than getting seriously drunk at the local pub. I've never bonded all that well with men, a throw back to my reserve when at school, I should think. Not that on occasion I wouldn't join in with the general carousing, but I'd rather have a cuddle than a drink, any day. Janet shared my love of swimming and our first date was to the swimming pool in Crewe. She was a long distance swimmer, and took it a little more seriously than I, but we did have that something in common. She also was interested in costume and design, so she joined the Dramatic Society as well.

Early on, however, I did find some real soul mates in the shape of a skiffle group. They were called Group 3, and there were four of them. I sat in whilst they practiced one day, and asked if I could sing a couple of songs. Now it so happened that Mike Thompson, one of the two guitarists, was a Lonnie Donegan fanatic, and I rather rated him too. In fact I'd liked him since the days he formed the group within the Chris Barber Jazz Band. So I got up and we did some of the old skiffle numbers like *Digging My Potatoes* and *The Rock Island Line*. The other guitarist was a quiet sort of guy called Ged Platt, and he played a very sweet acoustic guitar, but was very understated. The drummer, Derek McNaney was with me in Keats House, and became a good friend. The other guy in the group was their singer, John Knowles. Now, obviously he wouldn't have been keen on me because, not to put too fine a point on it, I was a better singer than he was, and he was the guy in possession! But, somehow, we managed to make it work. There was always potential for conflict, though, because John and Ged were very keen on "folk music" and Mike, Derek and I tended towards Rock and Roll. One number I did was always requested, and that was the old Gene Vincent number, *Be Bop a Lula*, but our audiences were just pleased to be hearing some reasonably good live music in college.

Peter Purves

Mike was also keen to electrify his guitar, and I had a tape recorder (one of those big old Grundig machines, reel to reel). We could, if we were lucky arrange the wiring so that it became a small amplifier; so Mike was able to go electric, we ran the microphone through the same amp, Ged strummed louder, and Derek walloped the skins. We were a band. In fact over the next two years we played two or three concerts and dances each term, and the students liked us. We were always the last act in the monthly lounge concerts, and we even went out on the road to perform a couple of gigs in halls in Stoke and Hanley. I was having the time of my life. Not doing a lot of work mind you, but who cared?

And the Dramatic Society went from strength to strength. My English tutor, Olive Donald, a delightful lady with a lovely sense of humour, showed an interest in what we were doing also. When I became president of the society in my second year, she pointed me in the direction of Arnold Wesker and Bernard Kops, and we did three major productions that year; Kops' *The Hamlet of Stepney Green*, *The Miser*, by Moliere, and Terence Rattigan's *The Deep Blue Sea*. Quite a variety and we also performed the farce, *Love in a Mist*. Add to that the pantomime (I played my first Dame), and the other lounge concert sketches, it is little wonder my academic assessments were poor. Save for the English, because I liked to read, and kept up quite an input of critiques that must have come up to standard.

A favourite moment during those two years was the annual lecture by the principal, to us all about being in "close propinquity". Or rather not being. I don't think any of us knew what he was talking about but we could make a pretty good guess. Our college was one of very few that was for both sexes, and we all lived in the houses on the campus. And there was a lot of close propinquity! I managed to find time for illicit meetings with Janet but the college regulations were very strict back in 1959 and 1960. Any man caught in the room of a female student would be immediately sent down, and likewise the girl. So we had to be very careful but it was taken right out of our hands on occasion.

Keats was on the opposite side of the campus to Janet's house, Shelley. I used to exit my house via the back door, and skirt the college in the dark, passing two tutors' flats on the way and then when I got to her block I would creep along, keeping below the windows, some of which may have been lit, tap on her window, which she would open and I would climb in. Some hours later I would repeat the journey in the opposite direction. Horror of horrors, on one very cold winter's night, it snowed heavily whilst I was in Janet's room and the snow fell to a depth of about two inches. When I went to leave I realised I would leave a track straight from her window to my house. I spent the best part of three quarters of an hour at about two in the morning making tracks all over the college, from door to door and from window to window, before escaping back to my own house. Luckily for us both, no one saw me. But the following morning the tutors must have been amazed at the apparent amount of nocturnal activity there had been!

Two years passed very easily, my Maths wasn't great, but my English was getting better grades all the time, and I really enjoyed the Education course. Naturally enough there came the time each year when we had to put our theory to the test and go out to various schools in the area for teaching practice. Most of the students seemed to dread it, but I really looked forward to it. Let's face it; teaching is an awful lot like acting if you think about it. You have to get up in front of the class and perform. As it happens I was asked to teach English at a secondary modern school in Hanley, and I decided I would do a modern day version of Shakespeare's *Julius Caesar* with them. They were not the top stream in the school, but a semi remedial group, it wouldn't be easy, but I had three weeks to devise the piece, and get them to perform it in front of the other five classes in their year. Without going into too much detail, I was able to break down a lot of the language and get them to express it in modern English for themselves. They lapped it up. They simply loved being the conspirators, and it worked for them like a dream. They attacked it with flair and enjoyment, and when it was finally performed, although there were mistakes and the occasional embarrassed moment, the others in their year loved it. I loved it too, and I discovered later that I was due to be failed, but teaching practice had taken me from that low point to a Distinction in Education in my final assessment. So maybe all the time I'd spent with the Dramatic Society had actually been very well spent after all. And my time with Group 3 wasn't wasted. I'd enjoyed the opportunity to sing, and it didn't do my ego any harm that I was really quite popular. The group stayed in touch, well four of us did. No one knew where Johnny Knowles went, but Ged, Mike and Derek and I went to a recent reunion of our year, and in October 2008 had our 50th anniversary reunion. Imagine my surprise when in walked the unmistakeable but somewhat larger round the girth figure of John. I'd taken some sound equipment with me, as had Mike, and so we played eight numbers or so from the old days. Both our voices held up, but I have to admit, the voice ain't what it used to be. Ged is as dry and quiet as ever, Derek still keeps an approximate rhythm, and Mike remains an excellent musician and a very good guitarist. And John and I got on fine. Another celebratory gig is planned for the autumn of 2009. The oddest thing was that on arriving at the hotel for the reunion, I immediately wondered, "who are all these old people?" before recognition began to dawn, together with the realisation that we all were now nearly 70 years old.

I never intended becoming a schoolteacher. As I said, I went to college to continue in education and to postpone my doing National Service. And three weeks before I left Alsager for good, National Service ceased. The government finally realised that keeping young men in the Army, RAF or Navy for two years, mostly doing things that didn't need doing was an expense and for all but a few, a waste of their time. I've known several people who thoroughly enjoyed themselves, but the majority felt they had been deprived of the opportunity of getting out to work and to start living their lives. I have no regrets about missing it, because I had spent so much of my time as a teenager away from home and learning to look after myself. What to do next, that was the question.

Chapter Five

A year teaching in London; Discovering Spurs;

The Renaissance Theatre Company calls me back;

More than 90 plays in two years;

Jazz, rock-climbing and best friends;

I get married

I realised that until I had completed a year's teaching, I wouldn't be fully qualified, and the whole point of going to Alsager had been to get a qualification behind me in case the acting thing didn't work. I could have taught anywhere I suppose, but at nearly 21 years old, I reckoned there was only one place to be and that was London. I applied to the GLC and was invited for an interview at County Hall. I found it all rather daunting, but I answered my interrogators as well as I could, and then went back to Euston to get the train back to Barrow.

A few days later I got a letter offering me a post as a Maths teacher (oh no!) at a school in Hackney, South Hackney Secondary School, and I wrote back to accept. One of Janet's friends at college, a really nice Jewish girl called Geraldine Cravitz, lived in Walthamstow, and she said that her parents would be pleased to give me digs, and that's where I eventually ended up. Gerry's dad was a bus driver on the old Number 9 route, and her mother did voluntary work for deprived East End children, of which there were many at that time. The East End was still to a large extent a bombsite, though some areas had been cleared and ghastly skyscraper blocks of flats had been built. It was a tough time for education too. There had been a lot of immigration from Pakistan, and there seemed to be no love lost between them and the Jews.

I made some good friends in the year I was in Hackney. I taught in the lower school annexe, now no longer there, in Lauriston Road. There were two Welsh teachers there, Stan Jones, and Rhys Davies, and I stayed in touch with them for some years. Stan and I went to every London football club to see First Division games, and in 1960 I went to my first game at White Hart Lane. I have been a Tottenham Hotspur supporter ever since. Stan and Rhys became my drinking buddies, though how we afforded it I do not know. I was earning £500 a year, and that included an extra £50 London Weighting. Out of that I somehow paid rent and fares and ate, and went to football and had some fun, and even backed a few winners at the bookies. And I did a bit of teaching too, though not much! In the school there were nine streams in the first year and seven streams in the second year. I was required to teach Maths to the bottom three streams in years 1 and 2 and swimming in two sessions a week. The trouble with that was that the children I was teaching needed a remedial skills teacher – many of them couldn't read or write so how on earth do you start to teach numeracy? I tried a number of things. I was able to lay my hands on some surveying equipment and took the kids outside to do a survey of the school buildings. That worked quite well. It wasn't in the curriculum, but who cared? It was getting through to a few of them. But mostly I made no headway at all.

I didn't really enjoy the work, there was so little to be positive about. Why do they give inexperienced teachers the most difficult tasks? And all the time I was thinking of what to do about my acting. I liked the Cravitz family immensely – they were a typical Jewish household, and the entire family came to visit on a Friday and all sat down to eat Gefilte fish together. I was invited too, but although I liked the company, I didn't like the food all that much, so every other week I would make my excuses and be out. At the end of the first term I decided to try to get a place of my own, and was lucky enough to have met a couple of guys who had a flat in Gloucester Road, and so I moved in with them. Duncan Rotherham was one of the chaps, and he, Stan, Rhys and I would often go out together for a few beers, and parties were in good supply. So whilst life was fun, work was crap. I still saw Janet a few times but she was teaching in an infant school in Wakefield. Long distance love don't work too well!

I started playing bridge and solo. It was a useful skill to have in the lunch hour, and Stan and I became quite good at it. Stan had been playing bridge for a few years and he taught me some basic bidding systems, and how to play the game. I had always played whist, and bridge is just a sophisticated version of that, I always thought and it came quite easily to me. He was a good partner, and after I moved to the Gloucester Road flat we would play at a Kensington bridge club. I found it all a bit stuffy, but the games were good. The problem was that the serious players all played for money, and I didn't have any. But at school we played for pennies only and the losses weren't too hard to bear.

London is so darned big, and you are always going to have to travel a fair distance to get to work. Gloucester Road to Hackney wasn't easy, so I decided to move. Duncan found it difficult too, so we started to look for a different flat, and we found it on the top floor of a semi in Kensal Rise, NW London. Actually for me it was ideal because I could get across town on the North London Railway to Dalston Junction and then a couple of buses took me to the gates of the school. The only problem was that my bedroom window looked out on the railway line, and it was a busy line, with a lot of goods trains on it overnight. Trains are the sort of noise you eventually get used to, but it took a while. Downstairs there were three New Zealand nurses, and the parties began again.

Stan shared a couple of rooms with his lady, Jo, in West Kensington (long before it became fashionable). In fact I think it was ultimately condemned, and if it wasn't, it should have been, but it wasn't a great distance from my new pad so we were able to stay in touch and my love of football grew and grew, particularly as it coincided with the start of Tottenham's great years of the 60's. Sadly it has been a team in transition ever since. Will we ever see their glory days again? Those were the days. No stand seats for us – we would queue and stand on the terraces, sometimes in crowds of 50 to 60 thousand people, and there was no better feeling in the world. Many years later when I was regularly in receipt of tickets in the stand, although it was still fun, it wasn't the same.

I even went to watch Arsenal a few times when my friend from junior school, George Eastham was playing for them, but the other team Stan and I regularly watched was Fulham. At that time it was the friendliest club in London, and the support was thin enough for us to change ends at half-time and still have a great view. These were the days of Johnny Haynes, and Jimmy Hill, and the unforgettable Tosh Chamberlain on the wing. I continued watching Fulham well into the 70's. The only club I really had no interest in was Chelsea. I would go to Stamford Bridge if Spurs or Manchester United were playing them, but only to watch them lose, or so I hoped. Some things never change.

But I am getting a little ahead of myself. After two terms teaching, I knew it wasn't for me, and I decided that I would quit at the end of the summer term and I did. I handed in my written resignation to the headmistress, the formidable Miss Beswick, and that chapter of my life was finished.

I knew I was taking a terrible risk. The salary I had been earning wasn't enough to have saved anything, and so I was broke, and out of work. I managed to sign on at the labour exchange, which was near Marylebone station, and queued up for the dole each Thursday. I put my occupation down as Actor, and they kindly said they would try to find me some work. Yeah right!

Then began the traipsing around town, wearing out a lot of shoe leather – the tube and buses were too expensive – climbing a lot of stairs and knocking on a lot of doors in an attempt to find an agent. I poured over *The Stage*, looking for potential auditions, and basically in five weeks got absolutely nowhere. My mum in the meantime, sent me a small parcel of food each week – biscuits, baked beans, coffee, and tea, that sort of thing, and to be honest, without it I would have been very hungry indeed. But then came a surprise. I received a telegram from Donald Sartain at Her Majesty's in Barrow. It was a simple message. "If you are serious about acting, there is a job for you here."

I didn't think twice. A regular job in a weekly repertory company was the most perfect offer I could have had. I stuck a fiver in an envelope and left a note for Duncan, packed up my meagre belongings, and caught a train the same day, having stopped to send a telegram on the way to the station. Again the message was simple. "Thank you Donald, I am on my way". The bonus with being in Barrow was that I would be able to stay at home rather than find digs, and I knew that my mum would not charge me a great deal. I telephoned her from Euston to say I was coming home, and she sounded absolutely delighted. What I hadn't realised at the time was that she had become a regular at the theatre, and knew Donald quite well through his being a customer at our shop. She had mentioned to him in passing that I had stopped teaching and was looking for work in the theatre, and Donald did the rest. I was flattered that he felt I had what it takes, though his company was a small one and had no spare money. But he needed a versatile junior leading man, and that was to be me.

Having already performed one play two years earlier, I had a vague idea of what the work would be like. I wasn't engaged to play any particular parts, just to be a member of the company and play as cast. What I hadn't appreciated was the relentlessness of weekly repertory. It did what it said on the tin – each week there would be a new play opening on the Monday night and playing six evening performances and one matinee on the Saturday. As it happened I was to stay with the company for two years, and in that time appeared in some 90 plays. It was the hardest work I have ever done, for the least money, but it was just about the happiest time of my life. It was what I had wanted to be doing since I was nine, and now it was my profession. I was a professional actor, earning £9 a week – even less than I had earned as a teacher – but the fulfilment just grew and grew.

The other actors in the company accepted me quite happily; Donald, of course was there, as was Bernard Gallagher, later to become well known as one of the stars of *Crown Court* on ITV; David Baillie whose career has had a recent revival in the *Pirates of the Caribbean* films; Alan Partington, who was a little older than the rest, or at least looked it as he was going quite bald; David Chant who was the set designer/painter and sometime actor; Charmian May, the leading lady, later to become a regular TV and film character actress; Gabrielle Laye, Madeleine Blakeney, and Gillian Emmett. And that was it. Talk about a skeleton crew. Obviously the company was augmented by the occasional student and other actors were brought in for special weeks when we had a larger cast, but for the most part this core group did the lot for the first eight months or so of my time with the Renaissance Theatre Company.

David Baillie and I shared a dressing room on the top floor of the little theatre, and we became pretty good friends and that friendship continued for a good few years. But at first, and I didn't realise it, he resented my presence. In fact I had taken his job. There is no question that David could act, he'd been through RADA, and knew his way about, but there was a stiffness about him, and I guess Donald was worried he wasn't versatile enough. But we got through that, and I really enjoyed his company. We bought a car together; a 1936 Ford 8 for £15 and felt like lords as we drove it around town. I painted the ban the bomb symbol on the doors and was banned from keeping it on the forecourt of my dad's shop. Very conservative, my dad.

Peter Purves

The schedule was very tight indeed. I started work some two weeks after travelling home. I cannot remember the first play at all – so many of them all blend into one, but in a typical week we would have opened a new play on the Monday night. Then on the Tuesday morning at 10.00am we would commence rehearsals for the next play. We would break after blocking the moves for Act One at lunchtime, and would have the afternoon to learn the lines. Then it was back to the theatre to perform the play that had just opened in the evening. At 10.00am the next day we would "block" Act Two, learn lines in the afternoon, and then perform in the evening. And on Thursday we would finish "blocking" the next play, learn everything in the afternoon and then perform again in the evening. On Friday we would attempt to run the play in the morning without our scripts, and again in the afternoon, and a performance again in the evening. At least after that the weekend was looming and time to rest. Not blooming likely. On Saturday morning we would run the play and if there was time we would tidy up the rough bits – and there were always rough bits. There would be a matinee in the afternoon, and the last performance that evening. Time to rest? Well, no because the set would have to be dismantled, so the set for the following week could be put up on the Sunday. On the Sunday there was always some frantic learning and going over the script, before arriving on Monday morning in time for a dress rehearsal of the new play.

And come what may, hell or high water, sunshine or tempest, at 7.30 that evening, a full house of 380 seats, (all at two for the price of one) would stand for the National Anthem, and then settle down into their seats for the first performance of the new play. Whether we knew the lines or not, we were on. Nerves, terror, excitement and pure joy were experienced by all of us in our own way in our pursuit of fulfilment and ultimately stardom and discovery.

And then on Tuesday morning we started to rehearse a new play.

It was an extraordinary way to live and work. Naturally in some plays one would play a small part, in the next a lead; some would be highly dramatic, some would be farce, some potboilers, and even the occasional musical. Weekly rep required the actors to be able to play a full range of parts. Occasionally you would be cast in a part that suited you perfectly, in others you may be totally miscast. I can recall one period when I played the 80 year old Professor Serebryakov in *Uncle Vanya*, and the following week a 12 year old in some piece of no consequence. Let's face it in 96 plays you could only be really good in a very few roles, and variably OK to awful in the rest.

Where I think I shone was in farce. I loved to make people laugh and people always said my timing was good. Bernard Gallagher and I made a very passable double-act in the Whitehall Farces, and these were amongst the most popular plays we ever performed – those and some of the Agatha Christie mysteries. Serious culture struggled, and if I am honest I wasn't that keen on Shakespeare. That was probably because it was just too difficult to learn in a week. I really had a hard time learning Malvolio in *Twelfth Night*, which is a great part in a wonderful play. I made a reasonable stab at it, and we were dutifully applauded by the full houses we had all week. That was because it was the Schools Shakespeare play for GCE O Level English that year. And it could be quite disquieting to hear half the audience saying the words with you on the big speeches. For that reason I was relieved to be only playing a small part in *Macbeth* the following year. One week we rehearsed Congreve's *The Way of the World*. Restoration comedy is every bit as hard as Shakespeare to learn, and for the most part we failed. Actually, David Baillie and I played the two fops, and we were the only members of the cast not to be ad-libbing like crazy most of the time. The biggest part was played by an actor called Alan Partington. He was a super bloke, and a good actor, but he wasn't good at learning lines. I don't think he knew his part even by the time we did the last performance on the Saturday. What the audience made of it all I can only guess!

Peter Purves

Luckily I was a quick study, and after I had a few plays under my belt, I was even managing not to have my head buried in a script all the time, and began to enjoy a little free time. In fact although it was really serious work, we all had a very good time. I was very taken with Gillian Emmett, a small dark-haired girl from Leeds, who covered her accent by speaking a little like Joan Greenwood. She had trained at the Guildhall School of Speech and Drama in London, and was a most energetic actress, and she and I spent a lot of time together during those first months. We would help each other with learning our parts, and began to socialise and go places together. She was good fun, and we made each other laugh. We seemed to like the same things and got on really well together, and gradually we fell in love.

We found a pub in town that had a Jazz band that played there regularly, and I had always liked my Jazz, spending a lot of time at Humphrey Lyttelton's 100 Club in Oxford Street when I had been in London. One weekend we were invited, together with a few others from the company to a party and the members of the band were there. I got into conversation with the trumpeter about Jazz and we didn't hit it off. Les Bull was his name, and he remains, possibly my best friend to this day, but at that party he thought I was talking through my backside. And I probably was, but at 21 you really do know everything about everything, and I thought I knew all about Jazz. There was another chap there, Keith Findlay, and the conversation got round to driving. I threw into the conversation that some idiot who hadn't a clue had failed me in my first driving test. "That was me," said Keith. I really didn't do too well at that party, and we left early.

The Furness Jazz College Seven was a very good band, and we went to see them after the show most Thursdays and Saturdays. Gradually a friendship blossomed and I started to sing with the band. I did a couple of good old Blues numbers and Les and I would duet on some funky version of songs like *We're a Couple of Swells*. I discovered that Les had been a professional trumpeter for a year with Mickey Ashman's Band when he had worked as a wine salesman in London, and he was married to a really pretty blonde girl, Eileen, whom I had watched many a time at various dances when I had been out on a Saturday night at the Rink or Town Hall in Barrow before I was a teacher. I had never asked her to dance as she was just too cool, and I'd never had the confidence. Les, Eileen, Gilly and I became very close friends. Their house was in the wonderfully named Paradise Street, and after the show on a Saturday night we would go round there for a drink and to watch *That Was The Week That Was* on TV. It was a truly happy time. They already had a son, Steven, and whilst we were still at the theatre their second son, Gavin, was born.

Surprisingly, after such an inauspicious start, we also made friends with Keith, the driving examiner, and remain in contact to this day. He's a lovely man, much older than I but very young at heart. And very witty too. He is the kind of man that brings a smile as soon as you meet him.

Then there was Smooth Sid. When we met him he was a shoe salesman at Freeman Hardy and Willis in Barrow. He too, was a jazz fan, and we got to know him through Les. Sid was a rock climber, and was responsible for Gilly and me taking it up during the second summer we were in Barrow. One of the Jazz band hangers-on was a platinum blonde girl, very flash, and we all knew her as Diamond Lil. Her boyfriend was in the Merchant Navy, and when he came home he always had tales to tell of exotic places. He climbed as well, and we began to go up to the Lakes on a Sunday and climb a crag or two.

The first time we went to the Langdales, and attempted a climb classified as difficult (that meant it was more than a scramble, and involved at least one pitch that required proper climbing) we climbed with two ropes, Sid leading me, and Gilly bringing up the rear. Having got to the bottom of the crag, Sid set off up the first pitch, belayed himself off, and called me to follow, which I did, and finally Gilly came up. The second pitch was pretty straightforward too. But the third had a couple of difficult moves, certainly for the beginner, requiring quite a significant weight change to get from one face to another. I managed it OK, but Gilly had a bit of a problem, as her legs were much shorter than ours. She made it in the end but it wasn't easy. Half-way up the next pitch there was a slight traverse to the right and then a couple of big steps up over what appeared to be very smooth rock face. Again, Sid went up, and called me to follow. At the smooth face I got stuck. We were some 150 feet up the crag and I couldn't find my next handhold. I was balanced really well, with both toes in small footholds, and one hand was gripping another hold, but I couldn't find anything that would advance me any further. Sid shouted encouragement from above, things like "Come on you silly sod", and "It's there, just reach for it" but I was stuck. I was able to lean back from the face and look around for the handhold that would rescue me, but without any immediate success. It was then, in this most perilous position, that I chanced to look to my left. About 15 feet away, on a grassy space sat a family, two adults and two smallish children, having a picnic. It made me wonder what I was doing there, when there must have been an easy route up. But, of course that isn't the point of rock-climbing is it?

After being stuck there for a good 10 to 15 minutes, or at least that's what it felt like, I did make a big reach up and to my left found the elusive handhold, and I was away and up to the top. Gilly came up with no problem at all behind me, though she used a slightly different route.

On another occasion I was climbing a much harder route with Sid, and after the hardest pitch on the climb arrived at the point where Sid was supposedly tied off, to see that on the edge of the ledge was a box of matches, with the rope tied round it, and that was the sum total of my protection, though to be fair, Sid was holding the rest of the rope fairly tight. I dread to think what would have happened had I fallen off.

Speaking of which, when we were climbing on Dow Crag near Coniston, there is a very difficult pitch called the Devil's Elbow which requires a climb up a short rock face, and then a long traverse over a sloping plate of rock, and a final climb up another face. The rope therefore runs at quite an angle, and as it is a long pitch, you could only have two people on the rope at a time. Gilly followed Sid, and was making good progress and just starting the traverse when she fell off. Sid was properly tied off, and held the rope firm, so Gilly swung in a huge pendulum, bumping against the rock face a few times as she went. Apart from some bad bruising she was fine, and it didn't put her off. I have always been told that you aren't a proper climber unless you've fallen off, so I guess I am not one, and she is. And all this was with no helmets and the old-fashioned hobnail boots. We both loved the freedom of the climbs, and I am sorry I didn't carry on with it as a hobby after I left Barrow, but there aren't a lot of crags round London!

We got into a great working routine, and in the summer months it was a great place to be. After finishing rehearsals at lunchtime we would go over to the sandhills on Walney Island, or out to the point at Roanhead, and lie on the beach, learn our lines and swim in the warm water of the Irish Sea. It was actually warmer than perhaps it ought to have been, because not far to the north was Seascale and the site of Britain's first atomic energy plant. Back in the late 50's there had been a serious discharge of radioactivity that contaminated the landscape there and meant that the milk supplies locally were damaged and poured away. I know my parents said they could smell sour milk in the air for weeks. But we also went over to skinny-dip on warm nights after the show. Often there'd be as many as 20 or so of us enjoying the warmth of the air and the sight of the phosphorescence on the water. I'm just glad nothing has fallen off as a result!

I suppose we were lucky to grow up when we did. It was when satirical humour was appearing in the mainstream for the first time, and the pill was about to revolutionise the way people regarded sex. The politicians were telling us we'd never had it so good and there was optimism everywhere. The

Beatles were about to take the world by storm, and British popular music was turning the tables on America.

The theatre suddenly found itself with a little money as the local council and Vickers Armstrong each decided to sponsor it with matched amounts (£1000 each) and the arts council also gave it a £1000 grant. It meant that mine and Gilly's money went up to £9.10s a week each. With that we decided to get married. My mother's comment was typical when I told her. "She's not pregnant is she?" And she wasn't, but I guess my mother knew me pretty well!

The wedding was in the late summer on a Saturday and Donald Sartain gave Gilly away. The theatre was due to close for two weeks and we would all have the next week off. The play that week was *Private Lives* by Noel Coward, and we played the two lesser characters. Having just got back to the theatre from our small wedding reception at a pub on Walney Island, the curtain went up to find us on the balcony of a hotel, and Gilly's first line was something like "Isn't it wonderful darling, here we are, married." The applause was deafening, and the show couldn't continue for quite a while. But it did, and we had a party on stage after the show, before setting off for a short honeymoon. By this time I had bought a 1939 Austin 12HP, a lovely car with walnut interior and leather upholstery. It had cost me £12 from George, the mechanic I had known when I was still at school. It took us down to London – a long journey in those days with no motorways apart from the Carnforth by-pass. I think it took us 10 hours but we made it. We stayed with Duncan Rotherham in his new flat in Gloucester Road, went to see a couple of shows and looked up old friends like Stan and Rhys, and then we set off back to the north via Stratford. We saw a production of *A Midsummer Night's Dream* with the most amazing cast – Judi Dench as Titania, Ian Richardson as Oberon, Ian Holm as Puck, Diana Rigg and Ann Beach as Hermia and Helena, and Nerys Hughes and Patricia Brake played two of the fairies. For the life of me I cannot remember who played Bottom or any of the other mechanicals. But it was the most magical production ever, and I don't think I have ever seen its like since.

We stayed the night at the Shakespeare Hotel and we had a supper of stilton and biscuits, washed down with a bottle of Veuve Cliquot. The perfect romantic honeymoon. We couldn't afford it, but I've never let that stand in my way!

And so we trekked back north to Barrow, the car finally breaking down as we turned off onto the Barrow Road at Levens Bridge with 35 miles still to go. This was in the days of unvandalised telephone boxes and I was able to ring my dad who came out in his car and towed us back home. Unfortunately it was the death knell for the car. MOT tests had just begun, and the garage to which I took it for repair said it couldn't be done. Apparently, as well as the mechanical failure, the iron chassis had a split in it, that meant the back axle was only held in place by the big fish springs. If they had failed, the car would have been in two bits!

But I needed a car. Gilly and I had rented a flat at the top end of town that cost us £4 a week, so we were pretty well off for the first time, and so I looked for another car and found a delightful 1938 Wolseley 16 for just £18. It had an MOT but it was an electrical death trap. Every time it started there was this smell that suggested imminent explosion, or at least burning rubber. But we persevered with it and it served its purpose for a good few months.

The plays continued with an experiment. A new director arrived called Derek Goldby who had a few notable successes in London in the 60's. He reckoned that a week was insufficient time to rehearse. Well that didn't take a Degree in Logistics to work out, but it was all the time we had. He suggested a scheme that would allow us to have fortnightly rehearsals and weekly playing. Donald Sartain decided to give it a go. We'd had a few changes in the company; David Baillie had left a few months earlier, so had Alan Partington and Madeleine Blakeney left during that season break. Frank Moorey, whom I had seen playing *Benedick* at Keele University when I was at college, and

John Kilby, who went on to work as an assistant producer on *Fawlty Towers* amongst other things, had come in, and there were others who appeared from time to time. We all attempted the new schedule. On the first Monday we began rehearsals of a new play. Rehearsals continued all week. OK so far. But week two got a little more complicated. On the Tuesday morning we started to rehearse a new play, and in the afternoon we continued rehearsals of the first play. Still OK so far, because we had some script-learning time in the evenings. It was in week three that it all started to go pear-shaped.

On the Monday, the first play had its dress rehearsal, and opened to a full house that evening. Great. Then on Tuesday morning we began to rehearse play number three. In the afternoon we rehearsed play number two. In the evening we performed play number one. And that was how the week continued. The subsequent week play two opened and plays three and four were rehearsed. By the next week we were all exhausted. We had no time in the schedules for learning the parts, and some of us were in all five plays and they weren't easy plays either. There was *Chicken Soup with Barley*, by Arnold Wesker; *The Giaconda Smile* by Goldoni (a most energetic Comedia del Arte piece); A Whitehall Farce; an Agatha Christie; and something arty and vaguely Russian I think. It was a nightmare time, everyone panicking and struggling, and after five weeks we went back to the still unsatisfactory, but much preferable weekly rehearsal and weekly playing. Never again was the fortnightly option suggested. The theatre could never support a fortnightly rehearsal and fortnightly playing – the audiences just were not there.

One show that brought a standing room only notice was a Sunday concert I organised for the Furness Jazz College Seven. The theatre was packed to the roof, and even after paying the band, the theatre made a tidy little extra sum. Donald enjoyed them too, and when he decided we should perform Brendan Behan's great semi-musical about the Irish troubles, *The Hostage*, he asked the band to play. Again it was a huge success – one of the better productions at Her Majesty's. I played the barmy self-styled Irish Lord, Monsewer, Gilly played one of the Irish girls, and John Kilby played the Hostage himself. It was a most touching performance and the show had a huge impact in the town I recall. The band was sensational. At a party a couple of weeks earlier, Gilly and I had met three girls and two men who had never been to the theatre. They were quite interested in what we did, and they liked us. We suggested they should try it out and so they came to see *The Hostage*. In the bar after the show, the one comment they made that has stayed with me forever was "That was fantastic. We thought it would be like church!" They became regulars for a few weeks, and enjoyed a farce, and an Agatha Christie, but then they missed a few weeks, came one more time and that was the last we saw of them. Sad really, but we had affected them for a while. And I believe that's what the theatre should do – it ought to move people and change them somehow.

One of the fun things about working in repertory is that you get quite well known about the town, there is an element of celebrity about the players and we were a little eccentric. I went to a local hairdresser to dye my hair blonde when I played the German piano teacher in Peter Shaffer's *Five Finger Exercise*. This was at a time when men didn't do that sort of thing. I have to admit it all came out a bit over the top – almost albino blonde! A few weeks later it went jet black for the part of Mick in Pinter's *The Caretaker*. The audiences felt they knew us, and liked the fact that we played a different part every week, and they also liked it when we got it wrong. There was mass hysterics not only from the audience but also from the actors in *Dangerous Corner*, when Madeleine Blakeney at one point got up from a chair at the front of the stage, crossed to the other side and walked upstage with a cushion firmly attached to her behind with a dress hook. Poor Madeleine had no idea what was wrong, until one of the other actors unhooked her. Her blush could be seen through her make-up.

The comments from the audience in some shows were to be treasured.

Peter Purves

"Who the hell remembers that?" said one old dear loudly in *The Wrong Side of the Park*, when the leading female character berates her husband for not remembering when they first went to bed together! "How did you like the play?" asked Madeleine of her landlord after one Monday performance. "You looked a bugger in that 'at" was all he said. And the pensioners' cheap performance on a Wednesday brought its usual clutch of odd folk. One old fellow used to sit on the front row every Wednesday and go to sleep. He must have slept solidly through every one of my performances. There was one regular who had to explain to her partly deaf friend what was going on, so we often got a running commentary, intermingled with the occasional, "Oh NO!" "Did he really" and "Has she?" And through it all we just kept on doing our best.

After I'd been in the company for a few months, a nice young man called André Tammes arrived as our stage manager, a luxury for us, because he didn't act on stage. He was really quite young, but rather pompously smoked an ostentatious Meerschaum pipe. Until then we had shared a number of the stage-management duties – though this usually only meant raising or lowering the House tabs, and sorting out stage props, and occasionally operating some lighting changes. But we also got a couple of acting assistant stage managers as the company began to get a little more affluent. A former child actor, David Langford, succeeded André as stage manager. I liked him a lot, and amazingly he was later to become a studio director on an obscure TV show on which I was to work, called *Blue Peter*!

Things started to change in the spring of the second year, when Stephen Berkoff joined the company for a couple of months. Make no mistake he was, even then, a very serious actor, and he brought with him some serious plays and ideas. But they weren't the kind of plays that the Barrow audience wanted to see and the audiences voted with their feet – not so much that they walked out, but didn't come in the first place. For the first time since I'd been there we seemed to be alienated from the town. And I can't say that I was surprised

– "we want to be entertained, we don't want all that stuff preaching at us" was the message we got loud and clear.

In March 1963 a major change in our lives was forecast when we discovered that Gilly was pregnant, and as the second summer came round we decided that with the baby due in October we'd better move on. It had been two years of unbelievably good times. Wonderful camaraderie, some good theatrical experience, hands-on working that must be every bit as good, if not better, than a drama school course, and a firm footing in the business. After two years of continuous work I could truly believe I was a professional actor. And London's streets would be paved with gold, wouldn't they?

Chapter Six

The streets aren't paved with gold; My son is born;

Touring, no money and a dreadful show

at the Palladium;

First TV work; Moving again;

A big break and a big disappointment;

Hello Doctor Who!

We left Barrow as the season ended in July. The old Wolseley had gone to the big car-breakers in the sky, and my mum scraped some money together to buy us an ex Post Office van. It was a pretty clapped out Bedford, and easily carried all of our belongings, including our only luxury, my granny's old wingback chair. She, incidentally, had died after a long battle with thyroid cancer in the spring. I think we both had deep misgivings about the move to London, because we knew it would be a long time before we would have such fun again. The memories came rushing in of the plays, the friends, the lakes, the sea, and the experience of being pretty big fish in a very small pond. We were about to become sprats in the ocean.

My old flat-mate Duncan let us move in with him for a while, as I tried to find us a permanent place to live. A top floor garret with no lift at number 49, Warrington Crescent in Maida Vale was the result of that search, and the rent was just about manageable at £4.5s a week. I had cashed in a small insurance policy when we got married, and there was still about £45 remaining of the original fortune of £127. But that small amount would have to keep us going for a while.

I signed on again in Marylebone, and with the National Assistance we could claim, we were in receipt of a fantastic £4.13s every week. Obviously I needed to get some work. Gilly was now quite heavily pregnant, and the 96 stairs to our flat were a real struggle for her. I call it our flat, but it was just an attic room, about 14ft by 14ft with sloping ceilings, and a small kitchenette through an open doorway. The Baby Belling cooker, a couple of pans and an electric kettle were our sole means of cooking. But we could, in the warm days of the Indian summer we experienced that year, get out onto a flat roof to sunbathe, overlooking the panorama of London to the east and south. And it was ours. We even had a really beat-up old TV in the corner that was well past its expiry date, but it gave us a hint of a flickering black and white picture – a touch of luxury. The optimism was bubbling out of us both, and Gilly stayed really healthy as the baby grew inside her.

It was a good hour's walk to central London, and I did that two or three times in the first two weeks, so I could trudge round agencies in the hope that someone would take an interest in my undoubted talent. After a couple of weeks I got lucky. I went to see Vincent Shaw. I think he was one of the first ports of call for most young actors, whether just out of drama school, or, like me, just back from a stint in the provinces. He had agreed to see me after a telephone call, and told me to come prepared to audition for him. His office was on the second floor in a grubby block on the corner of Greek Street in Soho. It was bright and clean enough inside, and Vincent, good as his word, watched from behind his desk, my attempts to be a convincing actor from a distance of no more than eight feet. I gave him my best Irish captain from *The Rough and Ready Lot*, and a piece from Pinter's *The Caretaker*. He was happy enough with what I did, though I cringe when I think of it now and he agreed to put me on his books. As I didn't have a telephone, I agreed to phone him twice a week to check on the progress he was making.

Well, I hadn't really struck gold. More like base metal. But after a couple of weeks, Vincent sent me for an audition with Arthur Lane and Audrey Lupton at the Wimbledon Theatre. They were casting for a short tour of *Witness for the Prosecution* starring the great Sonia Dresdel. I travelled on the underground out to the southern suburb, and with some fear, presented myself at the stage door. I was asked to read a scene from the play and to my surprise was offered the part of the doctor in the trial court, there and then. Arthur and Audrey said they would be contacting my agent with the dates and money and I went off back to Maida Vale with a real spring in my step.

The tour was a small matter of six dates starting at the beginning of September with a week's rehearsal. This was a critical time for Gilly and me because the baby was due at the end of October. Before starting work on the show, I had to find a hospital for the birth. Ideally I would be back from tour in plenty of time, but I wanted to get things sorted. It proved to be very difficult. None of the local maternity units had any space at the time we would need it, and we were put on some sort of citywide waiting list. As luck would have it, Bethnal Green Hospital in the East End was the appointment we got. Not the most convenient venue for us, but at least it was a guaranteed place.

With that settled I felt I could go off on tour, particularly as the money was considerably better than the dole. I got £15 a week, but out of that I had to pay for my travel, food, accommodation, Vincent's 10% and the London rent, and leave some money for Gilly. Hey ho the glamorous life!

At least the rehearsal and first week of the tour was in Wimbledon, and wasn't too expensive for me, but the only way I could make the tour fit the budget was if I lived in the van. So when the time came to go to the second date which was in Bath, I managed to get hold of an old straw-filled mattress from Duncan's flat and stuffed it into the back of the vehicle. That was to be my home for the next four weeks. In Bath I parked on a bombsite car park to the rear of the theatre, next to an original greasy spoon café. I managed a small breakfast there each morning, and they kindly let me use the sink in the washroom for my ablutions. And that's how it went for the rest of the tour, which took in Coventry, Westcliff on Sea (to which I could commute), and Hull. This was show business at its most gritty, but it was fun. I telephoned Gilly at fixed times every day – there was a payphone in the hall, and she seemed to be managing all right. But I knew that the stairs were hard for her.

One night in Bath, my sleep was interrupted by the police hammering on the side of the van. They grilled me about what I was doing and checked through all of my things – not that there was all that much of it – and eventually left me none the wiser. The next day I heard that there had been a robbery of the night mail train, and unusual vehicles were being checked by forces throughout the south of England. It was a crime that became infamous as The Great Train Robbery.

I enjoyed the tour, but I was glad to get home again to the garret and to my heavily pregnant lady. There was another small stroke of luck, in that Wimbledon Theatre asked me to play the lead in another play for them, starting immediately, this time only at Wimbledon and Westcliff. That meant I had another three weeks' work and I could work from home, and they paid me an extra £2 a week for it. Things were really looking up. Vincent also got me my first West End audition to understudy in *The Mousetrap*, but I didn't get the job.

Just after I finished the job in Westcliff, our son Matthew was born. Gilly's contractions had started and I drove her in the old van to Bethnal Green Hospital. But Matthew was in no hurry. Gilly was in a fairly painful labour for 36 hours in all. In the end I was sent home by the staff – fathers were not allowed anywhere near the birth in those days. I said I would wait, but was refused on the grounds that there was nowhere for me to wait, and I'd be in the way and so on. So I went back to Warrington Crescent and telephoned throughout the night until I've no doubt they were thoroughly sick of me. At last, when I rang at 5am I was told I had a son. I guess I broke all records for crossing London at that time, and rolled into the hospital to find Gilly with a lovely tiny boy in a small cot beside the bed. Gilly looked exhausted, as I am sure she was, and when I kissed her, she just burst into tears, and said "Never again". And she meant it. But the boy was worth it.

A few days after Gilly and Matthew came home, I had an audition as a singer with a group called the Derek Taverner Singers. This was a name invented for the chorus singers in a projected new show at the London Palladium, *Man in the Moon* to star Charlie Drake, and due to open before Christmas. A couple of days after the audition I was told by Vincent that I'd got the job. The show was due to run for a year, and rehearsals would begin in the middle of November. I was to be one of two top tenors in a chorus of eight boys and eight girls. And best of all, the pay was £32 a week for 12 shows. A fortune. I really felt I was on the way. But no one had asked if I could dance. Big mistake.

Two weeks later, with my job to return to, Gilly settled into the wingback chair in the back of the Bedford van, with Matthew in a small carrycot on the floor, and I drove us back to Barrow to show him off to my mum and dad. It was a long journey, but we made it in a little over eight hours, and we spent four days enjoying a relaxing time and some good home-cooked food. My sister, Judy was now nine, and took a real interest in the baby and I have to say he was a real beauty. Whilst there, we had him christened, Matthew Fraser Purves, in the same Methodist church in which we had got married 14 months earlier.

Gilly and I also went down to the theatre to see some of our old friends. A lot of things had changed – Donald and Bernard had left and the new artistic director was Giles Havergal, later to become a very well known director, and artistic director of the Glasgow Citizens Theatre. I cannot remember the play we saw, but we met Giles in the bar afterwards and we had a nice chat together. The chatter was insignificant, but unknowingly to either of us, he was to have a major impact on my life four years in the future.

I managed to fit in a gig with the Jazz band, which I found totally therapeutic, apart from the fact that there was a big fight in the pub that night, caused by a drunken heckler. Some of the band got involved, but I managed to keep out of it. It was great to see Les and Eileen again. They were the two people I had missed most, and our friendship was becoming, if anything, stronger. Les always claimed that Matthew was called Matt because he was conceived on their hearthrug in Paradise Street. And it may be true – I rather hope it is.

My mum was thrilled to see Matthew, and she shed a few tears when it was time for us to go back to the smoke. But I had a big job waiting and I was anxious for it to begin. On the way back, Gilly and I chatted about moving from our top floor cupboard, and on our return I contacted my old teacher friend, Rhys Davies. He had his ear to the ground for most things and I thought he might know of a flat we could use. Unfortunately he was in the midst of a divorce from his wife, Anne, a Hungarian refugee. But as luck would have it, he said she was looking for a lodger to help her pay the bills in her house on Hammersmith Mall. Sounded great, but in fact was a new small terrace house at the back of a filling station on the Great West Road. But we were to have a double bedroom, and use of the kitchen, bathroom and telephone for the same money we were paying for our other flat, and we jumped at it.

It proved to be a dreadful mistake. I started rehearsals for the Palladium, and many an evening I would get home to find Gilly, sitting on the end of the bed in tears. She and Anne really didn't get on at all, and although I was busy with the show, I did try to find us an alternative but that wasn't easy and took some time.

Peter Purves

In the meantime, *Man in the Moon* progressed towards the stage. As I said earlier, I had been engaged as a top tenor, and I now discovered that all of the singers were expected to be in the big production numbers and to dance, or at least to move! I'd always enjoyed dancing at the Jazz clubs and at earlier dances, but I was never much good and had approximately three left feet, so I was dreading the rehearsals with the choreographer. The singing hadn't been easy either. All of the rest of them could read music, and I had forgotten everything I had learned as a child, and had to listen very carefully to what the other top tenor, a much older chap called Lewis Henry, was singing, and try to learn it. Actually, once I'd got an idea of the tune I could follow the basic top line of the score, so I began to relax. But the first few rehearsals were so difficult; I was sure I was going to get found out and fired. It didn't happen and I got away with it, and after a week was beginning to enjoy it all. Mind you, the music was seriously awful, and although we hadn't seen any of the acting scenes with Mr Drake, we began to suspect it was a bit of a turkey. Then came the dancing. Michael Charnley, the camp Australian choreographer had the good sense to make sure that the singers were essentially at the back, so that his very good dancers could do their thing at the front. After two or three rehearsals, I can remember him walking round, watching various parts of one of the bigger numbers. He was saying complimentary things to some of his dancers, and then he came upon me and Lewis at the back doing what can only be described as indelicate musical gymnastics, and just said "Oh my God! It's Godzilla being done by King Kong!" And I think that was probably a pretty good summation!

Things progressed and the numbers sort of came together. The singing was pretty good – the male voices balanced well with two top tenors, two second tenors, two baritones and two basses. Sexually we were pretty well matched too with an equal number of gays and straights and the girls were pretty and sang well. Jenny Wren I remember particularly, she later appeared often at the old Players' Theatre under the Charing Cross arches, and has always been very friendly when I've met her over the years. One of the boy singers, David Rowley, became a good friend for a number of years until we lost touch. He was so nice to my little boy as he grew up and always asked after him.

Somehow I managed not to get fired, and the show moved towards opening. We never saw the actors or Charlie Drake until we got to the final stages of rehearsal, when we were added as extras to the various scenes. The director was Robert Nesbitt, a revered figure at the Palladium in those days, but he never even spoke to the chorus. We had met the principal singers. One was Eric Flynn, and another was the lovely Anna Dawson, who were both billed as the "Stars of Tomorrow". Eric was good fun, and there was nothing starry about him, or Anna for that matter. They were certainly very much a part of the company and not aloof from we underlings.

The show was a stinker. It had gadgets galore, it had a giant moon monster dragon, it had massive sets, it used the revolve stage, and it had a 30 piece orchestra in the pit, conducted by the legendary Billy Ternent. And it had Charlie Drake, and there lay the problem. No one else had a look in as far as the story went, and it was purely a vehicle for him to be not very funny. There were several other actors who had very small parts as scientific boffins and military people and newspaper reporters but that was it. They were sorely wasted, and I guess their only pleasure was in making up a four for bridge between matinees and evening performances; something that I was pleased to be part of too.

The critics panned the show, and the audiences stayed away in their thousands. At the start of the second half of the show, supposedly we were on the moon, and it began with a moon ballet which was quite stylish actually. We singers stepped out as the curtain went up onto the apron wings of the stage, and started to sing. Then the ballet started. We then had nothing to do except stand there for about five minutes as the dance went on. One evening

Peter Purves

I counted the audience. There were 167 people in the house, that's all, in a theatre that could seat something nearer to 3000. That size of audience wasn't unusual. On another evening there was a bit of a tangle with the microphone cables (no radio mics in those days) as we walked on, and I got tied back against the proscenium arch. The singer following me, John Gordon, took one look, threw his arms up and ran off stage. The eight singers on the opposite wing could see what was going on and burst out laughing, so did I and so did the girls on my side of the stage. And when the moment came for us to sing, only the first boy on my side was able to get out a note. Even the orchestra members facing us were in mild hysterics, and the only person not laughing was Billy Ternent who was patently furious. At that point on walked Eric Flynn to sing whilst the ballet continued, and when he got to centre stage he could hear the laughter that was now convulsing the audience, and could see some of the dancers were shaking. Before singing he looked down to check his flies. Chaos all round. The stage director was Dave Jackley, brother of a very famous act of the time, Nat Jackley. He gave us all a severe dressing down, talking about unprofessionalism and the rest, but I suspect he saw the funny side too.

The show was supposed to run for a year and had cost £75,000 to stage, which was a massive sum in those days. All but two matinees were cancelled after the first two weeks of the run and our money was reduced accordingly to £24 a week. The show limped through to Easter, when it was finally put to rest after a miserable three month run, and what had seemed like a wonderful year long job had been snuffed out in a flash. We were all thrown out onto the labour market again. I was beginning to learn about insecurity!

The only good thing that happened during the run was that I was able to find us a flat in Thurleigh Road, SW11, between Wandsworth Common and Clapham Common, now one of the more fashionable addresses in South London, but then still undiscovered and we were able to escape from the Great West Road. But now I didn't have a job and the rent still had to be paid.

Here's one I wrote earlier...

David Rowley and one or two of the other singers had got jobs in the chorus at the Prince of Wales Theatre in a new show starring the singer Max Bygraves and the chorus needed a dresser. He suggested me, and although I hadn't a clue what was expected of me, I accepted the job. At least it meant I could go for auditions and stuff during the day and could leave at the drop of a hat. All the job actually entailed was keeping the clothing rails tidy, taking articles for repair to the wardrobe department, and making sure that clothes were ready for the boys when they came for a quick change. Not too difficult really, but I was dreadful at it. One of the boys, Alan Hollidge who had also been with us at the Palladium, was a very good caricaturist, and he drew me in typical pose. I still have the drawing.

All this time, Gilly was doing a brilliant job of bringing up our little lad, and he was getting quite sturdy. We had even managed to buy a third-hand pram – one of those that nanny's use to wheel their charges round Kensington Gardens. It was most luxurious, and we were able in those days to park it outside the flat, with a fly curtain over it, and let Matthew soak up the fresh air. There was never a thought that he might be stolen away or would come to harm. And he didn't.

Round about June I went for an audition at the BBC to meet the director of an episode of Z-Cars, which was a hugely popular twice weekly series on TV. I was cast as a bus conductor who was interviewed by Brian Blessed (PC Fancy Smith) about a suspect who'd been on my bus. I was thrilled. It was my first television part, and although it was only a cough and a spit it was a foothold, and it was all adding to my experience. What was most daunting about it was that the show was "live", and you could cut the tension in the studio, before we went on air, with a knife. I remember when I got the contract, and I was seriously broke, going to the local bank at Clapham Junction. It was the Westminster Bank in those days, and I asked to open an account with them. Then I asked if, on the strength of my contract I could have a small overdraft. I was going to earn £30 for the role, and the bank manager agreed to let me have £10. I've been with the same bank ever since, though not the same branch.

I had parted company with Vincent Shaw by this time, and had another agent, and they started trying to get me other TV work. It didn't exactly pour in, and so, when I wasn't working, Gilly went to work at the National Film Theatre on the South Bank, where she had worked previously when she was at Drama school. So we weren't exactly broke, though we had very little to spare. I did get a few jobs on the shows that were the popular shows of the day. I was thrilled to be cast by the great Michael Mills, (the man responsible for legions of hit comedies for the BBC) to play a small comedy part in *The World of Wooster* with Ian Carmichael, who turned out to be a delightful man. Funnily enough, in later years I was to use his daughter Sally as the make-up girl on a number of corporate videos I produced. But comedy was what I liked playing best, although to be honest I haven't, over the years, had a lot of opportunity in that direction. Wooster was made even more exciting because we filmed the scenes at Ealing Studios, the former home of some of the greatest English film comedies. In the nearby pub, one lunchtime, I even met an elderly actor who was already becoming a legend of television – William Hartnell, who was filming for an early episode of a show called *Doctor Who*!

There were agents who specialised in work at particular studios. One man every budding actor had to visit was Ronnie Curtis who cast a lot of very low budget movies made at Merton Park Studios. I had been warned that when I went to see him, not to look over my shoulder. I didn't know what had been meant until I walked into his rather seedy office near Seven Dials. He had such a wall-eye that you were convinced there was someone behind you, and of course, I looked round. But he did cast me in an Edgar Lustgarten Mystery film whose name eludes me, and I earned a bob or two. I did another bit of something at Shepperton for a few pounds, and was in an episode of *Gideon's*

Way that was shot at Elstree. The latter was almost a major embarrassment. When I was cast, I was asked if I could ride a motorbike. Of course I said yes – even though my only experience had been of a bike owned by a student back at Alsager and I had fallen off it quite regularly. But there was no way I was going to miss out on a job by saying I couldn't ride. How difficult could it be anyway? Very difficult is the answer to that. When I arrived on the set I was given the few pages of script that would involve me. I read with horror the directions that described my riding along beside a van and trying to get on the running board of the van before riding off. No one had told me there would be a stunt man for that bit, so I spent a terrifying half hour at lunchtime trying to get to grips with the BSA 350 that I had to ride. All's well that ends well, and I got away with it, but I would think twice before saying I could do something that I couldn't. And I determined to learn to ride a motorbike! I also appeared in an episode of *Redcap* with John Thaw, and *The Saint* with Roger Moore, but unfortunately I never met him. One of the bigger parts I played was in an episode of *Dixon of Dock Green*. Vere Lorimer, a lovely chap and one of the legendary old school of BBC directors, directed it. He was easy to work with even under the terrible pressure of the schedule, and I had a very happy couple of weeks working on the show. The whole cast was fabulous, from Jack Warner at the helm, and Peter Byrne whom I was to work with again many years later, to the lowliest bit part player. I played opposite Helen Fraser, who was one of the up and coming young leading ladies of the 60's. Jack, himself, was a remarkable chap. I'd only ever worked with him on that one appearance, but whenever I bumped into him over the next few years he knew my name and greeted me warmly.

I changed my agent again because I felt I wasn't being seen for enough work, but nothing much changed. The house in Thurleigh Road was being sold and we had to move again, and we found a cheap flat in a 1940's block in Streatham. Not what we wanted, but we didn't have much choice. This move came in the autumn of 1964 but both Gilly and I knew it was only going to be temporary.

I guess our friends and social life was what kept us going through these fairly difficult months. In total I had only worked a few weeks since the collapse of *Man in the Moon*, and I was becoming quite a good househusband as Gilly kept a few pennies coming in from her work at the NFT. Whilst I was a dresser at the Prince of Wales, it turned out that one of the chorus, Alan Lynton had been at the Guildhall with Gilly, and he became a good friend. None of us had much money, and so we'd while away the time playing the odd game of Monopoly or other board games and occasionally go out for a drink. Gilly also had old friends out in Billericay, Essex who worked for Ford, the motor giant. Harry Worrall was a skilled mechanic, and had come up to Barrow to see Gilly in rep. He worked on cars that his good friend Rod Mansfield raced. They were a good team and over the years became very good. Rod was a works driver for a while and led a number of saloon car teams. He and his gorgeous wife Val have just celebrated their 50th wedding anniversary. Harry had met Madeleine Blakeney on the Barrow visit, and they became close and married, and had it not been for her tragic capitulation to cancer, they too would have been approaching a big anniversary now. We spent several weekends with them at that time, and always enjoyed their company. We would occasionally go to support Rod's racing, but twice at Brands Hatch we witnessed him come off the track in spectacular fashion, so I began to suspect we were a bit of a jinx!

Then, much to our surprise, my mum and dad decided they wanted to be nearer to us and sold up the business in Barrow and bought a small village store and post office in the village of Horton, just to the west of Heathrow Airport. That meant we would spend every other weekend there, eating well, and mum was able to enjoy Matthew growing up. They inherited a dog again, a black German Shepherd called Kipper, and he was a real beauty. We would take him swimming in the Thames at places like Runnymede and Windsor, and although we were poor financially, our life was pretty good. Dad helped me to buy another car so we could make the journey more easily. It was an old 1950's model Ford Popular and cost an astronomical £50, but it was a Rolls Royce to us.

Occasional work kept on coming in. Alan Cooke cast me as a confessional Monk in John Osborne's *Luther* for the BBC. It really was a cough and a spit, with a couple of days learning some Plain Song, and then three days rehearsal followed by a studio shoot. Alec McCowan, a most respected actor of the time, and a delightful man, played Luther himself. In an early scene in the play, when I stepped up to the altar to receive a rather large candle from him he quietly muttered "stick that up your arse!" And this was during the recording! I was totally nonplussed, and it was all I could do not to burst out laughing. Alec just carried on being pious!

Towards the end of 1964 I went to meet the director, Alvin Rakoff, who was casting for a new Armchair Theatre. This was a series of one hour plays produced by ABC TV (later to become Thames) at Twickenham, and was one of the principal drama series' on TV at that time. This particular play could not have been more appropriate for me because it involved a photographer from Blackpool who gets involved with a pretty girl and enters her into the Miss Great Britain contest at the Winter Gardens. It was written by Allan Prior, a Blackpool chap himself, and with whom I became quite friendly. I spent a couple of nervous weeks before Alvin eventually decided I was the man for the part. It was called *The Girl in the Picture*, and playing opposite me and also getting her first big break in TV was Nicola Pagett. Suddenly, for me this was big league. We rehearsed in London and then flew up to Manchester to film on location in Blackpool. It was a big unit, and we filmed for four days at the end of the illuminations, before returning to London to complete the show in the studios at Teddington Lock. The escape from Blackpool was dramatic – the illumination traffic meant that the roads out of town were terribly congested, and the production manager managed to get us a police escort with sirens and flashing lights out of town in order to catch our flight from Manchester Airport. It was all great fun, and I knew that this was what I had been waiting for all my life. I spent four days chatting up Nicola, who rebuffed my every approach, and rightly so. But we had a good chemistry on screen, and later, when the play was transmitted, we each received quite a complimentary review. However, that was a month or so away. I learned a lot from Alvin. He was a most experienced director and was very respected by his crew. In the studio he was immensely helpful, and gave me a lot of confidence. But it was just one job, and the money didn't last forever – I can't remember exactly the fee, but it was less than £100. So it was back to pestering the agent and looking for the next job.

Eventually it came. Peter Plummer was directing an episode of *The Villains* up in Manchester for Granada. I was cast as Mike Pratt's brother in my second leading role on TV. We were a couple of crooks operating a scam with a base somewhere on Saddleworth Moor. It was pretty violent stuff, and one scene which had me catching my hand on a spiked railing during a fight was so bloody that it was cut from the final transmission. The fight arranger was a professional wrestler called Tommy Mann, who also owned a big nightclub in the city. Mike and I spent several very boozy evenings in that club, and Mike became a long-standing friend until his very untimely death from cancer. The show was the first and only time I worked for Granada. It may have been my fault, in that I was dreadfully late for my first filming call. I was staying with an old school friend, David Johnson, in Fallowfield, which is a fair distance from the studio. Unfortunately, on the morning of the shoot it had snowed, and buses were thrown into chaos. In fact there just weren't any. David had no telephone, and mobiles hadn't been invented. There were no taxis on the streets, I couldn't find a serviceable public telephone and in the end I walked to the studios. Anyone who knows Manchester will know that it is not a short stroll. I eventually got a bus, and that got me to the studio one and a half hours late. The crew and the rest of the cast had already gone by coach to the moor land location and Mr Plummer was waiting for me at Granada with an expression of total fury. All I could do was apologise and keep my lip buttoned. As it happened the shoot was still completed on time, and was, by all accounts, very good. But any rapport I may have had with the director was gone. Still, none of that showed on screen and I was quite pleased with my performance.

After that things went very quiet. After several weeks, Caroline, my agent, asked me to go to meet a director on *Doctor Who*. Richard Martin was looking for actors who could "move" to play giant butterflies and moths in one of the stories. She had sold me on the basis that I had been in the chorus at the Palladium so I must be able to move well. Oh yes? Anyway, the audition was on a Monday, and it so happened that on the previous Sunday, *The Girl in the Picture* was shown on ITV in the prime slot.

When I got to the BBC, broke again as usual, I nervously waited for my appointment with Richard. As soon as I walked in he was most friendly and easy. He had seen the play the previous evening and commenced praising me for my performance. So I was convinced he would cast me in his new serial. But no! He told me that the parts he had on offer were not really speaking parts and that he wouldn't insult me by asking me to play one of them. Great as that was as a compliment, I really needed a job, so I was most upset that it wasn't to be. But Richard did say that when he was casting something more worthy of me, then he would get in touch. I took that with a pinch of salt. I thought he was just saying that to soften the blow. Actors do get lied to an awful lot, and it was never a good thing to believe everything you were told. My cynicism was growing.

I barely worked for a few months – I think I may have done a couple of episodes of Z-Cars, but that was all, and Gilly and I continued to struggle to make ends meet. Matthew was now well past his first birthday, and was walking and growing and money was a perpetual worry for us. Thank goodness for the NFT which continued to employ Gilly on a casual basis.

But then out of the blue, my agent got a call offering me a cameo part in *Doctor Who*. Richard Martin had been as good as his word, and had cast me, without an audition, as Morton Dill, an American Hillbilly visiting New York in episode three of *The Chase*. This was a 10 minute scene at the top of the Empire State Building, where a group of tourists are being given the guided tour. My character becomes detached from the group, in time to meet the Doctor and his travelling companions as they arrive in the Tardis. Later, I also meet the Daleks who have arrived in a pursuing time machine. The results were, and remain very funny. I never saw the episode when it was first transmitted, but it was shown at a convention I attended in Chicago five years ago and I was happily surprised.

We rehearsed in a Territorial Army drill hall in Acton, and I loved every second of it. I got on really well with Russ (William Russell), and Jacqueline Hill, the two original cast members who became Bill Hartnell's travelling companions. And Jacquie was married to Alvin Rakoff in real life. Small world, showbusiness! The younger girl companion was Maureen O'Brien, a lovely girl, who became a wonderful actress and writer. Bill Hartnell himself was friendly enough, if a bit crotchety – I refrained from reminding him of the one occasion we had met in the pub at Ealing. Richard directed sensitively, and gave me plenty of rein in the comedy playing. He toned down the bits that were too big, and encouraged me by laughing when I was funny. Always a help I can assure you.

What was most surprising was what happened next. We recorded the show as if it was live at the BBC's Riverside Studios in Hammersmith – not a bad venue and with a pub opposite that was known as Studio Three! The

My mother holding my baby sister, Judith, March 1965.

Me, aged 10, with one of our cats outside the pub in Derbyshire.

With Mum and Dad on holiday in Scarborough. I was aged 11.

Two college productions
We're no Angels...

And Moliere's
The Miser.

Bernard Gallagher and I in a farce/thriller called Wanted One Body (1961) for The Renaissance Theatre Company in Barrow.

My first publicity still. So moody (1961).

Playing
Professor
Serebriakov in
Uncle Vanya.
I was all of 22
years old!!

Early days on Blue Peter with Valerie, John, and a lot of dogs.

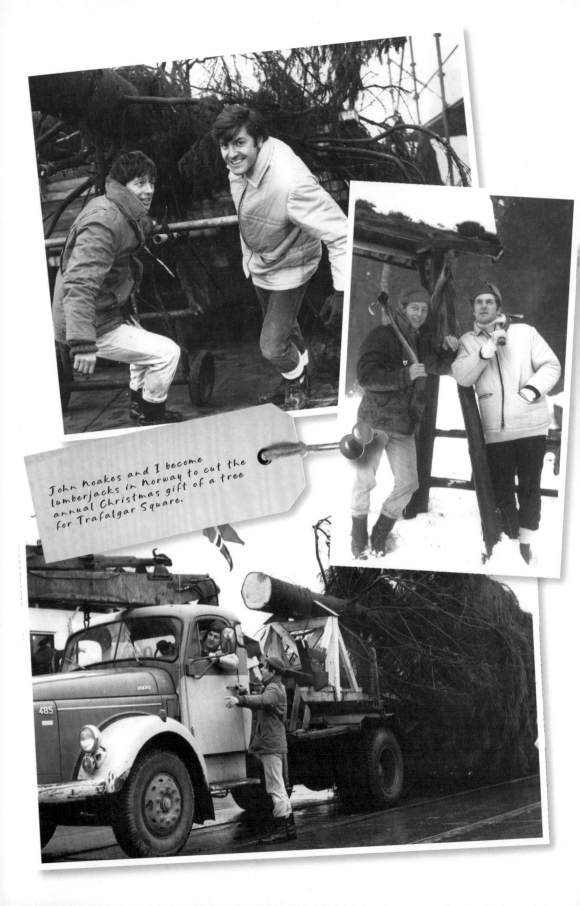

John Noakes and I become lumberjacks in Norway to cut the annual Christmas gift of a tree for Trafalgar Square.

One of the many Blue Peter painting competitions we judged, seen here with then Doctor Who actor Patrick Troughton, 1967.

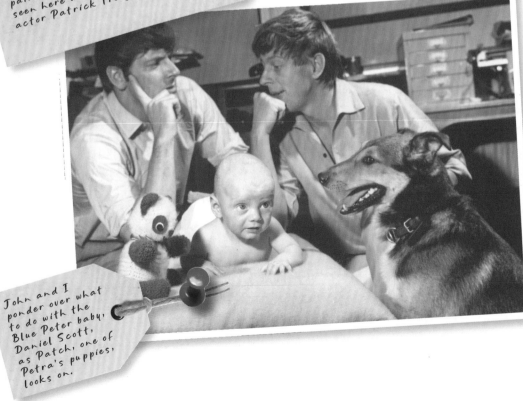

John and I ponder over what to do with the Blue Peter baby, Daniel Scott, as Patch, one of Petra's puppies, looks on.

I believe these were circus elephants from either Billy Smart's or Chipperfield's. Certainly this was not the famous Lulu incident.

In the studio
with Princess
Anne after the
Blue Peter Royal
Safari to Kenya.
The princess
was absolutely
charming.

Me attending a
Lifeboat day at
Port Isaac to
support one
of the Blue
Peter Inshore
Rescue Boats.

Close up of an
Ugly Sister,
and acting with
the legendary
'Arthur Askey'
together with
Noakesy and
Lesley Judd.

A studio "still" during rehearsals, circa 1974. Shep is now on the scene.

Attending a fete somewhere or other, in the 70s with a young Blue Peter fan.

John and I attend an old motorcycle rally near Cheltenham in 1972 or 3.

I think this was a Blue Peter birthday party, but I can't be sure.

I cannot recall a single thing about this rather gargantuan studio item. It must have been a hot-air balloon basket, but that is only a guess.

Lesley and I attend a massive fete in Portsmouth for HMS Collingwood.

COLLINGWOOD QUEEN

H·M·S COLLINGWOOD AUTUMN 1. PM to 5.30. PM - TO·DAY

Two studies of me with Petra, the first Blue Peter dog who lived most of her life with me and the family.

Walking the cable of the Forth Road Bridge in Scotland.

PETRA
1962
1977

Beside the beautiful bronze bust of Petra, by artist William Timyn (Tim). It stood proudly outside the main entrance to the BBC Television Centre for years. Now she is relegated to an overgrown and untended part of the Blue Peter garden.

Cindy and Buttons, two of the puppies I "walked" on the programme for the Guide Dogs for the Blind Association.

Once again I fall off my bike during the trials course I took with the Royal Signals, before finally being awarded an honorary White Helmet.

recording went well, nothing went seriously wrong, and we finished on time. As I prepared to leave the studio, the producer, Verity Lambert, whom I had met briefly at the technical rehearsal at the drill hall, and the story editor, Dennis Spooner, came up to me and said how much they had enjoyed my performance and asked if I would like to join them for a drink in Studio Three. Nothing very surprising in that, but I was flattered to have been asked. You can imagine my surprise when, after a brief moment, Verity asked if I knew that Russ and Jacquie were leaving the show in three weeks time, and then hit me with the bombshell question. "We wondered if you would be interested in taking over!" I nearly dropped my pint!

Chapter Seven

The ups and downs of a TV series;

The BBC pay me peanuts;

Bill Hartnell, a man of contrasts;

Bill's greatest gaffe;

Behind the scenes; Some pleasures and some

disappointments;

My contract isn't renewed

Would I? I was absolutely staggered, and replied without thinking that I would be thrilled to take over. Whereupon they expressed their delight, and Dennis asked me to come to the Television Centre the following morning at 11.00am and we'd talk things through. And that was that. To say I was euphoric, when I got back home from the studio after the Morton Dill episode, would be an understatement. I just hope that the delightful Richard Martin knows how much I appreciate what he did for me. And after meeting with Dennis and Verity, I felt the most wonderful optimism surge through me. Out of the blue, and totally unplanned I had gone in a moment from being a small part player to a regular character in what was to become one of the greatest cult shows of the past 50 years. The following morning Steven Taylor was born when

Here's one I wrote earlier…

Dennis took me through the character. He had written the first story in which I was to be involved, and had also handled the way in which Russ and Jacquie left, and I was introduced. I was to be a stranded space pilot from the future, and the Doctor and his team rescue me whilst bringing the serial, *The Chase*, to a conclusion. The odd thing about it was that I was to appear in episode six as Steven, having just played Morton Dill in episode three of the same serial. A quick growth of a stubble beard and some make-up made me look sufficiently different and three weeks later I was a regular in the series.

For the first time in almost two years I had a job that was just like normal folk! I worked Monday to Friday week in and week out. It was quite a punishing schedule in TV terms. We rehearsed from Monday to Wednesday with a full run through of the show on Thursday morning. On Thursday afternoon the technical crew turned up and we did another two runs for them, so that lighting and sound could make sure everything would work, and that the cameras could actually shoot what the director desired. The first technical run was always quite scary, because the crew were looking at everything but your performance. The whole exercise was so much more about the technical achievement than it had ever been in the theatre but it was still fun. Then on the Friday we would go into the studio and rehearse with the cameras. That normally took the morning and a fair bit of the afternoon and it could, after the first flushes of excitement, be quite tedious. There was so much to get right and as we had to record with virtually no breaks – the only breaks being for special effects or for the playing of telecine (the forerunner of videotape) – there were a lot of things that everyone had to rehearse with great precision. There were also the technical difficulties of making sure cameras moved from scene to scene at the right time. You could have one scene at one end of the studio with four cameras, and the next scene, also requiring four cameras would be at the other end of the studio. As we only ever had five or six cameras in the studio, that could require some very fast moves and the giant sound booms had also to be moved up and down the studio – remember no radio mics in those days.

Then with those rehearsals complete, there would be a break for the boffins to line-up the cameras, matching their pictures and output, and we were ready for a dress run. Into costume and make-up and the show was then performed as if it was the recording. Supper break came next and at about 7.30pm we would record the show. Normally I think the BBC schedules allowed two and a half times the programme length for the recording slot. As we were a 25-minute programme that meant everything had to be in the can by 8.45pm. Not much leeway in there, and it meant that we, the actors, had to get it right. Unless we made a truly dramatic cock-up there would be no likelihood of a retake. None of the *It'll be Alright on the Night* attitude, that seems to make every actor and presenter look totally incompetent. Mostly we got it right, rather than the other way round. Not always, however, but even Bill Hartnell's script errors were transmitted as recorded – his most famous line ever, being "I am not a Dog, a God" in an episode of the *Myth Makers* about the siege of Troy.

Unfortunately the BBC wiped a whole lot of the episodes in which I appeared. I made 44 episodes in total, and only about 15 still exist. That was because we recorded on two inch tape, and the cartridges were enormous and heavy. Storing them was a real problem, in terms of space required alone. So many shows had their tapes wiped in order for them to be re-used, with the loss of some gems on the way. But even though there were no such things as domestic video recorders at that time, there were still viewers fanatical enough about the "goggle-box" that they recorded the sound off air on reel-to-reel machines. In the case of *Doctor Who*, someone recorded every episode I made, and those tapes have in the past 10 years been found, remastered and digitised, and I have remade audio versions of each serial. The producer of the collection, Mark Ayres, was fastidious in leaving the original soundtrack untouched and unedited, so every pause and every mistake remains. I added commentary links to explain the visuals, which are obviously missing, and though I say it myself, they come out as pretty good radio plays. But that didn't happen until the late 1990's and right now I am still in 1965.

Two things happened early on that stopped the show being the pleasure I had hoped it would be. The first was the deal my agent struck, which was far from the best one ever. I was paid £30 per show, with an extra £5 for any filming work that may be needed so there was no way I was going to become rich on the show. But to put that into context, it was the mid 60's, when £1000 a year was a good executive salary, and I would be earning at least £1500, so I guess it wasn't too bad. The second was much more important. Dennis Spooner had talked at great length to me about Steven's character. He was a headstrong, brave young man, who had a lot of ability and skill – let's face it, I don't think a space pilot was likely to be dumb. He was also going to be quite argumentative, giving him a lot of opportunity to fall out with the Doctor. Bill liked that element in the character as well, because it would give him something to bounce off, and react to and in the first serial, *The Time Traveller*, that character came to the fore. I was having fun and I got on very well with the director, a hugely talented chap called Douglas Camfield. He and his wife Sheila became very good friends of mine and Gilly's and I always looked forward to working with him. Sadly he wasn't terribly well and had a heart condition that killed him whilst still comparatively young. We had a lot of laughs on that first serial, not least because there was another principal character called the Meddling Monk, who also had a Tardis, and that character was played by the wonderful Peter Butterworth, truly one of the nicest people in the business, and seriously funny. His timing was perfection, and it was a joy to work with him.

The second thing to upset me happened three weeks in, when we got the scripts for the next serial, which was *Galaxy 4*. Steven's character just didn't exist. The story involved a group of Amazonian women who capture Steven and he can't do anything about it, so for much of the piece he is a prisoner of these delectable ladies. Not, quite the heroic character I had expected to play.

The reason was simple enough, but it was never made plain to me at the time. It was a classic case of the left hand not knowing what the right was doing. William Emms, who wrote the script, had written it with Jacqueline Hill's character in mind, and when I was cast to replace both her and Russ, it was too late to seriously alter the concept of the story. In fact William told me later that it was only shortly before the first read-through that he had been told there had been a cast change. I fully understand now, but at the time I was mortified and I couldn't discuss it with Dennis because he had moved on, as had Verity. I'd been in the job three weeks and the two most important people in my professional life at that time, had handed over to two others, Donald Tosh and John Wiles.

I suppose I could have had a serious strop and threatened to walk out (both things I considered) but after expressing my disappointment at the read-through, I let it drop. No point in cutting one's nose off to spite one's face, an adage I have tried to live with all my life – not always successfully, I regret to say.

If I think about it, *Galaxy 4* was a pretty good yarn, if it hadn't been for Steven's impotence and we did have some fun with it. My friendship with Bill and Maureen was growing all the time and Bill began to take a sort of mentoring role with me – giving me little tips here and there about how to act on the small screen. He obviously thought I did everything a bit too big and tried to get me to tone it down. Actually if you watch Bill in the show, he does an awful lot of small hand movements up near his face, and that was because if he was doing a gesture he was damn sure that the camera could see it. It made the Doctor even more idiosyncratic.

The director this time was Derek Martinus, who had been a drama teacher at RADA. Sadly he was very inexperienced in the TV studio. On our first recording day we went into crew overtime when he got his cameras and sound booms seriously tangled up. It was one of the few occasions when we had to do some major retakes. During the second week his PA tried to show him on the studio ground plan how he could plan his camera and boom moves by attaching discs with string, clipped to the appropriate plug positions for each camera and sound boom. Then he could move the cameras and see how the cables would loop – bearing in mind that cameras were too heavy in those days to move them over another camera's cable.

Solved, or so you'd think. The next recording, cameras got tangled in each other's cables again, causing another unplanned recording break. I know that his PA spoke to him again, and asked if he hadn't tried out the discs and string plan. The reply was that he hadn't, because "the strings keep on getting tangled up"!! You have to laugh, and in fact I like Derek very much, and was pleased to use him as director on a very ambitious video I produced in the early 1990's so no hard feelings there. By episodes three and four he'd got the hang of it, and there was no more tangling of the cables.

We rehearsed each week in another TA drill hall at the corner of Shepherd's Bush Green, and that suited Bill perfectly. There were good restaurants on the Green at that time, and as Bill liked his food, his lunches were soon sorted. In fact he often would ask me to join him, and we would cross over to Bertorelli's, a lovely old-fashioned restaurant, with white tablecloths, and napkins, and waitresses in black satin with small white aprons and bob caps. It was so traditional, and damn good food to boot. Actually the original Bertorelli's had been in Charlotte Street and many a student or out of work actor had kept body and soul together by being given delicious minestrone at a special discount. But for Bill it was an opportunity for a good fillet steak and a glass of red wine and on the many occasions I joined him, he taught me to appreciate a very rare steak and wouldn't consider me paying either for him or for myself. Consequently Gilly and I repaid him by taking him out for an Indian meal occasionally, and every fortnight or so we would have him over to our new flat.

The contract had meant that Gilly and I could think about moving from our grotty little flat in Streatham, and we'd put out some feelers. As it happened, our former landlord in Thurleigh Road had a property at No1 Cornwall Gardens, on the corner of Gloucester Road, near to South Kensington and he had an available flat on the second floor. We took it. We had a West London address and things were looking up. To help pay the rent, we offered a room to Bernard Gallagher, one of our friends and colleagues from Barrow and he stayed with us getting on for a year. He also served as a very good baby-sitter on occasion!

With a decent flat and a very fashionable address, it was a great place to have a party, to which we invited Bill. Round about this time, Kenneth Tynan caused a national rumpus by using the word "fuck" on television for the first time. Bill was visiting us on the Monday after the weekend gaffe, and we were sitting with him and a couple of friends in the living room, and I asked what did anyone think of what Mr Tynan had said? Bill went off like a bomb. "It was disgusting," he ranted, "how dare he use language like that on television in the living room. You wouldn't go into someone's living room and use fucking language like that." And we nearly split our sides trying not to laugh out loud. He never realised what he'd said.

The series took a break for the late summer, six weeks I think it was, and so we parted company after *Galaxy 4*. We returned in the autumn ready for another season and more fun. Or so we thought. The first series after the break was *The Myth Makers*. It was a stunning cast – Max Adrian was King Priam of Troy, Francis de Wolf was King Agamemnon, Barrie Ingham was Paris – and the whole serial was the most exciting since I had joined the show but it turned out to be an unhappy experience for several reasons. Not least was the fact that we had a read-through of episode one and we got the three later scripts during the week, only to discover that Maureen's character, Vicki, was written out of the series at the end of episode four. She was to stay in Troy as "Cressida". When she received the script, that was the first time she discovered her contract was not being renewed. No reason was given, it was a fait accompli and she had been allowed to go away for a six week break without anyone informing her that she didn't have much of a job to return to. In addition, Bill got very funny with Max Adrian. Max was gay, which Bill would probably have found offensive, and he was Jewish. I can recall Max, whom I often gave a lift to a convenient underground station after work, saying to me "Peter, what is the matter with Bill? He won't speak to me, and I've known him for years." It was baffling to him, but I can only assume it was his sexual and religious orientations. Apart from when the script dictated it, I don't think Bill said a word to Max in the four weeks we were all together.

Francis de Wolf didn't get on with Bill either. Bill was beginning to have difficulty in remembering his lines, and in the second episode, when Bill had been quite crotchety and awkward – he always got that way when his memory failed him – Francis had to invite Bill into his tent with the lines "Come in Doctor, sit down and have a ham-bone". Instead Francis delivered the immortal "Come in Doctor, sit down ham, and have a bone". That did require a retake!

Our director for this serial was Michael Leeston-Smith, whose first loves were his polo ponies (he had two) and his families (he also had two, I think). He would turn up for rehearsals reminiscent of the silent-film director, Eric von Stroheim, in his jodhpurs, riding boots and with a cowboy hat. I thought he was fun – Bill didn't like him at all because he told me he thought he was a clown. But I had good chats with him, first when we filmed a wonderful swordfight between me and Barrie Ingham on location at Frensham Ponds, which served for the beach outside Troy. And he shot the whole serial with a genuine feel for the time and with great sensitivity. I think it is one of my favourite serials from my time on the show. But underlying it all was the fact that we were to lose lovely Maureen at the end. I think she was a great loss to the programme, but as the following storyline was largely led by a woman, that couldn't have been Maureen's character. Who in their right mind becomes an actor? You are always at the beck and call and dependent upon the whim of somebody else. I am surprised we aren't all gibbering wrecks.

So at the end of the serial we said our goodbyes, although Gilly and I remained in contact with Maureen and her partner for a couple of years, before we lost touch. By this time, Matthew was two years old, and an absolute delight. Gilly was beginning to get restless in so far as she wanted to be back acting again, but in our business starting again is as hard as it was first time. At least we had an element of security in that I was working full-time and the bills were getting paid. Our friend Bernard got work at the National Theatre so we were beginning to feel a quite successful household. Our social life was good, and I had been introduced to a really good actors club in the centre of town, The Buckstone Club, which served moderately good food, and the drink was served until late. One of the regular barmen or stewards at that time was the delightful Bert Kwok, many years before he struck fame as Cato in the *Pink Panther* movies. It was a good place to unwind late at night, and to meet ones friends in town.

Enter and exit the lovely Adrienne Hill. As far as we all knew, she was the replacement for Maureen, and she joined the Tardis from Troy. But not for long. Our next serial was a massive 12-parter called the *Dalek Master Plan*, and in episode four she was literally sucked out into space, and Jean Marsh arrived to take her place. It was getting pretty confusing for both me and for Bill – I was beginning to feel a trifle insecure myself, and Bill was the only constant. Having said that there were rumours at that time that the powers that be were looking at ways in which even he might be replaced, and he certainly was not in the best of health for much of that period.

Here's one I wrote earlier...

For such a rambling serial it needed a director well schooled in the world of *Who*. Re-enter Dougie Camfield. As previously he was just great to work with and he made the serial work. It was a terribly convoluted story with all manner of top-drawer actors being involved. The principal baddie was Mavic Chen invented wonderfully by the excellent Kevin Stoney. Nicholas Courtney, later to become the Brigadier with UNIT in later series', made his first *Who* appearance as Bret Vyon; Peter Butterworth's extraordinary Meddling Monk made a comeback; Terence Woodfield, and Bryan Mosley were there too – it was an epic. But until we reconstructed it as a radio play in the early 2000's I couldn't remember much about it. It even had an episode especially for Christmas in which we visited Hollywood and made a series of Keystone Cop style sketches, and even those were a mystery to me until the reconstruction!

What I do remember clearly however is that I had a short fling with each of the two leading ladies, Adrienne and Jean. The trouble with our business is that one meets really interesting and attractive people all the time, and sometimes it is hard to resist (if you'll pardon the expression). I was genuinely sorry that Adrienne was written out so soon, and she, like Maureen before her, had no idea that she wasn't going to be the regular girl in the programme. Jean was a different case, in that she knew her character would die horribly at the end of the serial, and she duly obliged. I met up with her again a few years ago when we worked together on a short film for *Blue Peter*, and I found her as lovely and as delightful as ever she had been.

There was one other thing. Until that serial, everything the Doctor could do had a certain logic about it. In episode eight or nine, the cliffhanger was that we couldn't get back into the Tardis – I think the Meddling Monk had damaged the lock or stolen the key or something. Calm as you like the Doctor pulls a magic screwdriver, that we had never seen or spoken of before, out of his pocket, which magicked the door open. Even Bill thought that was preposterous. When I look at the excellent modern version of the show, magic stuff like that is commonplace, but at the time we all felt it was a bit of a cheat. However, we had to get inside, and that was the way it was done. On that same episode, with Peter Butterworth in his most mischievous mood, Jean, Peter and I got a horrendous fit of the giggles. Each time we tried to get on with the show we started to giggle again until the producer, John Wiles, came screaming out of the control gallery and yelled at us to control ourselves. We just shrieked. It was a full 10 minutes or so before we could continue and to this day I can't recall what was said that set us off. It must have been very funny indeed.

Then came *The Massacre*. Of all the serials I think this was the best script of all, and in many ways it was the result of non-collaboration between the story editor Donald Tosh and the commissioned writer John Lucarotti. However the final script was arrived at and the result was a grim and brilliant story about a fairly obscure piece of French religious history. I loved it, because the part Steven had to play was the first bit of really serious acting I had done since joining the show. I believe it was the first time in the programme's history that the companion took centre stage. The director was Paddy Russell, an exceptional director, and she was so easy to work for. I think she got one of my best performances out of me, and we had such a good time together. We did a little location filming somewhere on the south coast, and the cameraman was Paddy's then partner, Tony Leggo, a brilliant cameraman with whom I worked many more times when I joined *Blue Peter*. I can't actually remember what scenes we filmed, but I do remember two excellent dinners!!

The Massacre was also a great opportunity for Bill to get his teeth into a more mysterious character. Was he the Abbott as well as the Doctor? And for a man who a few weeks earlier had been unwell and barely been able to remember a line, he reaffirmed his ability as an actor. For the first time, in this story, there was no female companion for the Doctor. There was a girl in the story, however, Anna Caplet. The diminutive and lovely Annette Robertson played her, and it may have been that she was possibly destined to stay in the Tardis, but the idea of a companion from the past created too many problems for the storytellers. In the end, a new character, supposedly a descendant of Anna's, Dodo, became the new companion for the following serial, *The Ark*.

The Ark was a very clever story, but physically, the Monoids were not a particularly good realisation of the author's imagination. The patently obvious man in a mottled rubber suit just reduced me to mirth every time I saw them. I couldn't believe that they would be convincing to the audience, and I was right. But it was an intriguing story, and Jackie Lane made a different, lively and funny debut as Dodo. Bearing in mind that the Tardis was supposed to be malfunctioning and that the Doctor couldn't control where we ended up – something sadly missing from the latest series, I think – it was a clever twist that we actually left the Monoid Ark at the end of episode two, only to return to it a thousand years later in episode three. The more I think of it, the more I like the fact that *Doctor Who*, as a series, was script led rather than character led, and that made each serial a real challenge for us all. It also kept the whole thing very fresh.

In the pre-filming for the series, we were on the sound stage at Ealing with a whole load of animals provided by Mary Chipperfield. We had snakes, apes, birds and a delightful young female elephant. In one scene we had to be concealed in the jungle as the elephant approached but the elephant didn't want to approach, and was coaxed from behind the camera in a sweet voice "Come on Monica, come on girl. Good girl Monica, come on." And eventually she did. She was gorgeous, but Monica? Funnily enough *The Ark* is one of the serials that exists in its entirety, and has been shown on occasion. The director on this show was Michael Imison, of whom I heard no more after the serial, except that his brother became, I believe, a commissioning editor for BBC radio drama. Then in 2001 I was at an event at Wingfield Arts

Peter Purves

Centre in Suffolk, and saw this chap who looked vaguely familiar. I started towards him and he did the same towards me. It was Michael. We had a nice chat and he told me that immediately after the final recording of episode four, John Wiles, the producer, had fired him before they left the control room, and he never worked for the BBC again. I had no idea there had been any acrimony, but something had obviously gone seriously wrong. I just said that I hoped it hadn't been my performance that got him fired! He replied that he really never understood what had gone wrong. When I look at the programme, I wonder if it wasn't the awful Monoids that had put the nail in his coffin, as it were.

I had always preferred the historical stories rather than the purely sci-fi stories, but *The Celestial Toymaker* bucked the trend. As an idea it had everything; great suspense, problems to solve, and a baddie to end all baddies. The Toymaker, as played by Michael Gough was pure evil. The back-story suggested that the Doctor and he had crossed swords in the past, and when in the power of the Toymaker, there was real peril for the Doctor. Bill, again, had been ill, and needed a rest, so this story gave the producers the opportunity to leave him out of most of it. By reducing him to a disembodied hand that was pre-filmed, Bill was able to take three weeks off, and the producers got the opportunity of seeing how the show might work without him. The story was a delight. The Doctor was set a problem by the Toymaker – the Trilogic Game. This involved a three-sided pyramid made up of 10 segments, the largest at the bottom and the smallest with a point at the top. There were three points on the table, and the pyramid starts on one of them. The object and rules of the game were straightforward. The Doctor had to move the pyramid onto one of the other two points, by moving one segment at a time, and never putting a larger piece on top of a smaller piece. But he must never repeat a move and complete it in exactly 137 moves. Sounds easy enough? Try it.

Whilst the Doctor's hand was trying to do the puzzle, Dodo and I were confronted by a Billy Bunter-type clown and a Doll clown (Peter Stevens and Carmen Silvera), who set us a number of difficult physical challenges. These involved negotiating all sorts of difficult courses, with death facing us should we get it wrong. It was an immensely satisfying serial, because Jackie and I had such a lot to do in it. Off the set I was fascinated by the Trilogic Game. It was a beautifully made piece, standing about 12 inches high, and painted a deep rich blue, with the numbers 1-10 clearly marked on one of the sides. I spoke with the designer, who may have been Ray Cusick who designed and gave life to the Daleks, and asked if he would save it for me at the end of the show. He agreed, and I was delighted to take it home as a keepsake. I have never kept memorabilia of any kind, and until I started writing this book I rarely gave the past any thought. But this was one piece that I thought would be nice to keep. I was wrong, but that comes later.

The next four-parter was one we should have all enjoyed but it didn't quite work out that way. Called *The Gunfighters* and written by Donald Cotton, it had all the ingredients of a great serial. In short we arrived in Tombstone in time to become involved with the Gunfight at the OK Corral, one of the classic western adventures. The director was Rex Tucker, one of the BBC's most esteemed directors of the time, but I always felt that he was unhappy at being asked to direct such low drama as *Doctor Who*. Perhaps he felt it was beneath him, I don't know, but he paid me and Jackie the least attention of any director who worked the show. It may just be that as he hadn't cast us, he didn't feel he had a responsibility to us. All I know is that it was an uncomfortable four weeks, and that was a shame. On revisiting the story recently for the audio book, I realised how amusing it had all been, at least from the audience's point of view. The Doctor was stuck with toothache and the only anaesthetic available was Doc Holliday's scotch. I was pretending to be the gunslinger Steven Regret until I came up face to face with the Clanton gang and the Earp brothers. One hilarious sequence in the saloon had me singing *The Ballad of the Last Chance Saloon* at gunpoint, whilst Jackie feverishly hammered out the tune on the upright piano. I also felt that Steven had been made a bit of a wimp in trying to get the humour out of the piece, and all the tough-guy bits were left to the visiting actors, who I must say were pretty good. Film star Laurence Payne came in as Johnny Ringo, and John Alderson, Shane Rimmer and William Hurndell made their mark too. A *Doctor Who* regular, David Graham played the bartender and was very funny in the small part and it was good to work again with Reed de Rouen, a Canadian actor who had been one of the scientist boffins in *Man on the Moon* at the Palladium, and one of our bridge four. It could have been so much fun, but there was an underlying unease throughout the month which may partly have been due to Rex also having an antipathy to Bill Hartnell. But we did get through it and the result on screen was a good sight better than it might have been.

The producer had changed again for *The Gunfighters*, John Wiles finally standing down in favour of Innes Lloyd (later to become head of drama at the BBC), and story editor Donald Tosh was succeeded by Gerry Davis. I really liked Innes and thought we were getting on really well, so it was a surprise to me when we started rehearsing the next serial, *The Savages*, that he took me to one side after recording the first episode to say that he was sorry, but that they weren't going to renew my contract. It was a bombshell to me, because, like Maureen and Adrienne before me there had been no hint that there was to be a change of cast. Bill was absolutely furious – he really had stayed very close to me throughout the year and he thought I was indispensable to the show. Not only was I totally dispensable, but little did he know that his days on the show were numbered also.

Chapter Eight

A difficult period ensues; I become a driver;

I get lucky on a Frank Sinatra film;

The Trilogic Game is binned;

Things happen fast and my life changes forever

The fact that *The Savages* was to be my last serial put a bit of a damper on what was a very good story. At the end of it, Steven decided to stay on the planet and help the people rebuild their civilisation but it was a sad end for me. Innes told me that it was now the programme policy that companions would only stay on the show for one year maximum, and my time was up. The storyline was very sympathetic to Steven, and director Christopher Barry gave me a lot of encouragement to get the best out of the part.

I was sorry to leave the show. We had really melded into a good team, and although Bill's health was not as good as it might have been, he, Jackie and I felt very much a trio. I certainly would miss Bill's lunches at Bertorelli's, and his regular faux pas in company, none quite matching his Kenneth Tynan moment, however! After a year of regular work it was time to readjust. In this business, nothing is forever, and there is no such thing as security. Nowadays, with the mega-bucks some performers are paid, it is possible after only a few appearances in a successful TV show to buy your security but not in 1966, after all, there were only three TV channels in the UK at that time, and opportunities for work were not enormous. Also at that time, there wasn't a great deal of kudos in appearing as a regular in a TV series. The theatre was still the main outlet and actors who didn't or hadn't worked in television tended to look down on it. That was soon to change, but it certainly seemed to be a prevalent attitude at the time. I was still only earning my £30 a show, so I certainly hadn't made my fortune, but although it was the end of an era for me, people were at least aware of my name. Now to cash in on my new found fame!

Fat chance!! I could still open the odd fair or fete for £50 a go, but the work offers that I had expected to come pouring in just didn't materialise and it wasn't too long before the money ran out. Actors could no longer draw the dole – we were classed as self-employed, and in any case it was going to be darned embarrassing standing in the line after having been in 10 million living rooms every Saturday night for a year! Too embarrassing in fact, so I didn't sign on. I scoured the *Evening Standard* for occasional work I could do that wouldn't be too restricting on my ability to go for interviews and auditions and there I got a bit lucky. I found a company in Streatham called the Drivers' Bureau. Once signed with them all you had to do was phone them on any morning you wanted to work, and they would send you where a driver was needed. There was no need of an HGV Licence in those days, so you could be driving anything from a cement mixer to a Rolls Royce, and in my time I did both of those. In fact I did a number of jobs through the bureau that were quite fun. On the first morning I was sent to a laundry off the Fulham Road, where I would have to drive one of the delivery vans. The dispatcher was a little Hitler, who described the job, and the workings of the old Albion truck. Then he started laying down the law about this that and the other, after which I told him to stuff it and walked out. The job had lasted all of 20 minutes.

Not great, but the following day the bureau sent me to deliver cars. That was really fun. I would go to a large field near Maidstone in Kent and pick up a vehicle. The first was an old Roller, a pre-war Phantom I believe. I had to deliver it to the East India Docks for shipping to the USA. What a delight that was, as I drove sedately from Maidstone to the East End in one of the ultimate classic cars. No motorway then, just good old fashioned English trunk roads. If only my old friend, Keith, the driving examiner from Barrow could have seen me. He had often described me in the past as an accident looking for somewhere to happen!! Then it was back to Kent to pick up another car. If it was late, I got to take the car home, and then deliver it to wherever the following morning. There were sports cars, old saloons, and one more Rolls Royce. I knew I was going to be driving that the following day, so I took Gilly and Matthew with me for the drive. We may have been broke but we drove like the king and queen. One night I got to take a VW Karmann Ghia home, so we took it out for a spin along the recently opened M4 as far as Slough. We were so flash!

Another laundry claimed me for a few weeks, during which time the five routes covered a vast area of London. They were based in Balham, but we had routes as far as Tottenham, Regent's Park, Stanmore, Wimbledon, Streatham, Croydon, Bow, Shoreditch, Holloway, and lots more. I quickly got to learn short cuts and routes all over the city that have been incredibly useful to me all my life. At that time I would have sailed through the black cab drivers' knowledge.

In between times there were the odd jobs. I appeared in another four episodes of *Z-Cars*, each time as a crook. In one of them I worked as the partner of Derek Ware, a fight director, with whom I made several films later on *Blue Peter*. He was a good friend, or at least a close acquaintance for several years. One of the directors was Gerald Blake with whom I had a great rapport. Gerry cast me a little later in a thriller serial called *The Girl in the Black Bikini*, where I had a leading part as the girl's boyfriend in the first episode, only to meet a dreadful end at the beginning of the second. The girl was Angela

Scoular, who had just completed a *Bond* movie – so I was moving in bigger circles, or so I thought.

I spent three separate weeks working for directors who were taking the BBC's colour course. Even experienced people had to go through the colour test in which they produced segments of stories in colour. Dougie Camfield was one of them, and he directed me as T E Lawrence in Terence Rattigan's *Ross*. It was a great experience for me, because the part was complex and challenging, and I had already learned that TV gets in really close. My somewhat overstated acting had been reined back considerably during my year in *Doctor Who*, and Douglas was very pleased with my performance.

Alvin Rakoff also used me again – this time in an episode of *Court Martial* out at Pinewood Studios, where I was horribly strangled to death before the opening titles!! But it was a job, and I was grateful that he thought of me for it. Secretly I was thrilled to go to the studios, and it really doesn't matter how experienced one is, there is still a feeling of privilege when one is admitted through the main gates. This is where the big boys work and deep down, I still wanted to make movies – the childhood pact I'd made with Philip Barker had not been forgotten.

I was sent by my agent (I had changed again) for numerous parts – this one at Elstree, that one at Twickenham or Shepperton, and I didn't get any of them. I went for an interview at Pinewood for *James Bond* (don't laugh) when Sean Connery left the first time. Actually a very good friend I had met at the Buckstone Club was Michael McStay, who was one of the two coppers – Johnny Briggs was the other one – in *No Hiding Place*, a cop series made out at Wembley for Rediffusion on ITV. Michael went up for it at the same time, and was shortlisted. I didn't get past the interview stage but Michael got close. Unfortunately for him the producers chose the somewhat less gifted George Lazenby who made just one film for them. I swear Michael would have been brilliant. He remains a good and close friend to this day.

Then I struck gold with the Drivers' Bureau. I was sent to Shepherd's Bush to drive the sound van for a location sound company. The sound equipment and crew were working on a feature-length movie called *The Naked Runner*, directed by Sidney J Furie. The star was Frank Sinatra and the production company was his, Artanis. I drove the truck. As it happens I only saw Mr Sinatra once on the first day, and even then he was a small figure in the distance, but I knew I was in the company of greatness. It was a big-deal movie, and we worked on it for several weeks. The hours were incredibly long, so I got paid overtime for driving by the location sound company. Then one day, one of the sound boom-swingers didn't turn up, and I was co-opted onto the crew. That meant the production company paid me again, and film crew overtime was seriously good money. That was the way it stayed until the movie was finished about four weeks later. It wasn't what I'd meant to be doing but it certainly let us put some money in the bank and I was learning about areas of the business that were hitherto unknown to me. I drove to locations at Duxford aerodrome for an aircraft arrival (that's when I saw Sinatra); we filmed a car chase and crash on the unfinished M40 near High Wycombe, a chase through some tunnels with Sinatra's double and interminable scenes in offices and aircraft hangers – most of which ended up on the cutting room floor. I had such a good time, but the movie was such a disappointment when I finally saw it in the cinema. I had felt it was a good story with a lot of twists, but the final cut gave away all the secrets, and there was no tension in it at all. The money I had earned on it kept us going for several weeks in comparative comfort but the lack of proper acting work was very depressing.

A few weeks later, I received a letter in the post from my agents that increased the depression even further. They told me that they had done all they could to get my career moving again, and as they had failed, they felt I should get another agent and they wished me luck. So I was back where I'd been in 1963, with no job, no agent and no prospects. With a growing family, I had started thinking I should perhaps do something else for a living. At this time in the 60's, there was a growing air of mysticism – people believed that shapes like Pyramids had great power, and the Age of Aquarius was upon us. When we'd had friends round to the flat I'd often shown them the mystical Trilogic Game that I had kept from *The Celestial Toymaker*. I was pretty good at it, and always got it right, but no visitor ever managed to do it correctly. When the letter arrived from my agent, I looked for things to blame. In fairly short time, I decided that the Trilogic Pyramid was the source of my misfortune. That same day, much as I liked it as an object, I put it in the refuse bin in the basement of our block.

The following morning I got a telephone call from my former agent, saying that although they didn't intend handling this, they had a request from a programme called *Blue Peter* at the BBC. They wondered if I would like to go along to meet the editor Biddy Baxter, and they gave me a telephone number.

As it wasn't a proper acting job, I wasn't sure I wanted to go for it, but in the end, I thought that it was better than nothing and I called the BBC. An appointment was made, and a couple of days later I turned up on the fifth floor in the East Tower at the concrete doughnut; the BBC TV Centre.

I was called into the office where I was surprised, first, to discover that Biddy Baxter was a woman. It just hadn't occurred to me that she was – apart from casting directors, every major player I had met so far in the business was male. I was also surprised to see how attractive she was, albeit with an overlying untidiness, particularly her hair, which was loosely tied up in a sort of bun. But she welcomed me gushingly, and introduced her two colleagues, the producers Rosemary Gill and Edward Barnes.

We chatted about what I'd done in my career to date, and whether I'd seen the show. I could honestly say that I had. Actually I had seen the very first episode way back in 1958, when it had been a short hobbies programme presented by Christopher Trace. I had seen it on several other occasions, notably when Valerie Singleton joined the show, and later when Gilly and I were watching it and she suddenly said "bloody hell, that's John Noakes!" as a small young Yorkshireman was introduced to the presenting team. Apparently she had been at the Guildhall School of Speech and Drama with him, and she and another chap had shared a basement flat (or underground cellar) in the Finborough Road with him. Small world.

Anyway, after 15 minutes or so, they said thank you very much and I was ushered out. A few days later I was invited to attend the TV Centre again, this time for an audition. In due course, maybe a couple of weeks later, I was back at the BBC, only this time having been sent a script the previous day, of a 15 minute programme. Learning lines had never been much of a problem for me, following my time in repertory so I had learned it pretty well overnight. The audition covered a number of the main elements that one may be required to deal with in a typical programme – talking straight to camera and giving some information; having a conversation with a co-presenter (I had gone weak at the knees meeting Val for the first time); demonstrating something (in this case a new kind of moped); and linking into and out of filmed inserts, with voice-over commentary. Pretty comprehensive, I'm sure you'll agree. I didn't have to bounce on the ubiquitous trampoline, but just about everything else was included. We rehearsed in a fully crewed studio, and it was quite an awesome occasion. Finally we went for the take, and at first all went well, except for the fact that try as I might, the moped would not kick into life for me to ride in. So I pedalled it in, and delivered the script as if it had been working, and then continued the demo whilst apologising for its malfunction. But deep down I thought I had blown it.

After the recording Biddy, Edward and Rosemary came onto the studio floor, thanked me for coming and said that they would be in touch. As I left the studio I caught sight of a well-known newsreader, Michael Aspel, going in with a researcher. As far as I was concerned that probably put the old tin lid on it. I left feeling pretty confident that I wouldn't get the job.

The exact time-scale fails me, but I believe it was only two or three days later that the programme contacted me and asked me to go into the TV Centre again. This time it was for a short meeting with the trio of producers and again we had a short chat in the *Blue Peter* office. After which I was thanked for coming and I left the office. As I was about to enter the lift, Rosemary Gill came quickly out of the office and asked me to come back. They'd had a quick confab and decided I was the right man for the job, and I was offered it there and then. I can't tell you the euphoria I felt. Although it was not acting in the sense I knew it, it was performing, and after the months of disappointments and lack of confidence, it was just wonderful to feel that my talent was being recognised at last. I accepted, and decided to get a new agent to handle the contract for me.

Gilly and I were thrilled and I think we spliced a bottle of champagne to celebrate. Only one thing disturbed me, and that was how the programme had known about me in the first place. I had never written to them, neither had my former agent, and it was quite a bewildering circumstance. In fact I had been even luckier than I thought, and it was some years before I discovered the whole story.

Apparently there was a lady at the National Theatre, whose job partly entailed replying to actors' letters when there was no work for them, and for filing their particulars. She was a friend of Edward Barnes, and they had been having dinner with a few others one evening. During the course of the dinner, Edward had put into the conversation the fact that he was looking for a replacement for Christopher Trace, *Blue Peter*'s original presenter. In fact he asked if anyone knew of any likely candidates. I had never written to the National Theatre so the lady couldn't have suggested me at that dinner party, as she had probably never even heard of me. A couple of days later, she was having dinner with some other friends, one of whom was Giles Havergal, whom you may remember was the artistic director at Barrow, and whom I met on the occasion that I took my son home for a short visit. During the dinner, the subject of the *Blue Peter* replacement presenter came up, and Giles suggested that I might be worth considering and the following day, the lady rang Edward Barnes and suggested me. The rest is history as the saying goes. It is often said that in show business you can have all the talent in the world, but unless you are also lucky, it won't happen for you. I guess I was lucky for the second time in my career.

One might have thought I would get a much improved rate of pay but the BBC operated a system whereby you graduated from one level of payment to the next, slowly and simply. There were different categories of show, and children's TV was somewhere near the bottom of the list, and in any case it was less than half an hour long. I had got £30 a show for *Doctor Who*. I was rewarded here to the tune of £35 a programme for *Blue Peter*, with an extra £5 per day for any additional filming. But as there were two shows a week, I was much better off than the last time I had been in regular work. I discovered a few years later, that they also worked on the principle that if you'd been on the show longest you got the most money. Consequently I was a fiver worse off than John, and a tenner worse off than Val. Later I would be a fiver better off than Lesley Judd! There would never be equality!

It was in November 1967 that I made my first appearance on the programme. One of the things I had discussed with Biddy and Edward was the fact that I was quite a good swimmer, having, amongst other things qualified as a Lifeguard whilst still at school with an Advanced Life-saving Certificate under my belt. So, for my introduction I went to Crystal Palace swimming baths and taught John and Valerie some basic life-saving skills in the diving pool and at the end, we all looked into the camera and said, "see you on

Monday, goodbye". I was, at last, a part of what has become, without doubt, the best and longest running children's TV programme in the world. It was a great feeling.

But the first studio appearance a few days later was a different kettle of fish. We were in Studio G at Lime Grove, and it was terrifying. I thought I knew about stage fright and nerves, but this was something else. Suddenly I was aware that there were up to 8 million people watching the show, and it was live, with no safety net; no autocue and very little time. I had received my script at home on the Friday evening and the show was live at 5.10pm on the Monday. I had one quite long item about space and the planets, with a large geo-map and model, and although I knew the words, it was totally nerve-wracking. After the dress rehearsal, Valerie, John and I were in the make-up room, awaiting Biddy's arrival with her notes and possible changes. I can't really remember if there were many changes to my pieces, but there were bound to have been some, and as I tried to absorb those, we were called back to the studio for the show. As we sat on the set and the title music started to play, I can honestly say I began to wish I hadn't signed the contract and could I please go home now! But I couldn't, and we did the show. And nothing in my life has ever been as frightening as that again.

Chapter Nine

Early days on Blue Peter; Lulu the elephant;

First foreign trips;

Accidents in Morocco; Extending the family;

Family holidays; Moving house

Blue Peter was already an established programme, but was about to enter what could fairly be described as its golden age. In 1967 there were only three TV channels in the UK, and colour broadcasting had not yet been introduced. Domestic video recorders had not been invented – in fact I recall demonstrating the first readily available Philips recorder on the programme in 1974 – and programmes were rarely repeated, certainly none of those that could be called current affairs or factual. If you wanted to see the programme you had to watch it when it was broadcast – there would be no second chance. Consequently children would rush home to watch at 5.10pm every Monday and Thursday; and during the winter, regular audiences of between 7.5 and 8.5 million were regularly achieved. In the summer, with the lighter nights the audiences dropped to between 4.5 and 5.5 million – figures that any prime time show would jump at today.

The show was aimed at seven to 12 year olds, but it was watched by everyone from three to 93. It was a genuine magazine – designed to entertain and although many say they enjoyed it because it was so educational, that was never the primary purpose. If, as a by-product, we educated children, then all well and good. The format meant it could go wherever it liked, and the items were always kept relatively short. If you weren't interested in an item, then you knew that in three minutes or so there would be something else. It was a highly produced show. We worked from a script that we had to learn, and be virtually word perfect. Although autocue was available in studios, Biddy Baxter decreed that it was not going to be used – and it wasn't.

At first I found the actual performances so daunting that it took me some time to register just how much control Biddy exerted, not only over we presenters, but also over the entire production team. There were one or two assistant producers and studio directors who could hold their own with her, but when it came to the crunch, Biddy ruled. It didn't take me long to realise that I was not necessarily living up to her expectations. I reckon it took me six months before I felt I was getting comfortable in the studio – I later discovered that it took almost two years before the senior producers felt the same! One of Biddy's regular notes to me on set was that I was too much like a schoolmaster. Maybe I was, but it had never been my intention to come across that way. I really did try very hard, perhaps too hard at times, but eventually it started to gel for me.

I guess that there came a time when the letters to the programme were more pro me than anti me and I realised that I had been put in a position, never explained of course, where I'd had to change the audience perception of me from being a person usurping Christopher Trace to becoming the *Blue Peter* presenter in my own right. Stupidly I had never really considered that implication of joining a long running show. I should have, because I had done exactly the same thing in *Doctor Who*, when I replaced two other long-serving performers. It takes time for an audience to accept you, and I now know that children particularly do not like change.

Mostly we worked from Lime Grove Studios in the first two years, with occasional forays to the old Riverside at Hammersmith, and even more rare visits to the TV Centre itself. Studio G at Lime Grove was on the second floor and a slow and smallish goods lift was needed to transport the larger items to it. One of the largest items came up in the lift just before the summer of 1969. It was a baby elephant called Lulu.

Our summer filming trip that year was to Sri Lanka (then still called Ceylon) and to reflect what we might see, Lulu was brought to the studio from Chessington Zoo with her keeper Alex, and his assistant, Martin. The item was straightforward enough. We would introduce Lulu, and talk about the work elephants do in Ceylon, what they eat and drink, how they live, and so on, and then, with a thank you, wrap up the show and trail our summer holiday. Simple enough you would think.

We rehearsed the whole show during the day, and everything went well at the dress rehearsal, which began at approximately 4.00pm. Lulu was quite compliant – she had a big chain around her neck that Alex held with one hand, and in the other he held a three-foot long stick with a bulbous end, and to emphasise what he wanted Lulu to do, he would tap her with it on the forehead. After which Lulu obeyed his instructions. But after we finished at 4.30pm, Biddy came down onto the studio floor from the production gallery and said to Alex that she thought the stick he used looked a little bit cruel, and could he do the programme without it.

At 5.10pm the show went live. I have no recall about anything else in the programme, but at the end of the show we came to the item about Ceylon and Lulu. Lulu walked onto the set with Alex holding the chain but without the stick. It started well enough, until we came to give Lulu a drink of water from a bucket. In went the trunk, the water went into the mouth, the tail raised and the pee came out in a fierce drizzle. In those days the studio floor was painted a neutral colour with water paint, and where the water went, it became like an ice-rink. In spite of the mess we carried on, and fed Lulu a couple of buns. So far we were still approximately on the script. Then we thanked Lulu and Alex and they started to leave. At which point, Lulu's back end faced our principle camera, and she pooed. John was close enough to have to move, whereupon Lulu trod on his foot, and he stepped back into the poo. I couldn't stop laughing, Johnny had no idea what to say and Valerie tried gallantly to keep the show going. By this time, Lulu had almost left the shot when she decided to turn round and come back to us. Alex could do nothing except let her come. She stayed a moment or two whilst we said a few more lines that were in the script, and we asked Alex to take her out again. He tried, bless him, but just when we thought they had gone, Lulu turned round again and came back towards us at a small run. Alex hung on gamely to the chain shouting "Martin, my stick", as he was pulled through the slippery pee and poo into which he slipped and was dragged off the set towards the swiftly moving back cameras. Somehow we managed to wrap up the show quickly and that was that. Biddy came rushing down on the floor afterwards horrified, but we were all, presenters, camera and sound crew, still in stitches. Poor old Alex was mortified, but he wasn't to know that his contribution to the golden era of television would never be forgotten.

For years I have honestly believed this was a "live" performance. I have to say that I am disappointed that my memory is wrong. Biddy Baxter has always insisted it was recorded and I have to admit she is right and my memory is at fault. In fact the entire programme was recorded as if it was live, on Wednesday July 2nd 1969 and transmitted the following day exactly as it all happened in real time. It was absolutely hilarious, and a later editor Richard Marson, confirms the fact of the recording in his excellent *Blue Peter 50th Anniversary Book*. But live or recorded, who cares – it was a wonderful piece of television history that could never have been scripted.

Before that, I had had my first overseas filming experiences with the programme. That was when I discovered just how difficult things could be. In the early spring of 1968, we went to Lech in Austria to make some pretty winter films. I had never skied in my life but as soon as we arrived at our location we were taken to an outfitters where we got fully kitted out. Val had skied before, and Johnny had been on the artificial slope at Crystal Palace, but for me it was all very slippery. We had a script, that involved us coming gently downhill, and I was determined to do it. I could barely manage a snowplough, but up the slopes we went, and with our cameraman strapped to a sledge, we filmed the downhill. I fell over a lot, but when it was all cut together we seemed reasonably accomplished. We filmed a magical sleigh ride at night, and enjoyed the après-ski immensely. I learned one of my first lessons, that *Blue Peter* presenters are expected to do anything, even if they can't. And if they can't they should have a darn good try! Actually the whole trip was really fun, and I could sense that I was really going to enjoy my stint on the show.

The second great film trip was in the summer of 1968 when we went on the famous *Blue Peter* safari to Morocco. This was at a time when comparatively few people were travelling abroad for holidays – the package tour was only in its infancy, and in a way we were quite pioneering. Also, in those days, it wasn't possible to shoot everything as it actually happened; we shot on film, and the equipment was much heavier than today's lightweight digital video cameras so our safari was very much a mock-up. Admittedly we filmed the departure of our safari Land Rover from London Docks, Hays Wharf to be precise. But in fact we joined a totally different Land Rover when we got to Morocco. A company called Minitrek was engaged, with driver Doug, to transport us around the country. Edward Barnes had been out to do a full recce of the trip, and the scripts were written. It was fascinating. We went to the Royal cities of Fez and Meknes, and to the ancient Roman ruins at Volubilis. We trekked to Rabat, and climbed the still incomplete Tour Hassan, and because it had not yet been completed, I went and worked with the mosaic decorators in the

Hassan mausoleum. We watched children working in the carpet factories – a sight I'll never forget, and some of the children wouldn't survive the dusty working environment – and finally we headed south to Marrakesh.

On the way we had an accident – a young local farmer was walking along the verge of the road, a narrow tar-topped highway, when his small flock of sheep and goats turned into our path and we ploughed through them. Carnage, but to our amazement, Doug didn't stop. It hadn't been his fault, the animals had behaved unpredictably, but that made no difference. He said that if he had stopped he may not have got away alive, and he certainly would have lost his passport and his freedom. He had unwittingly destroyed a very poor man's livelihood. Twenty miles further along the road, we stopped at a river where he washed the front of the vehicle, and we went on. I could do nothing about it, and I know that Valerie shares my feeling of guilt, even now, about the whole incident.

Marrakesh was everything I had hoped it would be and more. I don't think I have ever been anywhere since, that is quite as foreign, exotic, beautiful and very, very hot!! We had reservations together with the crew, in the lovely but unfortunately named Grand Hotel de Foucaud. It was just off the wonderful square, the Place DjemAlfn'a. All except Valerie stayed there – she decided the hotel wasn't up to her standards, and paid extra to stay at the fabulous Hotel La Mamounia. It is almost impossible to describe how it felt to wander in this magical place. There were storytellers, snake charmers, drummers and dancers from below the High Atlas Mountains, water carriers and a hubbub of chatter and sounds, and, unfortunately, smells. The all pervading one being eau de camel shit! But in spite of that I'll never forget the excitement it generated. We filmed in the Souk, the meandering market behind the square, and we drank mint tea in pavement bars. It was one of the best experiences of my life. And the bonus with Valerie being at the best hotel in town, meant we could enjoy the swimming pool there!

Here's one I wrote earlier...

There was a downside. Noakesy and I had bought our duty free booze at Heathrow, and chose one night in Marrakesh to drink it on the roof of our hotel. We played poker until whatever time it was, and tumbled down to bed having consumed a bottle of Jack Daniels. We weren't filming the following day, which had been our excuse, but we did have to travel quite a distance to the next base, Tinherir. I swear I have never been so ill; I was a greyish shade of green, and travelled in the front seat of Edward Barnes' hired car, suffering in silence and with silent disapproval from my producer. I have to say that Edward could have taken a much more critical view of my behaviour but he let it go without recrimination.

Two nights later we went as a group to an old fort that provided dinner and dancing, Moroccan style. Again it was a fabulous experience. There were 12 of us in the Land Rover; Doug driving as usual, four film crew, producer, director, PA and the three of us, plus our stills photographer, Charles "Tom" Walls. It was a bit of a squeeze, and for the 10 mile return journey, John and I said we'd travel on the roof, in the luggage rack. It was a beautiful night, and the breeze was just fantastic. There was a bright moon and it was a delightful journey but as we passed by a small mud hut village, a dog shot out in front of the vehicle and Doug had to swerve quite violently to miss it. John and I, on the roof, seriously had to hang on for dear life. There was no enquiry from below as to whether we were all right and so I suggested to John that when we got back to the hotel we should get off before the van stopped and then they would think we'd fallen off when Doug had swerved. There was a ladder down the back of the Land Rover, and so, as we drove into the front drive of the hotel, Johnny went first, and as the van slowed he stepped off, and as I followed, my foot went into a hole and over I went. I guess we were travelling at about 15mph. I had quite a fall, tumbling over and over, seriously grazing the whole of my left side and getting a lot of sand and gravel in the wounds.

Convinced I was about to lose my job on the show for being irresponsible and jeopardising the filming, particularly in the light of my drinking spree two nights earlier, I asked John to help me to my room, so I could clean up the wounds. He then went off and brought Tom Walls back who also helped me dress the damage. I have to admit it looked pretty bad, but bandaged up with a lot of savlon, I hoped all would be well.

The following morning, "Nurse" Walls again helped me dress the wounds, and luckily they didn't seem infected, but there was no way I could leave my arm open to the elements. For continuity, I had to wear the same short-sleeved shirt I had worn in the previous safari sequence, and so the bandage was in full view. No escape. My shorts concealed my seriously grazed hip, and the various other abrasions were not really obvious. Edward was pretty annoyed, but there was nothing he could do, and so I filmed in the Gorges du Todra, one of the world's truly beautiful places, in extreme pain. The storyline involved the vehicle breaking down in the middle of the river, and Johnny and me having to fix it. I think the cold crystal clear waters of the river helped me to heal quicker than would otherwise have been the case, and it also eased the pain.

I am a quick learner and decided to take the whole job a bit more seriously. There are a legion of stories one could tell about that trip. We went down below the High Atlas and to M'hamid, the southernmost outpost of the desert patrol. It was also a Camel Souk on the edge of the big dunes of the Sahara desert. Edward had difficulty negotiating with the locals because the last time a film unit had been there it was David Lean and the whole crew filming *Lawrence of Arabia*!! Things like that do tend to push up the prices. In fact the following year we followed in David Lean's footsteps again to Ceylon, where he had filmed some of *The Bridge on the River Kwai*, and we suffered a similar expensive fate!

In the town of Ouzazarte, John, Valerie and I stopped for a bite to eat at a small café, and were threatened by a man with a gun. In pidgin French we managed to discover he was the husband of the girl running the café, and no, we couldn't call the police, because he was a policeman himself. He seemed very drunk, which is unusual to see in Morocco, and he abused his wife quite badly before leaving us to finish our small repast. When we next passed through Ouzazarte we saw him on duty in his uniform, with the evidence of a severe beating on his face. His wife's brother was a senior policeman, we heard, who had sorted him out!

In the town of Zagora, also a long way south, we were booked into one of the Grand Hotels du Sud, only to discover, on arrival, that all of our rooms had already been taken by the Moroccan Army, who had commandeered the whole place. There being no other hotels in the town, I slept in a chair in a hall and Edward had the manager's office, sleeping on his desk. I think Valerie had a room, lucky girl, and the rest squeezed in where they could. The Army did move out the next morning and we finally got our rooms. It was scorching hot, but the hotel did have a beautiful swimming pool, and John and I were never out of it. In fact on one day, just before we set off to film, John pushed me in – I was fully dressed ready for filming in shorts and shirt – and by the time we boarded the van 10 minutes later, my clothes were bone dry.

We were caught in a sandstorm in the Camel Souk, when suddenly everything was battened down, shutters went up in the windows of the few houses, the camels got down on the ground, and the people covered themselves in their robes. It was dramatic stuff as the sky darkened, the breeze came up and a wall of sand approached. We took cover in the house we had been using as our base, except for our assistant cameraman, Nick, who stood outside watching the approach of the sand. His last words before vanishing in the dust were "It's all strangely beautiful..." He was engulfed as we dragged him inside and was actually sent home a couple of days later suffering from heat stroke.

There were two other moments on the trip. On his reconnaissance trip, Edward had used a local guide called Brahim. He had set up, amongst other things, a trip for us to go up a mountain on mule back and to have a meal in a private house at the top of the trail. The place was called Imlil. But by the time we'd reached Marrakesh, Brahim had been so stoned that Edward sacked him and got us a new guide and interpreter, called Moulay. He took over the itinerary that Brahim had arranged. First up was the trip to Imlil. When we got to the foot of the mule trail, there were mules waiting for us, and we filmed us getting up on them and riding off up the hill. As we were doing so, a group who had been on a ride earlier, returned, and one girl, who was extremely large, said as she dismounted, "I'll never be the same shape again!" It became a catchphrase for the day.

At the top of the hill it was all rather disorganised, but the elderly Berber fellow who lived there, and didn't seem to be too aware of what was going on, eventually provided a meal of chicken tajines for us all that was really lovely. We were now seriously behind schedule and only just got back to the bottom of the trail before dusk. I've often wondered what the poor old fellow thought about that day, as we discovered later that we had gone to the wrong Imlil. Somewhere at the top of another mule trail our meal was waiting. The fact that mules had been waiting for us was pure coincidence. Not Moulay's fault of course, but a splendid cock-up.

It had been intended at one point that we would spend a night in a Bedouin's tent, but that never transpired as the nomad had moved on, and, possibly somewhat relieved we were allowed to go back to the hotel. What I remember most clearly about the whole trip, apart from the wonderful and wild natural beauty of the country, was how quickly one adapts to being away from the luxuries of modern day living. M'Hamid was as far south into the desert as we could have gone, and on the way there we had registered the small towns that were quite primitive, certainly Zagora and Ouzazarte fitted that category. But after our riding with the desert patrol, being caught in the sandstorm and Valerie falling off a camel – "It's a bit much in this heat", she had complained – (and it was incredible heat; the thermometer in the crews' van peaked at 132°F) we greeted each place on the return journey as if it was a major city. So you can imagine that when we finally got back to Marrakesh, we thought we were in heaven. Actually we were pretty close, I think.

It was a fabulous experience, and, as it was my first *Blue Peter* summer filming trip, one I will never forget. By the time I left the programme 10 years later, I had visited some 27 different countries worldwide, and I still feel immensely privileged that I was allowed to do that.

Meanwhile, back in the real world, life continued to be very pleasurable. I was heavily into music at that time, and had regularly gone to the Albert Hall to see a whole range of wonderful bands, from Queen to Steppenwolf, Eric Clapton with Delaney and Bonnie, and Credence Clearwater Revival. These were all brilliant concerts that still cause a frisson of excitement when I think of them. Gilly and I saw a lot of shows in the West End, mostly plays, but we'd seen Barbara Streisand in *Funny Girl* at the Prince of Wales, which, I believe, was one of the first musicals to extensively use radio microphones. Unfortunately the technology wasn't all that great, and the mics were turned up so loud you heard a lot of extraneous sound from backstage, and the occasional taxi. But it was still a spellbinding piece.

Matthew was now five years old, and was an only child. In the summer of 1969 I opened a fete for the National Children's Home at Alresford in Hampshire, and Gilly and I got to thinking that maybe we could adopt a child. In fact we agreed, after vetting from a delightful social worker, to foster with a view to adoption, a little Chinese girl from Macau, called Lisa. At first we would travel down to Alresford to collect her for weekends and then later we were able to have her at home with us in London. With their birthdays just three days apart, Matthew and Lisa got on really well from the start, and the fostering continued for a year and a half. She was a lovely child, but she had her problems – she'd been taken into care by SSAFA, the forces welfare organisation, because her natural mother, from Macau, and her stepfather, who was in the airforce in Germany, had not treated her too well. Eventually a place had been found for her at the NCH and that's where we first met her. She wasn't a difficult child, and seemed to fit in well with our established family. My parents, and Gilly's mother and grandmother, thought she was a wonderful addition to the family, and we proceeded to adopt her, and that finally went through on her seventh birthday in 1970. She was now officially Lisa Jasmine Purves, having chosen her middle name for herself.

As a family we would spend time in the Lake District with our friends Les and Eileen and their two boys, and took lovely summer holidays in the sun. In fact the first time we went to Ibiza was in 1969, when it was a largely unspoilt island. Our friends Rod and Val had been there twice before, and asked us to join them, which we did, and we stayed in a small farmhouse near Las Salinas. Other friends of Rod and Val, Eyke and Peter, were staying there too. I hadn't seen Eyke since that time, yet I discovered that she lives with her lovely Deerhounds, approximately 10 miles from where I now live in Suffolk, and we have become friends. Small world.

At that time the airport building was a small, Bougainvillea covered cane and bamboo-roofed affair, and you arrived from London, via Valencia, having completed Immigration formalities on the Spanish mainland. Ibiza, itself was a treat. There were fabulous, small, and not too commercial café bars and restaurants dotted along the quayside at the main harbour in Ibiza town, and you could get great food on even the smallest beach. Big tourist beaches with hotels were unheard of, except perhaps in San Antonio, and we would find wonderful deserted coves where you might find a fisherman coming ashore with fresh lobsters that he would cook for you on the beach, and which we could wash down with the local wine we had taken with us. Rod had an inflatable dinghy with a high-powered outboard motor, and we all had a go, with varying success at water-skiing. We also met another couple who lived on the island, Gordon and Angela Sillars. He was a retired Marine major, and she a painter. They lived in a farmhouse at Santa Gertrudis, a very rural part of the island, and they had a small finca on the estate, and in later years we would rent it for a couple of weeks. They were good company and we had nice meals with them, and met some of their friends, notably Denholm Elliott who also had a villa on the island. The only sad moment on that trip was when we returned home, Lisa had to go through the aliens' customs at Heathrow with her Portuguese passport, whilst we went through the UK nationals' gate.

But in 1971, when we went again, she had her own English passport. This time we rented a villa from a friend, Susannah (Suska), a small finca at the top of a hill not too far from Santa Eulalia. I had rented a small car and it struggled to get us up the hill to the finca. On one occasion, Les and Eileen were with us, and as we approached the top of the hill, we got a flat tyre. The spare was missing, so we had no choice but to take the wheel down the hill to a garage that was a couple of miles away. Les and I took the wheel off, and whilst the others went on up to the finca, we set off down the hill. Always handy with a good idea, I suggested that instead of carrying the wheel we should bowl it down the track like a hoop. Great idea, except that a few feet in front of us, the wheel hit a small rock, turned left and went off the track and over the edge. It took us a good hour to get down to where it ended, and then to carry it back to the road and on to the garage.

In that year we made friends with Jon Pertwee and his wife, Ingeborg. They owned a villa on the hillside overlooking a bay, and we had some good times there. Jon was always making films and he made special adventures, in which he always starred, for his son, Sean. Gilly and I appeared in a couple of them – in one he threw us off the roof of a villa. Luckily there was a swimming pool beneath the roof, so the landing was soft, if a little damp. The children all played together, and a good time was had by all. Jon was excellent company, and a good raconteur, and he and Inge remained friends for some years whilst we lived relatively near to each other in London. Funnily enough I met her and Suska again recently at a dinner party hosted by a mutual friend in Suffolk. They were both as delightful as ever, but sadly Suska succumbed to cancer in November 2008, and it is a great pity that neither she nor Jon are still with us.

Round about this time, the owner of our flat in Gloucester Road sold the property to a local company who immediately put us on notice to move. I decided to stay put, and told the new owners so. They weren't happy, but they didn't push the issue. But after a couple of weeks we heard that they might offer us some money to move. I weighed this up and realised that I could probably get a mortgage on a house, if I could persuade them to pay us enough for the deposit. As it happens, that is what occurred. They did put a time limit on it, but provided we could move within three months they offered us something in the region of £1500 to go. Then, all we had to do was to find a house, and get into it before the deadline. Actually that proved easier than we thought it would, and all in good time we moved to Morella Road in SW11, the very next road to the flat in which we had lived in Thurleigh Road a few years earlier. We knew the area and liked it, so we were delighted with the move. It was the spring of 1970, and the house, a six-bedroomed Victorian villa, cost us £8750. I believe that the last time it changed hands in 2006 it cost £1.1million.

Chapter Ten

I lose the nation's best-loved pet;

Getting to know John Noakes;

And falling out with him;

Nature walks with Graham Dangerfield;

Trip to Ceylon – Too many chiefs – not

enough Indians!

Apart from wonderful events and trips, there was another new experience that I hadn't expected. On joining *Blue Peter*, I inherited a pet. Petra had joined the programme three or four years earlier, and she became my on-screen dog. She was regularly brought to the studio by a lady from Sussex, Edith Menezes, who had looked after her from the start, and also looked after Jason, the Siamese cat. Petra had never been fond of the studio – she was quite a highly-strung dog, and she really didn't like being on the set. Obviously that's where she had to be, and Biddy came up with the idea, that if she actually went home with me, and I was to bring her to the studio, she might find that continuity more acceptable, and she might start to be more relaxed. So I took on the role of Petra's owner, and she came to live with me, and the family, on the edge of Wandsworth Common.

I was appalled to see a recent article in the *Daily Mail*, showing a picture of me and Petra, and the caption said "Peter Purves simulates liking Petra". There was no simulation there at all. I loved Petra, although she wasn't a very nice dog. She had been bought from a pet shop, a ringer, in fact, for the first puppy that died after one appearance on the programme. She developed distemper as a puppy, and when her second teeth grew, they were pretty spongy and fell out. She was also quite aggressive towards other dogs, and always wanted to be top dog. When we had other dogs in the studio, she had to be watched like a hawk; otherwise we could have had a fight on our hands. Most viewers thought she was a German Shepherd, but actually she was a sort of Collie/GSD, and not a very good example at that. Having said that, she was lovely with me, and I took her most places with me when I was filming, just as John did with his dogs, Patch and Shep. Patch, by the way was one of Petra's puppies, and had a similar temperament. Petra also settled in well with my family, and was a fantastic house guard, something to be applauded as I had been burgled a couple of times in 1967 and '68, and I doubt that anyone would have ever entered the house with the apparent Hound of the Baskervilles in residence. I hope I gave her a happy life, and in later years when she developed diabetes, and poor eyesight, I gave her the medication, care and love she deserved. She was the nation's pet, and I applaud the programme, and Biddy in particular, for creating the idea of a surrogate pet for all those children living in properties where pets were disallowed. It was a great idea, and I was proud to be a part of it. Edith Menezes was a wonderful support in all this. She loved Petra, possibly more than anyone else, and when I was abroad, or away with the family, she always stepped in and took Petra home with her. It was the best of both possible worlds for the dog.

On one occasion we took her with us to stay with friends in the Lake District. She wasn't totally reliable off the lead, and had to be kept under control when we were out where there were sheep! In those days there was quite a propensity for farmers to shoot dogs that worried their animals. God forbid that would have happened to Petra. But we went with friends to picnic in Borrowdale, under the shadow of Black Crag, a most stunning location. There were four adults, four kids and Petra, who had the best time imaginable. She ran this way and that, dived into bracken and up over the rocks. Then she'd come back for a treat from the picnic. But suddenly, one minute she was with us, and the next she was gone. There was a moment of terrible realisation that she was no longer around. I called her, and whistled, and the friends and children set off in different directions, all calling for her to come back. After a good hour, I suggested that the others made their way back to the car and I would carry on looking for her. I searched everywhere, hardly seeing another human being – there were a couple of climbers on the crag, but they hadn't seen her. And after two hours with visions of the newspaper headlines, and dreading having to tell Biddy and Edward that I'd lost not only their dog but the nation's dog, I started back towards where we had left the car. I still kept on calling her and whistling, when suddenly I heard a bark in the distance. I called again, and the bark was closer, and again and again. You can imagine my relief and delight when I saw her, in the distance, on the other side of a small river, coming back towards me. She was soaked, bedraggled and absolutely exhausted; yet she still almost jumped into my arms when we met. It had been a frightening experience. She'd been gone over three hours. I have no idea where she had been, but she was back.

After that, I even managed to train her to do distant control, like the obedience dogs do at *Crufts* dog show. She was really quite good at it. She helped me to understand dogs better than hitherto, and that later helped me in my career with dogs. It was also a nice touch that a friend of the programme, the artist and cartoonist William Timyn, was approached to produce a bronze bust of her. It required us to go for a couple of sittings in his studio, and then the programme followed the production of the bronze. It is an amazing likeness, and for a few years she stood on a plinth at the very entrance to the BBC's concrete doughnut in Shepherd's Bush. She now stands in the *Blue Peter* garden, but not as prominently as I think she ought to be. I was genuinely very upset when she died, and I reiterate my stance, that there was no simulation in my liking for her. She was my dog, and I loved her.

During my time on the programme I presented a number of different dog-related items, and officially I was the puppy-walker for two Guide Dog puppies, Cindy and Buttons, that were provided by appeals to *Blue Peter* viewers. I must say here that had it not been for the assistance of the late, wonderful Angela Mulliner, these items would never have been made. She did all the preparation, and in fact did most of the puppy training. The programme had been responsible to a large extent for the growth in interest and popularity of the Guide Dogs for the Blind Association. Before my time on the show, Honey, the first BP Guide Dog had been provided after viewers collected tons of milk bottle tops and silver foil. It was probably one of the first examples of mass recycling. I always enjoyed making the Guide Dog films, and had a particularly good rapport with Derek Freeman, who at the time was the puppy-walking manager for the Association. I must have made a dozen films or more with him, and have maintained my relationship with the Association to this day. I regularly attend their Gala day, and have presented the Guide Dog of the Year Award three times, and even give after-dinner talks to some of the senior staff. In 1980 I was asked by Gollancz, the publisher, to write a book in collaboration with the renowned photographer, Fay Godwin, to celebrate the 50th Anniversary of the Association, and although it is out of print now, it did make the best-sellers list for a couple of weeks in 1981.

All this dog stuff was well into the future for me. John and I had an excellent rapport. Temperamentally we were very different, but we soon built up an understanding. He is naturally quite a shy man, and as an actor had always enjoyed hiding behind the character he was playing. As a presenter, there is no character to play, and so Johnny invented his own "John Noakes", an on-screen persona very different from his private one. Once I got used to that, I found I almost knew what he was going to say or do in a given situation, almost before he knew himself, and we began to play off that.

We made several films together that allowed us to be slightly amusing – one being the testing of Army equipment. I had always felt that comedy acting was my forte in repertory, and enjoyed making people laugh. And this way of playing together started to be a part of the filming repertoire. In fact during the second season I was with the show, we must have made well over 20 films together, everything from being chimney sweeps to playing water polo, and we had a ball. There were a number of different assistant producers who researched and produced our films. One in particular was Tim Byford who was exactly on our wavelength and it brings me full circle to the prologue of this book. He decided to make a film that incorporated some of the things we had already done on the programme, and *The Waiters' Orienteering Race* was born. We had a wonderfully good time filming, and there were a lot of very good sight gags that were developed on location. As I said at the outset, the film required the different pairs of waiters going round the orienteering course and serving a variety of food at the checkpoints. We were in full black tie waiter's clothes, and one gag had Johnny running along with me beside him, when he tripped, and the tray of drinks was thrown to me. I caught it and we carried on running without a pause.

The final edited film was transmitted, but what I didn't know was that Edward Barnes had absolutely hated it. It gradually filtered through to me that he had found it disgraceful, and that it wasn't a *Blue Peter* film and so on. Over the next few weeks I was not engaged to make any films, and John was always filming on his own. For some inexplicable reason, I assumed that John had said something behind my back and I had been struck off the filming list accordingly. He seemed to be making lots of films that I would have liked to do, and the outcome of that was that our relationship soured for several

Peter Purves

weeks and unfortunately the rapport we had been developing was not allowed to flourish. In retrospect I think Edward and Biddy were worried that our budding "double-act" was taking the programme in a direction they didn't like, and they took firm actions to prevent it continuing. I can't remember how long afterwards it was that Tim Byford left the programme, but it wasn't too long, and he went to a senior position running Czechoslovakian TV!!

I think it is a pity that things were never quite the same again, but there were many really good moments, and over the years we generally got on extremely well. That has continued and I've worked with John several times since we left the show, and we have a genuine fondness for each other. I think, when we work, I give him confidence, and I have to say I find him a useful foil. He is still capable of going into "John Noakes" mode, but I know what he's about and I find it endearing. Because he now lives in Spain I don't see him as often as I would like.

In the early days of my time on the show, we were blessed with several good studio directors who really knew what they were doing, in particular Alan Russell, and John Adcock. Alan went on much later to devise and produce *Record Breakers*, and John moved on with Rosemary Gill, to produce *Multi-Coloured Swap Shop*. They both helped to make the difficult programmes in the first months easier than they might otherwise have been. They were calm, efficient, and very likeable. Whenever we had music items on the show, Alan was a superb man to have at the helm, and that always gave us confidence as presenters. Bear in mind that we never had an earpiece talkback from the gallery, and all instructions were delivered by signal, given via the floor manager. We had some good floor managers too, thank goodness. It is hard to pick out highlight moments. I have excellent recall of almost every film I ever made for the programme, but can barely remember most of the studio items, even when there are photographs to jog the memory.

Most viewers seem to remember the studio "makes". I made very few because in all honesty I wasn't very good at it. A very clever lady from Cornwall, Margaret Parnell, devised the majority of them. It was five months before I was set loose on one of them, the Sea City. It was spread over three consecutive programmes, and I can remember being all thumbs, and didn't make the best model you've ever seen! Funnily enough I wasn't often asked to do those items in the future.

During that time I made a number of films that became almost traditional. One such series were the nature programmes I made with the wonderful Graham Dangerfield. He was the most splendid naturalist, and a man with a very dry and similar sense of humour to mine. We got on so well and it was always a pleasure to see on the schedule that I had to go to his house in Wheathampstead where he had what amounted to a small private zoo. People would take injured animals and birds to him, and he would take them in, look after them and nurture them until they were fit to return to the wild. He is probably responsible for my love of the countryside. Graham had numerous large cages in the garden, which held everything from foxes to cervals. He had coypus that had almost become extinct, and I can remember one lovely short film I made with a litter of badger cubs following my wellies all over the garden. We would take recovered foxes out into the countryside and set them free. And as farmland disappeared and barns were converted, and golf courses proliferated, he was responsible for introducing the idea of providing nest-boxes for everything from barn owls to kestrels.

If you look carefully, in the background of many of those nature walk films, somewhere you will usually see a heron. It was a blind bird that Graham looked after, and when we went filming, he would always put it in a big basket and take it with us. He would then plant it in a stream or watercourse, where it would happily spend its time wading about, until we went home again. It could never be released, because it couldn't see to feed. Graham kept it, with many other damaged birds that couldn't be released, in his aviary at home. He was the most humane man, and I respected him immensely.

On one occasion I was in his kitchen looking at a glass fronted case which had dormice in it, when to my surprise, and no little concern, a cerval, which is a small, wild, North African cat came in through the window, looked around, went through the door to his office and out of that window back into his cage. They weren't tamed animals; it was just that they were used to people, and to wandering through his house.

My friendly rapport and banter with Graham was another element that the programme wasn't thrilled with! Edward felt we were too familiar with each other, and I was severely reprimanded for a sequence at a small lake in St Albans, where we had been looking at swans and other wild birds. I had fallen in (intentionally I have to say) and when Graham, who was in stitches on the bank, offered me a hand to pull me out, I jerked his arm, and in he came too. Well we both thought it was funny, but it ended on the cutting room floor!

My second major foreign filming trip was the expedition to Ceylon, and it was another wonderful experience. We stayed in a wonderful old colonial hotel in Mount Lavinia, Colombo, where you could believe you were back in the days of the Raj. The food was sensational – though John would disagree. He could tour the world on steak and chips, and didn't go in for anything exotic. The hotel seemed always to be serving food, including a typical English afternoon tea if one wished to have it. Edward and I struck up quite a good friendship on that trip and got along really well.

Johnny got a bad stomach on one day, and that meant I took over his film, which was one of the high spots of the trip – going out on a sail outrigger for some sea fishing. We went out from Negombo on a most beautiful day. Our local fixer, George, was actually a filmmaker in his own right, and he organised it very well. The boat itself was a slim affair with a wide outrigger on its port side, which was connected via rough wooded spars, and with a heavy duty rope net, a little like a scrambling net, covering the wide gaps. There were three Singhalese in the boat crew, with me making up the four. Our film crew on the boat was just the cameraman and Edward. All three of the others had me running this way and that, shouting orders at me, and I nearly fell into the water on more than one occasion as we sped across the sea. Eventually I turned to the camera and said "There are too many chiefs on this boat, and not enough Indians!" That ended on the cutting room floor too! We almost lost George at one point when he lost his footing and was left hanging onto a spar with most of his body in the water. I think he was worried too, as there were sharks in that ocean. But it made a nice film and I had a marvellous time. Standing on the outrigger with the wind in my face under a blue sky was something I'll never forget.

I think I could probably write a separate book on the summer filming trips alone, there were so many real highlights. There is an annual procession in Kandy when huge tusker elephants in magnificent adornments parade to the Temple of the Tooth, which is where an ancient relic, Buddha's Tooth is kept. It is called the Perahera. Unfortunately, it takes place earlier in the year than when we were there. So Edward cleverly arranged for us to have a mini procession all of our own to reflect what traditionally happened. When we arrived at the Temple, our elephant was waiting for us. Actually he was chained by one of his front feet to a very strong fixing in the ground. He was also, for some reason or other, pretty cheesed off! Anyway, Edward talked to the Mahout, and then started to brief us on what would happen. He had his back to the elephant, which seized the opportunity to pick up a large bamboo branch from the ground with its trunk, and then took careful aim, and whacked Edward in the back with it, nearly flattening him. Not a good start, but ultimately the simulated Perahera made another spectacular film.

We had a slightly better experience riding some elephants down into the river near Kandy where we could give them a wash. Apparently they liked to be rubbed with coconut husks, and Johnny and I obliged. The Mahouts were pretty amused to see that John's elephant was doing its best to catch my leg with his trunk each time I was near. We got well and truly drenched and it was good fun, but on our return to the UK we heard that an English tourist had been killed by an elephant at that same spot a week or so later. It had just picked her up in its trunk and thrown her to the ground. You can never be too trusting on these occasions.

Before setting off for Ceylon, we had introduced a lovely couple of Singhalese singers on the programme. Eranga and Prianga were just lovely – she was tiny and he was tall and slim, and they were both incredibly shy. I made friends with them, and on more than one occasion Gilly and I visited their home in Kilburn where we were fed royally. Unfortunately they returned to Ceylon when their cabaret engagements ended and I lost touch with them.

The memories come flying back – Johnny digging for gems in the mines, and us drinking a most ghastly fermented alcoholic concoction made from king coconut milk called Toddy, the monkeys scuttling around on the roof of our corrugated-iron-roofed hotel in Kandy, flying kites on the seafront in Colombo, and Valerie looking wonderful in saris. Most of all I remember going for a pee in the middle of the night in the Mount Lavinia Hotel to see a pair of eyes looking up at me from behind the toilet bowl – an enormous rat! I think it was as scared of me as I was of it, when it took off at a huge speed, up and down the curtains and out of the open window. What a trip.

Chapter Eleven

The drive to Marrakesh; Mexico;

Riding in the charreada;

My first experience of real wealth

Immediately on my return from Ceylon, Matthew went to stay with my mother and father in Horton, and I took Gilly on a trip of a lifetime. The Moroccan trip in the summer of '68 had been such an exciting time for me that I wanted her to share in it. And so we drove to Marrakesh. Actually we took a car ferry to Bilbao from Portsmouth, and that really got us off to a great start. The night crossing of the Bay of Biscay was a delightful cruise, and when we disembarked in Bilbao we were like two excited children. I'd planned an itinerary with stops in Vitoria, Madrid, Granada and Algeciras. Actually we stayed three days in Madrid and three days in Granada, and did all the touristy things that one reads about. The museums in Madrid, particularly the Prado, were fantastic, and Granada remains one of my favourite places in the world. Our transport was a very trendy 2-litre sports car, a Bond Equipe, which I had bought three months earlier. It was very light and quick, and driving it with the roof down was, for me, one of the ultimate delights of the trip.

There were some lovely moments on the trip south, including listening to the Segovia version of Rodriguez' *Concierto de Aranjuez* as we drove through the town. Magical. As we travelled we kept on seeing billboards that said Beba Valdepenas, with a picture of a bottle. And as we crossed the plateau just after noon, suddenly there was a sign that indicated Valdepenas was just 2km to our left. So we turned off, had lunch and did Beba Valdepenas – both the red and the white variety. The wine was delicious, and to be honest we drank a little too much of it, and had to have a full Spanish siesta before moving off again. Eventually we got to Granada quite late, following our climb of the Sierra Nevada, to find the most beautiful Spanish hotel, oddly named the Hotel Inglaterra. Nothing could have been less English, and our three days proved to be too short to really enjoy everything the town had to offer. We explored the Alhambra and the Generalife with our eyes and mouths wide open. The Moorish architecture was a good preparation for our crossing over into Africa three days later, and we just loved it. We ate so well there – something we would not do very often for the next two weeks!!

A couple of months earlier, I had been with some friends that included the actor, Walter Gotell. Walter had starred as a senior policeman in *Softly Softly* (with Frank Windsor and Alan Stratford Johns), which was where I first met him. He was just beginning to make his mark as a regular villain in the *James Bond* movies. He owned a villa adjacent to Algeciras, and had offered us accommodation for the night before we crossed to Tangiers. We had gratefully accepted and he had also offered to get us the ferry tickets for the crossing. Fantastic. But the best-laid plans have a tendency to let us down. After the wonderful drive from Granada, down from the mountains to Malaga and Torremolinos (still unspoilt at that time, though the first two skyscraper blocks of holiday flats were in place) we arrived at dusk in Algeciras. Could we find the villa? Try as we might, after retracing our various routes and following the instructions, we thought, to the letter, we eventually at 11pm gave up, and set about trying to find somewhere to sleep. It was the height of the tourist season and there were no hotel rooms, and we finally wound up renting a smallish tent on a camping site at San Roque, and got our heads down for about three hours sleep.

We had the additional problem that we didn't have our ferry tickets, and so we set off to the docks early to get in the queue. We were also about 20 years too early for the "hole in the wall", and all we had were travellers cheques that would not be acceptable at the ticket office. The banks in Algeciras didn't open until half an hour after the ferry sailed, so we were suddenly in a bit of a fix. We got chatting to a young French couple who were also going on the morning ferry. My schoolboy French was better than their schoolboy English, but I managed to convey our problem to them. To cut a long story short, they had no reason to trust us, yet they agreed to lend us some Spanish currency, and in return I handed over all our travellers cheques as a guarantee that I would pay them back when we got to a bank in Tangiers.

There was great relief for us, followed by acute embarrassment. We were right at the front of the queue, and I bought our tickets when the office opened. But when we boarded the ferry, and parked the car, I realised that they had to travel in the very crowded tourist section, fenced off from us in the somewhat more luxurious first class. I'd never thought to ask about that. Anyway we got to Tangiers a couple of hours late, and I went to the bank and got some currency and paid them back. To ease my conscience a little we took them for lunch and I paid.

Then our adventures began. We had a long drive ahead of us (Gilly didn't drive, by the way) to the Imperial Royal City of Fez. I had planned the trip carefully, but rather overestimated the distance that it would be reasonable to travel in a day on Moroccan roads. Consequently we were absolutely exhausted when we finally drove into the forecourt of the Palais Jamais Hotel in Fez at almost midnight. We were greeted by the manager who profusely apologised that the swimming pool wasn't built yet, and took us to our room. We were hot, tired, dusty and a little fed up so we didn't take anything in as we were escorted to our room and with a further short disgruntled gripe about there being no air-conditioning we fell asleep.

Peter Purves

I awoke in a magical room, with a delicate frieze at the top of the walls, two beautifully shuttered windows, which overlooked trailing vines and hibiscus in a terraced garden. It was one of the loveliest places I have ever stayed, and it transpired that if we wanted to swim, we could go to the new hotel a minute or two away which was owned by the Palais. We were treated like kings, and really enjoyed ourselves. I was able to take Gilly to see some of the things I had seen the previous year, and we had a memorable day at the Roman ruins of Volubilis, and at the other Royal City, Meknes. It was nice to just be a tourist without the pressure of filming. Our tour took in Rabat, Casablanca, and Marrakesh on the way south. By that time the delicate engine of my little sports car was beginning to suffer, and in the end it failed to start altogether. As it happened there was a small team of British motor engineers staying in our hotel – not the Foucaud this time but the legendary Hotel La Mamounia. They worked for Rover, and had two prototype Range Rovers with them that they were putting through the paces in the scrub desert surrounding the city. Needless to say, they were able to clean up the engine a bit, and got it to kick into life and to get us off and running again.

The La Mamounia was heavenly. We had booked a small suite, and it overlooked the orange groves at the back of the hotel – the quietest and loveliest of places. We spent time in the Souk and the Place DjemAlfn'a, and I managed to contact our guide from the filming trip, Moulay. He worked as a guide for the Marrakesh tourist board, and was based, funnily enough at La Mamounia. He greeted me like an old friend, and I asked if he could stay with us for the five days we were there. I fully intended paying him, but in the end it was hard to make him take anything. He invited us to his house for a meal on the second day, and we went and had a wonderful time. It was a typical small Moroccan house, comfortable cushions on the floor to sit on, and a small kitchen and bedroom. The only problem was the loo that was a simple porcelain hole in the floor. But, when in Rome… He also had a lady-friend, an American girl from New York, who came for the meal too. She was a lovely person, but she was a big girl. She was in her element because Moroccan men found her very attractive. She and her friend had been touring the country, and her friend had gone home again, but Naomi had stayed on. The only problem with her relationship with Moulay, apart from the fact that she was Jewish, was the toilet arrangements. So he arranged a short camping trip for her in the hills near to a big reservoir that served the city. We went with them for the day and left them there together. And that was fine, because al fresco toilets were OK! Naomi stayed in touch for a short time after she got back to New York, and I wrote to Moulay a couple of times, but eventually we lost touch.

The journey home was a little more difficult. We travelled from Marrakesh to Essaouira and El Jadida on the coast, staying one night in each. By this time we were beginning to get slightly bad tummies, Gilly worse than I, and we decided to head back north a day or two early. Back in Tangier, with the car coughing just a little, we changed our return booking and crossed back into Spain. As we came through customs we were waved to one side, and the officials descended on us. They searched us, and then opened the boot and got our cases out. They went through them with a fine-tooth comb, and then a chap arrived with a big tool kit and they started to remove panels. But just then a rather wrecked VW camper van with several young people in it drove up, and was waved to the side behind us, and we were left to pack again and go. They wouldn't have found anything even if they had continued with the search, but I wouldn't bet that they didn't find anything in the camper van!

We'd planned to stop in Seville and Cordoba on the journey home, but we weren't feeling well enough and after escaping from the bed-bugs in the motel in Seville, we fled north as fast as the roads would let us. In fact, with one stop just short of Bordeaux, we made the ferry in Calais in two days. The trip had lasted a whole month, and although we had got ill, I don't think either of us regretted any part of it. But it made me realise that a month's holiday is at least a week too long. I like the UK and I like coming back to it, no matter how exotic the place I have been.

I never clocked how many miles the car travelled, or if I did I have forgotten what the total was but the car was never the same again, and I got rid of it a month or so later.

The summer of 1970 took the programme to Mexico. Each year seemed to top the previous one, and this was no exception. We flew into Mexico City, a vast sprawling urbanisation on a plateau, 2500 metres above sea level. Two years earlier, there had been considerable unrest there, with students demonstrating round the university, and the military had opened fire on them, killing several and wounding others. Our accommodation was in a tower block overlooking where the shooting had taken place. The Presidential Election was due to be held the day after we flew in. Admittedly things were a lot calmer, and the soccer World Cup had been hosted there in June but there was an extraordinary police presence all over the city. On the election morning, Johnny Noakes and I went for a walk downtown as we coped with the jetlag, and were astonished on approaching a square that hosted a polling station, to find several busloads of blue-helmeted police, parked just round the corner. They were all carrying arms. We were told that there were machine gunners on the roof of the polling station, but that whilst being prepared, no trouble was expected. I don't know whether they were lucky or not, but everything passed off peacefully, and President Echeverria was re-elected. It was somewhat different from my experience up to that date of policing!

Mexico City was full of contrasts, most notably being the extreme wealth that existed in the Blue Zone, the equivalent of London's Mayfair and Park Lane, and the extreme poverty that could be seen almost everywhere else. Nothing brought the wealth aspect more to light than the days we spent on a ranch. Actually it was a huge estate owned by a brewing millionaire. In

Here's one I wrote earlier…

1970, a million was a lot of money, and this chap had many of them. We arrived along a cactus-lined drive, well over a mile long, and drove up to a hacienda style house. We were welcomed by a member of the staff and given a short tour that took in the chapel that had an altar and other tables and was largely made of gold. I have never seen so much gold – really opulent – it was quite amazing. Then we were called to film. The shoot involved us learning to be cowboys with the polo ponies on the ranch. I made a reasonable fist of lassoing John, and we enjoyed ourselves immensely. We were told that we could ride the horses if we wished, and Valerie and I took up the offer. John declined – horses are the only things, I think, of which John is scared! The ponies were just so wonderful. We had big American saddles, a bit like sitting in an armchair, and the responses were perfect and immediate. It was one-handed riding – you brought the rein to the right, and the pony turned right; left and it turned left; back and it stopped. Val and I had an hour on these lovely beasts, and even raced each other along the mile-long driveway at full gallop. It was quite exhilarating, particularly as I had only ridden once before in a film I made for *Blue Peter* at Corfe Castle in Dorset. When we returned to the corral and gave the horses back to the real cowboys, we became aware of a presence. The owner was there on a fantastic black stallion. He was dressed head to toe in black with a black sombrero. The hatband was made up of several silver horses' heads in pairs, nose to nose. His trousers had a similar silver motif all the way down the outside seams, and he wore a gun belt, with a pair of pear-handled silver revolvers. He absolutely dripped money. It was like something out of a film.

He was absolutely charming, and expressed pleasure that we were enjoying ourselves, and that we were getting some good film. He then told us we could make use of his swimming pool during the afternoon, bade us farewell, and that was the last we saw of him. It was a day I'll never forget, and was a perfect example of us "going beyond the rope", a phrase Valerie used to describe the way we worked on the show – imagine a stately home with the rope-barriers that prevent the public from going further – we always were allowed "beyond the rope". It was certainly my first experience of millionaire lifestyle. Our producers on the trip, John Adcock and the lovely Rosemary Gill had really done us proud. Mind you they'd had a bonus, because on the recce they had been lucky enough to get tickets for the England v Brazil match, that we sadly lost, but had some of the best moments ever of English football, including Banks' unbelievable save from Pele. I really envied them that!

But the ranch wasn't the end of our cowboy exploits. Rival ranches hold "charreada's" – these are rodeos where the ranches compete in a number of skills, from wrangling the steers, to fancy riding, and even riding wild bulls. We were invited to a local one, and suddenly found that we were expected to take part. Thank goodness for the previous experience at the polo ranch. I did a couple of rides into the ring, and saluted the "royal" box, I spun my horse around on the spot, both left and right, and even managed the fast ride in and bringing the horse to a dead stop, followed by getting him to walk backwards. I was rewarded with a cheer, and a cry of El Beatle, because of my hairstyle that was getting longer by the day. Never to be outdone, I think Johnny actually rode a horse too.

Mexico is a strange place, with extraordinary history and we explored a lot of it. We climbed to the top of the Pyramids of the Moon and Sun in the old Aztec capital of Téotehican; we watched the fertility rite of the Flying Men of Papantla, we went to Yucatan and saw the ruins at Chichen Itza; we visited Acapulco and stayed in a fantastic hotel, Las Brisas, which consisted of lots of small bedroom chalets all the way up the hillside overlooking the bay. Each chalet had its own small pool with rose petals floating on the surface, and room service was delivered by jeep. I can remember thinking; it doesn't get much better than this. I learned to water-ski properly in the bay, and John went paragliding. Actually we nearly lost our cameraman, David Feig, whilst filming that. After John had been up, David put on a helmet camera, and went up to film John's eyeline. Unfortunately, the boatman didn't pay careful enough attention, and turned a little too tight. It meant that the tow rope went slack, and David descended. Just as his feet hit the water, the rope went taut again and he was whipped over onto his face, with the heavy helmet camera making it even more dangerous. He was lucky, but he wouldn't go up again!

We also made a very lyrical film on a large lake in central Mexico; Pazcuaro I think it was. The trade there of the locals was fishing, and we went out with them in their boats. They used butterfly shaped nets with great skill, and we tried to learn the technique with limited success and inevitably, John had to fall in. As he hit the water, hundreds of water snake heads appeared, like miniature Loch Ness monsters that swam away from him as fast as they could. I have to say he was out of the water and back in the boat faster than anything I've ever seen!

For some reason lost in the mists of time, Valerie and I had a serious falling out, that meant we wouldn't talk to each other, unless the script demanded it. We were supposed to be having fun in Chapultepec Park, riding the roller coaster – at that time the biggest in the world – and so on. John had to act as mediator, so Valerie would say, "John, would you tell Peter...," whatever it was, and I would reply "Would you tell her..." So childish, and it went on for several days. Neither of us can recall what had been the cause, and it was probably something really trivial. Eventually we made it up, and got on with the job of enjoying ourselves (sorry, I mean making films!)

One thing had nearly scuppered our whole trip. At Heathrow on the way out, we had checked our bags and gone through the passport control and were waiting for our flight in the departure lounge, when suddenly we were called back to customs. When we got there we were taken into a side room where our baggage awaited us. Our bags were searched and our hand luggage, and eventually we were allowed to go back to the departure lounge. I later discovered that a telephone call had been made saying I was carrying a quantity of drugs out of the country, and the customs boys acted on it. At that time I had been having a bit of difficulty with a stalker. Actually it had been my fault, in that I'd had a short *affaire* with a lady, and when I stopped seeing her, she made life pretty awkward for Gilly and me. There were constant calls blocking my telephone line at home, and one morning my car was covered in white paint. Amazingly Gilly stood by me through it all, and reading between the lines I guess the phone call had come from the same source.

Chapter Twelve

Some memorable Blue Peter films;

Rock-climbing; Stunt driving;

Having a smashing time in cars;

Near disaster on the Severn Bore;

Beautiful evocations of an earlier time;

Walking the cable of the Forth Road Bridge;

A tree for Trafalgar Square;

Survival course in Norway;

Training for the Royal Tournament;

Renaming the 532 Blue Peter

The best thing about being a *Blue Peter* presenter was that you got the opportunity to drop into the best parts of other peoples jobs. If you fancied driving a train, flying a plane, sailing a boat, riding a horse, you just did it and you were able to do it without having to serve a long apprenticeship. It was a huge privilege to work on such a show. I can clearly remember almost every film I ever made for the programme, yet my memory of studio items is very slim. I think that is because of the way I learned the scripts. Once you had finished a show, you had to get straight on with the next one, and I think my mind cleared out the things I didn't need to retain, so that I could more easily remember the new stuff.

I couldn't possibly tell a chronological story of the films I made, so I am just picking out some highlights. As I said earlier in the book, I loved rock-climbing, and consequently found myself making a number of films on various crags. One of the most exciting was when I went out with the Mountain Rescue Team from RAF Valley in Anglesey. The story was that Johnny was a pilot who had bailed out and was stuck at the top of a crag in Snowdonia, with a broken leg. The team arrived at the bottom of the crag on a fairly misty and damp morning, and after roping up, began the climb. During the ascent we experienced every type of English (and Welsh) weather. The mist cleared and out came the sun, quickly drying off the rocks. Then the clouds rolled in and it began to rain, followed by hail, then snow, and as we came to the last pitch it froze hard. As it happened the last pitch was classified as severe in good weather, but involved using the clenched fist in a crevice to climb up the last part of the crag. By the time we got there, there were two inches of ice covering the rock surface, and the climb required artificial aids, which we weren't carrying. So the climb was completed by the support crew, who had taken the easy route to the top, dropping a rope over to us so we could scramble up.

Then came the really difficult bit, which was for two of us to abseil down the rock face with a stretcher between us. Poor Johnny was strapped onto the stretcher, and he was unable to do a thing except lie still in a state of mild terror. He does admit to have been scared, but in the end we got him down to terra firma in one piece.

One thing Johnny discovered after several years of our working on the show was that we had not been properly insured by the programme for the quite dangerous work we sometimes were asked to do. We never questioned the insurance cover, and at the time there was little if any interference from the health and safety police! Actually I am not sure they existed then. They would certainly have had something to say when I joined the destruction squad, a team of stunt drivers from Leicestershire. The idea was that I would perform a stunt, driving a saloon car through a furniture van.

When I arrived at the disused aerodrome where the stunt was to be performed I found that the car selected for me to drive was not fitted with seat belts at all. It was an absolute wreck of an old Morris, I think. I naturally assumed that there would have been a protective harness of some kind, and that my legs may well have been packed in things like egg boxes. No such luck. Two guys who were to do other stunts told me that everything would be all right and that a seat harness would be fitted in time! In the meantime I was verbally taken through what I should do. I was to drive from a flat field onto the hard standing area, and drive straight up to a Pantechnicon parked at right angles to my line. There was a wheel ramp placed at the side of the van which, when approached correctly at 70mph would throw me and my car up and through the side of the van. I would come out the other side, and would probably turn over in the air and then crash into a pile of old wrecked cars that would provide a cushion and stop me. Nothing to it, they said!

I immediately went to have a closer look at my car. The belts had been fitted, which was a bit of a relief, but I decided to put a bit of pressure on them, and to my horror they pulled straight out of the rusty floor of the car. So it was back to the drawing board for the amateur mechanics. This time I stayed with them whilst they tried to find a strong enough point into which the bolts could be fitted. Finally it was deemed safe enough for me to use.

It did make a great film, but I was nervous. At 70mph with a slightly dodgy car, whose steering may or may not have been accurate, there was always the danger that I could miss the ramp and embed myself into the chassis of the truck. I won't pretend I wasn't nervous, but something like this cannot be rehearsed. I did rehearse the run up several times, and it seemed OK but 70mph was out of the question – the engine just wouldn't go that fast. It was agreed that I'd go as fast as I could and that if I didn't get up to at least 60mph then I would have to abort. That was easier said than done, because the brakes only worked at about 20% of what they were designed to do. In the end I just went for it.

At just over 60mph I hit the ramp, and at that second I wished I was anywhere but there. The car jumped up and through the truck we went. It didn't turn over and as it had been slightly deflected to the right, we missed most of the cushioning wrecks, and we skidded over the tarmac, metal wheels grating as the tyres had burst on landing. But it all ended safely and although I was a little bit shaken I was very proud to have done it.

One of the regular team was going to make a record-breaking attempt at jumping over 16 parked cars. The ramp this time was a car transporter with the ramps down. His route was similar to mine, but he had to make a slight turn on leaving the field to get in line with the ramp. The tractor for the transporter counted as one car and there were 14 other old bangers lined up. For the last car they asked me to put my own private car in the line-up. I refused. They said it was quite safe because it would be the first car in the line-up, right up against the tractor, and he was going to jump 16. I still refused, and so the stunt driver put his own car in that place and then set off to practice the run-up.

He made three trial runs, just pulling out to the left at the last minute, and then he went for the record attempt. The drive across the field went well enough, and as he hit the tarmac he made the slight turn to get in line. There was a fraction of a skid and then he was on his way. But he didn't hit the ramp properly, and the rim on the side of the ramp ripped his tyre from his front nearside wheel. The car slowed and just made the top of the ramp before toppling over with unerring accuracy onto the roof of his own car! It would have been mine had I agreed to put it in the line. I don't know what his insurance company would have made of that!

We made a lot of driving films from grass track to single-seater racers, and on one very silly day we went banger-racing in Warwickshire. It was a great day, and John and I took part in a couple of races after we'd been given some instruction on film. In the second race, we were really going hard at it. John half drove me off the track and I hit a marker barrel and was thrown into the air, and ended up straddling the barrel with no wheels on the ground. Then John met a similar fate and neither of us covered ourselves in glory. But we'd had a lot of fun – there's something therapeutic about smashing cars. At the end of filming I got into my car, which was the same Bond Equipe sports car I had driven to Morocco, to head back to London, and reversed it into a low pillar I hadn't seen, seriously damaging the boot. I was choked. But on coming into London down the A1, I stopped at the first set of traffic lights, and a car drove quite hard, straight into the back of me. No one was hurt, but the other driver was liable for the now even more extensive damage to the back of the Bond!

My first horse ride was quite something too. Apart from the donkeys on Blackpool beach, I had never ridden, and I was to make a film about Corfe Castle near to Swanage in Dorset. One of the stories was about Cromwell's Army arriving to take the castle during the English Civil War. I was Cromwell's Army, and I had to arrive at the top of the steep hill behind the castle, and then descend on a narrow path. Never having ridden, I didn't realise how difficult this was supposed to be. But I got up on the horse, and he was quite a big fellow, and had a short practice, and then I was called to film the arrival and descent. It was only when I was sitting on the horse at the top of the hill that I realised how steep the pathway was. Someone must have been on my side, because I came down with great ease – and amazingly was still on the horse's back by the time I got to the bottom.

Experiences like that make you feel a bit invincible, and I was delighted every time I was asked to ride after that. I made one film with the Royal Veterinary Corps at Melton Mowbray, and was schooled, together with some officers, by a former Olympic rider. All went well for half an hour or so, when suddenly my horse jumped sideways, and I was nearly thrown. But I managed to get him under control and kept my seat. The sergeant called out, "Well done, Peter", and I swelled with pride. As I rode past him he whispered, "You were the only person here who didn't know your horse was going to do that!" I felt suitably chastened, but I didn't know then what he meant, and he never told me. You can be too confident.

We also made several really beautiful films. A superb young director joined the programme called David Brown. He had such a lovely imagination, and set about making a short and very lyrical film about the canals. Val, John and I dressed in old bargees clothes, and we took the dogs, Petra and Patch with us to Braunston. The opening shot was sensational. It was a tight shot of cars on the M1, and then it pulled back as an express train passed through, and the camera continued to pull back to find the head of a beautiful Shire horse being led by me along a towpath, pulling a painted narrow boat with Val and John aboard. We filmed going up a long stairway of Locks, and John and I "legged" the boat through the Braunston tunnel. That was quite hard and we had to balance on our backs on a plank tied across the bow of the boat, whilst we walked along the walls of the tunnel, propelling the boat slowly forward. Val had taken the horse over the top of the hill to join us at the other end. It was totally authentic, quite beautiful and a wonderful reflection of a time long gone.

Another evocation of time long gone had me learning to drive a Coach and Four. This was a beautiful old Stagecoach, pulled by four matched horses.

The lesson was so much fun, and sitting on the coachman's seat, it was extraordinary to feel the strength and power of these animals. It was only 4HP but it felt like I was driving a Formula 1 racer. After the lesson we came to the second piece of the film that had Lady Singleton in all her finery boarding the coach. As coachman I helped her aboard and then I got up on the driver's seat and we set off up a delightful tree-lined country lane. I am pretty certain the real driver was sitting beside me, but I had the reins.

Halfway up the lane we were stopped by Highwayman John. He was sitting astride a jet-black horse, holding his pistols and issued the warning "Stand and deliver". So Valerie had to disembark and hand over her jewellery and the last shot was to be of Highwayman John wheeling his horse and riding off up the lane with his booty. The only problem was that, as I've said earlier, John hated horses and didn't fancy that at all. Some clever shooting masked the fact that the highwayman wheeling away and riding off was me in John's ill-fitting coat.

We set off one spring to make a film of the Severn Bore, the natural surge of water that causes a mini tidal wave to sweep up the River Severn. It can be quite fierce and the tides suggested that this was going to be quite a big surge. There are always canoeists and surfers wanting to ride the bore, and we decided that John would be in a canoe, I would be in one of the two boats with the camera team and I would do a reality commentary on what happened. It was carefully planned, because on the water, things can go wrong. John was to wait in his canoe and catch the wave as it surged past, and the camera boats were to face the bore and then speed away upstream keeping just ahead. The cameramen were Peter Middleton and Bob McShane and we had made many films with them. I was in Bob's boat and we faced the oncoming surge. Our boatman had practiced the move off three or four times, and all was set for a spectacular film. And so it was, but not in the way we had anticipated. As the bore approached, the water beneath us seemed to flow even faster downstream to meet it. At the very second that we had to move, it all seemed to go shallow, and as the boatman gunned the outboard motor, the prop dug into a small sand bar and we failed to move round. Instead the engine cut and we turned side-on to the bore. I just had time to see John pick up the wave in his canoe before we were overwhelmed. The wall of water must have been between four and six feet high, and the boat went over and under. We were wearing life jackets but with the churning water and sand and mud that were being whipped round it was easy to lose one's orientation. I hit the bottom and kicked to the surface, but I didn't make it, as I was hit first by a paddle I think, and then by a boot, and down I went again. I was being swept upstream with the speed of the bore, and I bounced off the bottom, kicking up again. This time I surfaced, and almost immediately up came the boatman. The upturned boat narrowly missed my head and Bob was nowhere to be seen. The water was still surging upstream and I looked round as well as I could whilst treading water – John was still heading upstream in his canoe, the other boat was concentrating on looking for us in the busy water. Where the hell was Bob? I ducked under the surface but could see nothing in the murk, and I came to the surface again.

The boatman seemed to be managing, and then to my great relief a body broke the surface. It was Bob but he was obviously completely disorientated. His life jacket had brought him to the surface, but he was lying face down, and not appearing to make any attempt to turn over. I fought my way to him, and pulled his head up. He had swallowed water and was absolutely out of it. What none of us had realised was that he couldn't swim. To cut the story short, I was able to nurse him to a mud bank and get him to the bank of the river where he could sit without the water bothering him, and he began to recover. It had been a terrifying ordeal for him, and thanks to my life-saving skills, I had been able to get him to safety.

The camera, of course was lost, but interestingly some boys out looking for crabs and such saw a piece of chrome sticking out of a mud bank some days later, and it was the shoulder support of the camera, and the camera was recovered. Amazingly the film in it was undamaged and it recorded everything up to the moment the bore turned us over, so we were able to transmit it on the programme. Bob, sadly no longer with us, was so grateful he bought me a gold money clip from Aspreys, and I really treasured it, until some petty crook burgled my house in Wandsworth and stole it together with a lot of other jewellery. I've never kept jewellery since.

One of my most spectacular films was made on the Forth Road Bridge. I had previously clambered all over the iconic Forth Railway Bridge, in the steps of Richard Hannay but this was something different. I spent a day with the bridge inspector, part of whose job involved walking the cable of the suspension bridge once a month. The bridge is a big one, and standing on the ground where the massive cable is anchored, it is a most impressive sight. Naturally I assumed we would be tied onto a safety rope or something, but no. Part of the bridge's construction are the tight hawsers placed every 50 feet or so that tie the cable down to the road deck below, and had we been fastened to the handrail we would have had to unfasten ourselves at every hawser so the safety line could then be re-attached at the other side of it. Very fiddly and potentially dangerous. So we were to climb without the proverbial safety net.

We were lucky that the day was bright and sunny, and there was only a slight breeze when we set off. It was a bit stop start at the bottom, because we had to get several shots from different angles of us walking on the cable, and at this point we were no more than 20 feet above the road. Then the climb began in earnest, and it was a strange sensation. I'd always had a good head for heights (from my rock-climbing) but as we climbed, the reference points with the ground began to leave our sight. It was quite scary to look left and see the roadway disappear, then the roadside lighting disappeared beneath us, and then suddenly there was nothing on either side except an expanse of sea. At that point I was unable to tell how high I was, and all the fear left me.

Peter Purves

I've tried to find out the bridge inspector's name, with no success, but we got quite chatty on the way up. We'd been told that the crew would film us from various angles, as we climbed, but that when we were halfway up we were to stop and wait whilst the camera moved to a spot down on the riverbank a good half-mile away. It was beginning to get a bit breezy, and so at this point we did fasten ourselves to the handrail with a climber's carabina and waited. Eventually, way down to our right we saw the crew ready, and they signalled us to move on. The camera had a very long lens and the shot started quite close on us and then kept on pulling back as we went higher and higher. Then we had to stop again, whilst the camera team came back to the bridge and went up (in the lift!!) to the top of the first main support column. Once they were set up and ready we continued the climb to the top, and it provided a spectacular finish for the film. It was no cakewalk – at the top of the bridge, the cable gets quite steep, and is approaching an angle of 40° – so it looked wonderful. The film was cut together with George Robeys' *Keep right on to the end of the road*, and was received very well. On *Blue Peter* we were often given film challenges that take a bit of courage to complete, and I was so proud and thrilled to have done such a spectacular film.

I also made a couple of other good climbing films – the programme had made a friend of the great Chris Bonington, who was in the process of organising expeditions, eventually successful, to climb Mount Everest. On a smaller scale he took me to climb Black Crag near to Derwentwater in the Lake District. The climb was called the South Pinnacle Direct, and was classified severe. In those days that was the highest classification before a climb needed artificial support. In fact there was only one severe pitch; the others were just darned difficult. Our cameraman was the brilliant Mick Burke, who free-climbed the entire route, with an Éclair camera, and a bag of film magazines over his shoulder, and he didn't miss a thing. Chris led me up the climb that we completed in five stages. It was exhilarating, even though at one point I got stuck. Whilst I pondered how to make the next move, Mick called instructions from behind me. Looking through the camera viewfinder, and perilously perched on another huge rock slab, he had time to say, "you've got to reach for it Pete, it's just above your left hand..." and so on. I was indebted to him for his help, and it was with great sadness that we heard later in the year that he had died whilst on the descent from the summit of Everest. Two other mountaineers who made the top had passed him as they came down, so although his body was never found, we like to believe he was one of the then very few to have reached the top of the world.

Every year Norway gives London a Christmas tree that stands in Trafalgar Square, and in 1968, Valerie was asked to switch on its lights. Before that, the tree had to be felled, and John and I were dispatched to the forests north of Oslo to cut it down and ship it to England. Actually it was an uneventful trip apart from the fierce "potcheen" that the woodcutters made at their campsite. It really was the ultimate hot toddy and knocked your block off. We were with the lumberjacks for three days, but only risked the hooch once! But down came the tree, and it was loaded onto a long truck and we drove it to the docks for shipment to London. It was an honour to have been involved in one of the iconic post war ceremonies, but as we did the work, we reckoned we should have switched on the lights!!

In 10 and a half years I must have made a couple of hundred short films for the programme, not including the summer filming trips. Some were straightforward factual pieces, and some were logistically almost impossible. Like, for instance the snow survival course with the Marines in Norway. We finished the programme as usual on a Thursday at 5.35pm, with me riding out of the studio on a motorbike. Even back in the 70's London traffic was appalling. It was taking me to Heathrow to catch an SAS flight to Oslo at 6.15pm. They had promised they would hold it for us, but it involved a scary ride on the pillion, and a desperate run through terminal two to board the plane. I made it, just, and as I boarded, the doors were shut, and then we were off. Once in Oslo I had to change flights and go north to Bardufoss, via Narvik. This was darkest winter and the weather was atrocious, but the pilots did an excellent job and we made it. A car was waiting for me and took me then on a two and a half hour drive to the hotel where the crew were waiting. I think I got my head down at about 1.30am local time.

The film was another wonderful learning curve for me. We went off into the hills in full winter survival kit, in temperatures (with wind chill) down to minus 40°F and with a fresh deep covering of snow. The Marines donned skis and were towed across a huge lake as we went further and further into the wild. It was a spectacular location, made even more so as the sun came out, and the sky was blue. I learned to make a snow hole for survival overnight, how to fish through the ice (it's amazing the sort of equipment they carry for such a contingency), and hardest of all, I learned how to cross-country ski. The Marines were fit, far fitter than I, and had the exercise been for real I would have struggled, but the men were great company, and we had a fantastic two days working with them. The problem was that I couldn't get back to London on the Sunday, except late at night, again with a couple of flights back to Oslo, and then an early morning flight to Heathrow. A car awaited me this time, and I got to the studio at 10.00am having had no sleep at all. A bed had been made up for me in my dressing room, and I got my head down for a couple of hours, before being woken and called to the studio for rehearsal, and at 5.10pm, a bleary-eyed Purves presented his bit of the programme, live, as usual.

We made films about vintage cars – twice we went on the Veteran Car Run from London to Brighton – vintage motorbikes, casting bells, and fancy dining, butlering, learned to be toastmasters, you name it we did it. Another very exciting film I made with John was the preparation and training with the Fleet Air Arm field-gun crew for the Royal Tournament. The training was the hardest circuit training I've ever done. We had driven down to Portsmouth to a land ship, HMS *Daedalus*, where we joined the teams. The training involved normal circuit work, plus the manhandling of a giant medicine ball that totally sapped your energy. I was absolutely exhausted at the end of it, but when you start on the actual field-gun, you realise why the level of fitness has to be so high. To be selected for the field-gun crew was a great honour for the men – huge pride was involved, and it was the same with the other two competitive crews, the Royal Marines, and the Royal Navy, who would have been going through the same selection process at their own bases.

There were to be two crews, one being the reserve for the first team. Each man on the team had specific jobs to do, and if you have ever seen the Royal Tournament, you will know that it involves running a field-gun and limber into the arena, and on the gun, they have to dismantle it, raise a rig to carry the parts over a wall and a simulated river crossing, over a second wall, reassemble the gun, run it fast to the end and fire a round. I can tell you it is bloody hard and there are plenty of opportunities to cock it up. John and I were given the task of carrying the wheels over. That is actually the first part of the gun to go and involved us each having a wheel over our shoulder, attaching ourselves to the rope and cross, unhooking ourselves and getting in position to await reassembly. In the meantime the rest of the crew are breaking everything down and moving the heavy gun over the obstacles. There were injuries – a fair bit of blood and flesh gets cut as the team speeds up. I guess that's why they have reserves, because the training doesn't stop when you lose a crew member. But we completed the course, keeping well out of the way of the serious work because these guys were very competitive and we didn't want to cause them any grief.

The director was a young chap called John Prowse, who was a newish member of the team, and he was very happy with the piece as a training film but he wanted to see the gun crew run at full speed in the smart kit, their white fronts, they would use at Olympia in the Tournament. The trainers had both teams lined up, as Prowse talked to the film crew, and then he turned and very politely asked the men if they would kindly go and change into their Y fronts!!! Total hysterics from 70 guys.

A favourite film was immortalised in one of the *Blue Peter* annuals – the *Escape from Hever Castle*. It was a film about stunts and stunt sword fighting. The instructor was my old mate Derek Ware, with whom I had worked on at least a couple of *Z-Cars* episodes. He gave me instruction in the swashbuckling sword-fighting style of Errol Flynn and Douglas Fairbanks. After the initial training we set up a scenario where I had to fight my way down from the battlements to the drawbridge and escape. It was a super film, and I "killed" a good half-dozen of the stunt team on the way down. At the end, a chap on the drawbridge, who was actually Derek Martin who went on later to have great success in *Eastenders*, confronted me, and with consummate skill I despatched him over the side and into the moat. Whereupon I was greeted by Derek Ware, and I said, "So what about that Derek, very Douglas Fairbanks, don't you think?" And he replied, "More like Mary Pickford, I thought."

Every now and then we would make a film that brought home to us the popularity of the programme, the Veteran Car Run being just one example. But more than anything else that brought about the realisation was when we renamed the locomotive, *Blue Peter*. This was a wonderful old Pacific steam engine that had gone out of service and into disrepair following the end of the steam era. A millionaire, who had spent a fortune on restoring it, had bought it privately and we had been covering its restoration. It was to be renamed in a special ceremony – rather like re-commissioning a ship I suppose – in Doncaster. We announced on the programme that we would be there at 11.00am on the following Saturday for the renaming ceremony. It was an event that could easily have got out of hand. The local police had been informed of the event and a token group of police were ready to direct traffic and so on, but no one envisaged that over 50,000 people would turn up. It was the most stupendous event that took everyone by surprise. We had to make a film of the renaming, but it was difficult for the cameraman to get into good positions. However, the massive crowd was so friendly and happy just to be there, that what could have been a really difficult situation, passed off really well. It was where a very nice chap first made contact with me – he introduced himself; "Hello Peter, I'm Laurie McMenemy, I'm the manager of Doncaster Rovers" – and over the years we have been in touch from time to time as I watched his rise through the echelons of football power in England. He was, and no doubt still is a delightful man, and I've never forgotten that first meeting.

But that wasn't the end of the story. I had taken Gilly and the children with me to Doncaster, and because we'd announced our presence there on TV, my flat was severely turned over by burglars whilst we were away. They had broken in from a balcony at the back, but couldn't get out that way with the TV and radio and lots of other bits, so they had used some antique knives that I'd brought back from Ceylon, to literally hack the door down. Not a nice sight to return to, but the memory of the day remains untarnished.

I had a big record collection at that time, and all of them were taken, even the only pressing I had of the band from college. It was a terrible recording, but it had some good music on it. It would have been thrown out by anyone else, but it was a part of my life that I thought I couldn't get back, but recently Mike Thompson, the band's guitarist, has sent me a CD of the tracks, so I now have my own record again.

And somewhere in the midst of all this, I managed to find time to have a short fling with Miss Singleton. I only mention this as she divulged the fact in her own memoirs in a national newspaper, so it would be churlish to ignore it. It was one of those things – after filming all day and after a drink or two in a congenial atmosphere, the inevitable happened, and to the best of my memory it was most enjoyable. 'Nuff said.

Peter Purves

Chapter Thirteen

Exit Valerie, enter Lesley; Iceland;

Hot Geysers and singing Lapps;

The land of the Midnight Sun; Denmark;

The ultimate summer trip to the South Sea Islands;

Another near disaster in the Sugar Plantations;

Toy town palaces and devout people

In 1972, Valerie decided it was time for her to move on – I think she had been talking to *Nationwide* (the first programme to link up the regions) and realised there would be a life after *BP*. It meant that we had to audition potential replacements, and I was engaged to be the supporting presenter on the set. There were several very good contenders, but one girl was quite outstanding. She had a natural friendliness and sense of fun about her, and she quite openly said to me she didn't expect to get the job, but thought she'd give it a try. I don't think she'd even seen the programme more than once or twice. I seriously kept my fingers crossed for her, and she didn't let herself down. Lesley Judd made her first appearance in May 1972.

Now that was a film I'd rather forget. Lesley had been a dancer with The Young Generation, and her introductory film was to choreograph and teach us a dance. Now I'd always thought I was an OK dancer, but when I started everyone laughed, including the cameraman, Patrick Turley. Pat later married my friend Nerys Hughes, and I was his best man. I think making me look reasonably good was his biggest ever challenge, and considering he was the cameraman responsible for the documentary series on the *Ark Royal, Sailor*, I think that says a lot.

But it was a perfect introduction to the programme of a girl who became a very good friend for the next 10 years or so. She also joined at a fantastic time with the summer filming trip looming. Actually the previous year's trip had been a bit of a botch-up. We had planned to go to Russia, then of course, the Soviet Union, a vast country on the other side of the Iron Curtain. The first stop was to have been Stalingrad (now St Petersburg) and the trip promised all sorts of excitement for us. However, there was a serious tit-for-tat political spat that ended in British and Soviet diplomats being expelled from each other's country. Our visa's never materialised and Rosemary Gill and John Adcock had to scrabble around for another destination, one on which they would barely be able to do a reconnaissance. They decided on a cold trip – and we ended up in Iceland, Norway and Denmark.

I was hugely disappointed not to be going to Russia, but I have to say, the alternative was an absolute delight. We swam in an open air pool in Reykjavik, with the air temperature barely above freezing, we travelled to see the fabulous waterfalls at Gullfoss, and the geysers with the hot springs, and were dive-bombed by angry Skua's protecting their eggs when we wandered unsuspecting onto their nesting site. The Icelandic nightlife was extraordinary. At that time you couldn't buy spirits in the main nightclub in the capital, and I can remember chatting with a Swedish guy and girl for about an hour, watching him gradually get more and more drunk, before finally sliding off his chair and collapsing under the table. He had been drinking from a coke can, but what I hadn't realised was that he'd filled it with vodka, and was absolutely smashed.

Then we moved on to Norway, and filmed the Kon-Tiki museum where

Peter Purves

Thor Heyerdahl's raft was displayed. We also filmed, but never transmitted a film about his Ra expedition. This was the papyrus boat that he said Egyptian explorers would have used to travel the world. I found it fascinating – the boat was kept in an inflatable hangar at Oslo's international airport, and kept at an exact temperature or it would disintegrate. Johnny filmed at the top of the huge ski jump, built for a winter Olympics, in the hills to the north of the city, but even he wasn't stupid enough to try it out. Actually it was really warm and there was no snow anywhere in the south of the country. In fact there wasn't much in the north either. We travelled up to Tromsö in the Arctic Circle where I saw a sight I will never forget. One memorable midnight, I stood on the top of a hill overlooking the city and out to the horizon, and watched the sun sinking in the sky and gently touching the horizon before rising again – the Midnight Sun. Actually perpetual daylight is a weird phenomenon, and it wrecks your sleep patterns, just as perpetual darkness, which is what they get in the middle of winter, is equally disturbing. When I'd filmed with the Marines in Norway, there was only about five hours of good daylight each day, and I found that pretty odd, too. But Johnny and I had a great time as we filmed fishing in the fjord, and then spent a couple of days up near both the Russian and Swedish border as we went on a Lapp hunt.

We found the Lapps and they were on the summer pastures with their reindeer. These nomadic people follow the reindeer wherever they go, and the animals provide them with everything; food, warmth, milk, and the skins make their clothes and cover their wigwams. And that, we thought was how they lived all year round. Actually the truth was a little different. In the winter, they move the herd into the lower lands and they tend to live quite a luxurious lifestyle with beautiful log lodges, all mod cons, cars and snowmobiles. What we filmed was how they used to be, and they were happy to allow our intrusion. We had a pretty disgusting stew with them in one of their huts and the smoke from the fire really got to us all. I don't think I got the smell of it out of my clothes for months. One of the funniest moments came when we had to sing to the herd. No really. Actually it's called yurtling, and the chief herdsman yurtles to his herd as he tries to move them. I like to think my yurtling was a little better than John's, but I am not sure what the Laps made of it!

For some reason, Val didn't come on the trip to Norway and we met up again with her in Denmark. I think she had been making a couple of other films whilst we were away, and in any case, I don't think that Rosie and John could find enough items at short notice for all of us to be involved. Eventually we got to Copenhagen and I loved it. Rosie and John had set up a couple of great films there, one involving the chocolate box soldiers guarding the Royal Palace, and the other was an exploration of the Tivoli Gardens. This is a big park in the centre of the city, with theatres, restaurants, open-air shows, and a funfair. It is good fun during the day, but at night it springs into life and nightly throughout the summer, the evening ends with a great firework display. Because we were filming at night there was quite a big crew – we had lights, and the full film kit with tracks, plus the personnel and our team, so we were about 12 people and a lot of big boxes. Waiting outside the Tivoli main entrance for our transport, an American girl sidled up, looked at the kit and the 12 of us, and said, "What are you doing?" I answered, "We've been making a film." After a minute she said, "Is it a hobby?" They do walk among us you know!

The cameraman and I had chatted to a couple of girls who turned out to be stewardesses on Icelandair, and had arranged to meet them for a meal one evening. We had a nice meal, and they were good company, and we walked down the main pedestrian street to get them a taxi back to their hotel. At this time there were a lot of sex emporia on the drag, and the girls said they'd never been in one, so we took them in, and were confronted by the gamut of toys, films and magazines that had so enraged Lord Longford. As we looked though some of the stuff, suddenly a voice said "Oh! *Blue Peter!*" Startled I looked round, covered in embarrassment. The voice had come from a girl who was working behind the counter, and it transpired that she had been an au pair in London. You just couldn't get away with anything, even abroad!

The last film we made in Denmark took us to Billund, the home of Legoland. It was a fascinating place, and at that time was the only one in the world – one of the original theme parks. Noakesy and I were like a couple of kids there. We'd often in the past had large-scale Lego models in the studio, and this was just an extension of that. Great fun for the kids, and everything made as if with giant Lego blocks. It was a toy my son thoroughly enjoyed as a child, and he made great things like airports and so on. You can never have enough Lego!

As a makeweight summer break, it had been a huge success, and I have to say that I loved the whole Scandinavian experience. But back to 1972. With Valerie now only involved with a *Special Assignment* series, Lesley, John and I set off on one of the best trips of all. We flew first to San Francisco and spent a week enjoying the sights and sounds and smells and everything that was San Francisco in the early 70's. We visited Fisherman's Wharf, went to Sausalito, and filmed in Muir Woods with the giant redwood trees, and we enjoyed our open-topped Chevy as we filmed on the Golden Gate Bridge and the highways that were so much bigger and better than anything we had back home. I loved the city, and its surroundings, and Lesley and I even found time to go off swimming in the surprisingly cold sea. We also took a look at Haight Ashbury, the flower-power centre of America, but were disappointed at how run down and seedy it was, totally devoid of any atmosphere. But most of all we all enjoyed filming on the famous cable cars. We spent a day riding them up and down the hills, demonstrated how they worked with the underground cables, and rang the bell as we rode. The driver, Mac, was thrilled that these "stars" from England were filming on his car, and we chatted about all sorts of things, and discovered to our horror, that he was paid approximately $10,000 a year more than we were! What an eye-opener for us.

After the first week we flew off, via Hawaii, to the island of Fiji. It was a strange place in many ways. In the south where the international airport was at Nadi, it was mostly vast areas of sugar plantations. The capital city, Suva, was in the north, and we would later be using that as a staging post on our way to Tonga but first we had a film to make about sugar. The plantations were mainly worked by the Indian population rather than the native Fijians and we were going to cut and transport as much cane as we could to match their incredibly fast and hard work. To get to the area where the cutting was going on there was a small train travelling on a fairly uneven track. It was soon obvious why; the track is freshly laid to take the train to wherever it is needed to collect the cut cane, and after a session of cutting we were going to be the railway tracklayers.

The track came in sections rather like a model railway, fairly narrow gauge, with each section being about 12 feet or so long. There were four permanent sleepers attached to the rails, and the laying system was very simple. I was to stand between the first and second sleeper, and John stood between the third and fourth. We then would bend down and pick the whole thing up. It was quite heavy, because it was made of iron, but it was manageable. We would then carry it to where the line ended, and John would drop his end and I would push back and the end of the section would slip into the groove on the piece already laid. Then I would drop my end and step out and we'd go for another section. We were filming this for a little while and we'd already laid five or six sections when disaster struck. As before, Johnny had dropped his end into place, and I dropped the front end. Unfortunately, on this occasion, the second sleeper that was a solid metal crosspiece, landed on my heel. I was only wearing trainers, and they didn't protect me much. The pain was excruciating, and I limped away very fast. When I looked down and raised my trouser leg, everything was red with blood. I didn't know what damage had been done, but I sat down and was afraid to remove my shoe – I really thought I might have cut my foot off. It meant I had to get from the cane field to the road, and then Rosie Gill could take me, very quickly to the hospital in Nadi. Once there, the nurse, an absolutely lovely Fijian, cut the trouser leg away and gently removed my shoe. I have to say that the anticipation of the pain was far worse than the pain itself. I think the heel and ankle had gone pretty numb as a result of the damage. The wound was cleaned up, and it was deep and ugly, and without any anaesthetic she carefully put in seven or eight stitches. So my third day in Fiji ended up with my having to use a crutch to walk. Not the most auspicious start to a film sequence. Lesley hadn't been with us in the cane fields so she was horrified to meet me back at the hotel with my ankle severely bandaged and limping badly but I had been very lucky. I think that the spongy back of my shoe had just stopped the sleeper from digging in and cutting my Achilles tendon.

It meant that unless I was sitting down, I wasn't going to be filming for a while. I desperately wanted to go on to Tonga, and was fearful I would be sent home, but I wasn't and the trip continued. A couple of days later, we flew north on the island to a hotel in its east coast, where we were going to film some firewalkers. Actually it wasn't so much fire walking as very hot stone walking. The native guys came from an island about two miles offshore, and surprisingly for such a strange Pagan ritual, they were all Catholics. Our 10 seater plane was almost overloaded with all of us, our luggage and the camera kit, and we landed quite heavily on a small grass strip between two large palm covered hills. The pilot, a young cheerful Australian just said after we'd disembarked, he wasn't sure we'd get out again. That was encouraging!

We met up with the firewalkers, to discover a deep pit that was full of big rounded stones that were being baked by fire. It was hot. Rosie and John talked to the "fixer" and the story was explained to us, and we began to film. The fire was now out, but the heat from the stones was quite intense. We didn't know what to expect, but assumed they would dash over the stones barely touching them. But they didn't; instead they almost danced on the stones, making full contact with the whole of their feet. The three of us were fascinated by the whole thing – it was hard to believe that there wasn't any trickery involved.

Immediately after they finished we were allowed to examine the underside of their feet. No one had any damage, and more amazingly their feet were not hot; they were really quite cool. We got chatting with one of the principal walkers and asked him how they achieved that. He explained that it was all in the preparation. He denied that they used anything to soak the feet or as a barrier to the heat. Instead, they all had to be celibate for a month before walking on the stones, and then they would be all right. And what happens if you are not celibate we asked? "We get burnt" was the reply.

The pilot had his reservations about us getting out of the narrow airstrip, loaded up as we were, but he went for it, and we took off slowly lumbering up and over the hotel and out to sea. We then turned right. My geography has always been good, and I looked over at Rosie, and said, "We are supposed to be going to Suva, aren't we?" She replied in the affirmative, so I tapped the pilot on the shoulder and said that we ought to be going the other way. No one had told him we weren't going back to Nadi.

Suva was purely a stopover, and the next day we flew to the island of Tonga. There was a funny incident at the airport. We were sitting on the runway in our old DC3 (the Second World War Dakota's were the same plane, and this may well have been one of them) waiting for take-off, when we were able to watch a fire drill being carried out near the airport main hanger. A group of firemen rushed out with a long hose, took up positions and the hydrant was turned on. As the water gushed out, they realised that they hadn't connected the hose to it. You couldn't make it up. Then we took off.

Dakota's were, even then, old and slow, but actually they are a lovely way to fly. We cruised somewhere round about 5000 feet and at about 180mph. Just perfect really. We could see islands clearly below, and ships, and were gently carried over the southern pacific to an island I will never forget. We landed on a grass strip again; the international airport there wouldn't have a tarmac runway for many years. And I honestly think of all the places I have been, I have the most affection for this most friendly island. It was totally unspoilt, and had an unreal toy town feel about it. We were to make some spectacular and original films there, though the first one was not so exotic. The following day, Tonga was playing Fiji at Rugby Union. John and Lesley made the film, because I was still incapacitated with my ankle, but I did, at least get to the match. South Sea Islanders are big fellows, and they are incredibly fit. It was a tremendous match because there is a tremendous rivalry between the two islands resulting in Fiji being triumphant. And the Tongan crowd still smiled.

A couple of days later I was walking quite well, and could abandon the stick, and so work began in earnest. We filmed in a village, where we helped the locals build a house for the new pastor. When we arrived there was an empty space on the hard mud caked ground with a small pile of furniture. Quickly a wooden framework was put up, and the ladies plaited palm fronds, which were then placed on the roof and sides. A hole was left for a window, and door, and basically that was it. The furniture was moved in, and four hours after we started, the pastor had a new home. It was lovely, if extraordinary, that everyone helped, and that seemed to be the way of life there.

On another day we were invited to have a feast at a village. It sounded wonderful and it was. When we arrived, the feast was still running about – several little suckling pigs. It wasn't a good day for poor Rosie – she was vegetarian. I had made a film at Smithfield Market a few weeks before we came away, and she had been the producer for that too, and I can remember she wasn't too thrilled with it all. But, we had a film to make. We dug the ovens in the ground – just a few holes a couple of feet deep. Into those we put some kindling wood and a log or two, and then lit it. On top of the fire, rather like the hot stones the Fijians had walked on, we added stones. Once the stones were giving out a lot of heat, palm leaves, which were wrapped around the sweet potato and other vegetables in tight packets, were put in, and finally the top sods of earth and grass were put back sealing it all in. And then it was left. I am relieved we weren't asked to kill the piglets, but when the feast was finally ready, I forgot all qualms. There were four roasted piglets along the centre of the table – actually the table was the floor and we sat cross-legged along the length with almost the entire village – and the vegetables just looked mouth-watering. I can honestly say I have never tasted anything as succulent as the roast pork. The crackling was out of this world, and I now know why the Tongans are so big!!! We drank Cava, which was a slightly anaesthetic tasting drink, and it tended to numb the mouth a little, but we never found out what was in it. It certainly wasn't fermented, and produced no alcohol. But it wasn't unpleasant. Some dancers – both the girls and the men in hula skirts – royally entertained us and I don't think I've ever had a more perfect day.

We filmed on the coral reef to the north of the island, and it was the experience of a lifetime. There were beautiful fish of every hue, and we were only using snorkels. John and I are good swimmers and we had a ball, but Lesley had never admitted to anyone except me, that she didn't really swim. It was one of the bravest things I've ever seen when she slipped over the side of the boat and into the ocean. I stayed near to her at first, but she gradually got her confidence, and when she knew she wasn't going to be allowed to drown, she began to enjoy it, and in the end it made a lovely film.

On our day off we all went off, early in the morning, on a lovely small sailing boat to a genuine uninhabited south sea island that was probably 10 miles offshore. We had taken a giant picnic and were in heaven. My injured ankle was now only covered by a small plaster, and Lesley and I went off to explore the island. It took less than half an hour to walk all the way round it. It was almost like a cartoon drawing it was so small. It had a lovely sandy beach, jungle in its centre and azure blue water lapping gently all round. The swimming was a delight, and the day passed by in a haze of lovely sensations. I doubt that any one of us will have forgotten that idyllic day. We got back to the main island just as the sun set.

Sundays were sacrosanct on the island, and everyone went to church. So as not to offend our fixer and our friends we went too. The principle religion was Methodist, though there had been a huge increase in support for the Church of the Latter-day Saints that was beginning to transform the religious patterns. Our fixer, Painee, was a very devout Methodist, and all he wanted, in life, was a proper organ for his church. I think he thought that we might have been able to help him in this, but sadly, we were unable to do so. I can still hear the wonderful sounds of the congregation singing beautiful harmonies in the church – like their dancing, the South Sea Islanders' voices have a particular quality you don't hear anywhere else. Painee was an influential chap and he did his best for us. He arranged for us to go to interview the Princess Pilalevu, daughter of the King of Tonga at the palace. The palace was a white wooden building with a pretty red roof, and looked like an illustration in a fantasy. We performed the interview with the delightful lady in a small gazebo on the palace lawn. I was so thrilled with just being there, that I cannot remember a word of what was said. But the event stays fixed in my mind forever.

The following year was an equally interesting trip but had fewer highlights – we flew to the Ivory Coast in West Africa. There were issues with permits and money having to be paid to senior officials before we were allowed to film anywhere, and for the first time on any of our foreign jaunts, it didn't feel safe to be out on the town on one's own. But when we made our films it was delightful. One of the films involved us going out with the local fishermen. That particular part of the African coast has huge surf, and the boat had to go out through it. John and I mucked in, and we did as we were told. Sitting amidships we pulled on the paddles as the boat went out into these huge waves. But it wasn't a successful voyage – what we couldn't see, but the camera could, was the locals abandoning ship as the waters crashed over us. Eventually we realised everyone had gone just before the boat capsized, throwing us into the sea. We were approximately a quarter of a mile offshore and the sea was very deep. That wasn't a problem for either of us because we were both strong swimmers, but as the massive breakers threw us back towards the shore, the boat was swept past us, narrowly missing my head. And as the big wave ebbed back, the boat was thrown around and back again. The safest thing was to get as far from it as possible, because a blow from it would probably have killed us. In moments we had made it back to the shore. But it could have been a real disaster. I do seem to attract them, don't I?

We had fun looking for elephants and hippos, but with minimal success, and we went on a jungle walk near an inland town called Man. We finally ended up at the president's village, Yamoussoukro. His palace turned out to be the most opulent place with huge grounds, and there was a hotel that rivalled the best in the world at that time. The village itself was a very poor affair, and I wondered what the locals made of the contrast. It was an embarrassment to be in such luxury, whilst the local population seemed to have so little. The palace grounds had a large lake with small mud banks near the retaining walls on which slept several crocodiles. There were one or two tourists, and to entertain them, and us, the palace guards would throw a chicken down onto the bank. That roused the crocs, which moved pretty fast, and then the guard would pull on a long string that was attached to the chicken's leg and the chicken was reprieved. When the crocs had settled again the poor chicken was thrown in again. Needless to say we didn't film that – hardly a *Blue Peter* film.

Chapter Fourteen

Christmas appeals and the Blue Peter Stampede;

The birth of my atheism;

Thailand; Turkey – the extraordinary trip;

Brunei and Jungle survival;

Brazil, Iguaçu and the girls from Ipanema;

Time to move on

In the spring of 1974, several years before *Live Aid*, we became aware of a famine in Ethiopia. Now *Blue Peter* had, since 1965, held annual appeals for convertible currency in aid of various charitable causes. The first had been when the nation went silver-foil crazy collecting milk bottle tops to buy a Guide Dog for the Blind. The success of that was amazing, with four dogs being provided and all of their training being paid for. And every year since then the appeals have continued, ranging from providing hospital trucks during the Nigerian Civil War, to raising an incredible £4million for Cambodia in the 1980's. At the last count, *Blue Peter* appeals had raised an estimated £100million for good causes, and all without ever asking for money. The programme was probably the original recycler! The appeals were something I was always pleased and proud with which to be associated.

The famine in Ethiopia was the 1973 Christmas appeal, when the audience was asked to collect stamps for the *Blue Peter* Stampede. This was held in conjunction with Oxfam and it touched the nation's heart. We had been made aware of a district called Dinser, that didn't exist on any map. Starving refugees had flooded into a small town called Dessie, and they all came from Dinser. It transpired that a Sheikh Dinser feudally owned the large area, and all of the small villages owed allegiance to him. At least that was our understanding. The location was eventually pinpointed, and the appeal was launched. Apparently all of the crops had failed the previous year, and any seed that should have been planted had been eaten, and the cattle all died. Without a cow the land couldn't be ploughed and nothing would grow again, and then everyone in the area, and it was a big area, would starve.

The aim of the appeal was to re-supply the area with seed, and cattle and ploughs so that the people could return to their villages and become self-sufficient again. It was a huge success and in due course the cattle were purchased plus the other elements, and there was even enough money left over to provide wire gabions to fill with rocks and stones that would help to protect watercourses and keep some of the valuable liquid. The big problem in the country was that it didn't rain very much and if the rains fail then you have a famine. Even if it rained hard, the water rushed down the dry watercourses and was gone – there were virtually no irrigation schemes, and no way of retaining the waters.

Lesley and I were dispatched to Ethiopia to report on the progress of the appeal and to see for ourselves what was being done. It was an eye-opening and heartbreaking exercise. The country itself is so arid and in many ways inhospitable, that even if you are fit and well, life is extremely hard. We had flown to Addis Ababa and then on, via a light plane to Dessie where the herd of replacement cattle were being held. The idea was that we would lead a cattle drive from there to the desolate area from which the refugees had come. All was going according to plan, when, of all vicious turns of fate, the cattle contracted foot and mouth disease and in one disastrous moment the rescue plans were destroyed.

I had been so optimistic that what we were doing was going to make a huge contribution to the survival of these poor people but what we saw on the ground was far bigger and more devastating than anything we had expected. The refugee camps in Dessie were full to overflowing with tired and dying children and adults. They had trekked for miles from their villages, and at the end of their journey, many of them would still die, in spite of the best efforts of the handful of nurses and doctors from various organisations who were fighting to save this rising tide of desperate humanity. I cried a lot of tears.

The Oxfam representatives said they would still take the seed and ploughs into the area where they were needed, and we went along with them. We were able to ride on mules, and there were pack mules carrying sacks of seed. Everything we would need for at least four days in the midst of nowhere also had to be carried with us. I have to say it was an exhilarating expedition – we slept under the stars and we could hear the wild dogs and occasional gunshots because this was bandit country. Ethiopia's unrest was already beginning, and that would end in the collapse of Haile Selassie's kingdom, and in the deaths of most of the royal family, some of whom we had met in the build-up to the appeal.

We travelled with one doctor and nurse, a Peace Corps water engineer, several local guides and helpers and, that was that. It was a wonderful experience and truly enjoyable – very hot during the day and quite chilly at night. We camped out and cooked on an open fire, and we slept in the open with just a sleeping bag, and the stars so clear and close one felt one could reach out and touch them. There were shooting stars every minute, and the clarity of the air and night-light was something I had never experienced before, nor would ever again. Eventually we reached our destination village, a small collection of round huts made of mud and straw, each within its own sort of fenced corral and there we stayed for an intended two days. When we awoke the following morning, we saw that quite a number of people were quietly sitting on a nearby bank. Word had got out that we had medical support, and they had come for some treatment. The doctor and nurse worked solidly for two days, dispensing whatever they could to help these poor folk who seemed quite resigned to their fate. It was a vicious circle – they couldn't plough because they had no animal, therefore they couldn't plant the seed; they had no crop to harvest, and they had no food. How desperate can you get? On the second morning we distributed a lot of the ploughs and seed, and sadly watched a small group who had carried their friend on a sort of primitive stretcher for three days to get to where we were. The doctor diagnosed something awful, and had no medicine to treat him at all. His only chance lay in them carrying him to a small mission house, which was where we had started our cross-country trek. It would take them at least three days to get there and their friend needed urgent treatment. There was nothing more we could do. The following morning, they were still sitting there on the bank. The poor man was doomed. The next day they had all gone.

We were supposed to be airlifted out of the area by a German Red Cross helicopter, and on the extraction day we heard it, but it couldn't find us. At one point we saw it in the distance but couldn't make it see us. Luckily we had a few toilet rolls with us, and we used them to make a giant "X" on the ground, and on the following day it did find us and we were able to leave. Once we got back to Dessie, which seemed remarkably like civilisation compared to where we had been, the situation with the refugees was getting worse. We talked to a local official who said his town was being swamped and didn't have enough food. I have never felt so helpless, and not to put too fine a point on it, I felt we had been "pissing in the wind". When Bob Geldof and the rest made the world even more aware of what was happening to this once glorious country, I remember thinking that sadly, no matter what we do, the plight of these people would always be on an absolute knife edge.

I have always felt proud that we tried our best, and we made children aware that not everyone lives in reasonable comfort, that even the poorest people in the developed world are like kings and queens compared with the hardship and basic survival level of the poor in the third world. We must always try to help, but for some particularly harsh parts of the world there is no long-term solution. I think that the whole Ethiopian experience is what caused me to become an atheist. There is no God I can worship who can allow this to happen to people. If we survive in this world, we have been lucky.

Thailand in 1974 was another exotic experience, but one where we weren't able to do a great deal except look at things. I enjoyed our trips into the Hill Country near to Chiang Mai, and the elephant training school near the Burmese border, but it was a trip without any real highlights for me. Except for the food, which was absolutely sensational. And of course, as a tourist it was spectacular, with the floating market in Bangkok well worth a second look.

There were two interesting events. We had been filming up near the Burmese border at an elephant farm, and had been warned that there was an ongoing situation in the north, partly diplomatic, and partly because of the drug runners from the Golden Triangle. When we got back to Chiang Mai, there did seem to be a greater degree of security than one would expect. It didn't cause us any problem but we went out as a group to a French restaurant in the town. It was immaculate and delightful, and was run by a very erudite Frenchman who spoke very good English. He chatted quite freely to us, and was interested that we had been up towards the border, and with the hill tribe people. He seemed far more inquisitive than a normal restaurateur would be, and I was interested to know why. The following day, I was told, by our interpreter, that he believed the man was the local CIA representative, keeping an eye on the activities of the drug barons in the area.

The other was when we first had been in Bangkok. There had been reports of some civil unrest in the city, and that a police station had been attacked. My imagination of what a Thai police station would be like was very much along the lines of *Dixon of Dock Green*. How wrong can you be? These police stations were like Army barracks, with large accommodation blocks and even a parade ground, and high spiked railings. There were guards everywhere, and it didn't look like the kind of place where you'd go to report that you'd lost your dog! John and I went walkabout, in the evening as we often did on arriving anywhere to try to get a sense of the place. As we wandered in the main part of the city, not too far from our hotel, suddenly people seemed to leave the street in front of us. We turned to see a small truck coming along the road, and in the back were a number of men with firearms and a mounted machine gun. As it drew alongside, the gun was brought to bear on us, and stayed pointing at us until the truck had gone 20 yards past, whereupon it focussed on another group of people further up the road. We decided to cut short our walkies and returned to the hotel. It was the last of the unrest, but it was an uncomfortable moment.

Turkey the following year made up for it. We filmed on the Bosphorus Suspension Bridge (I wasn't asked to walk this cable), which joins Europe to Asia, though even that had its problems. Rosie and John had got all the right permits, and so onto the bridge we went. There was one very nervous soldier in a sentry box at the apex of the bridge, the actual border between the continents. He waved his automatic weapon at us, and the permits were proffered. He certainly didn't trust us and as he patently could not read, the permits were worthless. We didn't like the way he waved the gun about, and he certainly wasn't going to let us film. In the end we had to beat a retreat and go right back into Istanbul to the interior ministry office to get someone to help. Three hours later, we were able to film on one of the most spectacular bridges in the world, but the soldier, who had been given a bit of a dressing down by an officer, still looked as if he had any excuse we'd be dead!

Peter Purves

We went to Ephesus, and although I claim to being an atheist, there was something very special about standing on the spot where it is alleged St Paul delivered one of his epistles to the Ephesians. Like Pompeii in Italy, the ruined city is one of the most beautiful places on earth – well kept and thrilling to walk through. The history of 2500-2000 years ago is a most fascinating period to me. I love the myths of Greece and Turkey and the ruins allowed my imagination to run wild. Further into the interior, there is a ruin at the cross roads of the ancient Silk routes called Hierapolis, and this has to be one of the most extraordinary places on earth. The Roman ruins are completely submerged in crystal clear water that emerges from fissures in the rocks and comes from the centre of the earth. It is warm, very warm, and tastes like champagne, and I doubt that I've ever had a more delightful swim in my life. Except for Pamukkale, which is a mere half-mile away. Here the water runs down the hillside, but has so much calcium in it that it forms pools all the way down the hill. They are known as the cotton castles, and swimming in the upper pools you could swear you were swimming to the edge of the world. Both of these wonderful places provided a unique and fulfilling experience. And our schedule allowed that we stayed there for two whole days. What joy.

I keep on using the word extraordinary, but Turkey really does have more extraordinary places than any other I have visited. In Cappadocia, you can explore the history of the rampaging wars that crossed and re-crossed the land, forcing whole nations to live underground or in troglodyte caves, in some cases for centuries. There are rock churches with the most stunning frescos still surviving, and one wonders how on earth these places were created. There are several underground cities, and one we visited went down five stories, and a sixth and seventh were being excavated. How far they will have got 40 years later, I dare not think.

The abiding memory I have of Istanbul, apart from the smells and the wonderful harbour with the busy ferries, and the Blue Mosque, is the sound of crunching metal as cars regularly clattered into each other. We were warned not to hire a car and drive it ourselves because the reputation of Turkish drivers went before them. We weren't stupid, we obeyed, but I don't think I left the hotel once in a week without hearing or seeing an accident. Two other memories bring a smile each time I think of them. The first was the visit to the Turkish Baths, where John and I were stripped, bathed and beaten by two very burly guys, and I can remember Noakesy muttering after one very harsh thumping and slapping "If he does that again I'll kill him!" The other was sitting at an open-air table looking over the Bosphorus after a lovely lunch with Lesley and John, and being offered coffee – Turkish coffee, and asking how we should have it. And the answer was "Hot as Hell, Black as Night and Sweet as Sin". Sounds like a recipe for life to me!

Brunei in 1976 was the least interesting trip for me – though it had its moments. There was a large ex-pat population there with the oil companies, but it was a very industrialised coastline, and not very pretty. We made our mark a couple of times – we appeared in a special programme on Brunei TV, in their wonderfully equipped and professional studios. The government had a programme of ensuring that the people in the villages in their long huts all had TV, and had a major launch of the TV station just prior to our arriving. Each long hut had a government observer in attendance when the service opened. Included in the opening night's entertainment was an episode of *Rawhide*, or one of the old cowboy programmes. In the long hut we visited apparently the head of the village had said he found the opening very interesting, but did not know that Bandar Seri Begawan (the capital city of Brunei) had so many horses!

John and I had fun with the charcoal burners in the jungle, we cut down sago trees, and we went on a short survival course in the jungle with an English major and a troop of Gurkhas. That was a real experience. We flew by helicopter into a jungle clearing on the bend of a river, to be greeted by no one until the whole edge of the jungle got up and came towards us. The camouflage was something else. Major Phil Pash and his men then proceeded to teach us how to set up camp, and what to look for to eat. Bamboo shoots and other fruits and so on were in abundance, and we were shown how to make use of bamboo for all sorts of things, including making drinking vessels out of them. We went along narrow jungle tracks and were shown how to spot animal tracks, and consequently where we should place our traps for catching food. This was real jungle, miles from anywhere, near to the border of Brunei and Borneo, and there was no pretence about it. The film story was that we would build a raft out of the bamboo and vines, and then we could float down the river towards safety. In between times John and I had a good swim in the river, being careful not to be swept too far downstream as that way were the alligators. We didn't need telling twice. The raft got built, and a fine seat was constructed at the back for Lesley. The soldiers helped us, and we just got on with binding the bamboo together until we had what looked like a very good ship.

Lesley got onto it, sat in her luxury seat, and the raft was launched out into the river, where it immediately began to sink, and then turned over and threw Lesley into the water. We'd discovered in Tonga that swimming was not what Lesley does, at least not well, and we could see she was beginning to panic. The good major reacted quickest and dove in and brought her to the gravel bank. The upturned raft continued apace down the river. I've often wondered what the local former headhunters made of this strange craft that appeared out of nowhere from the darkest jungle. A few of our bits and pieces were lost on the raft, but not the camera or crew, and we carried on filming. I think the original idea would have been a closing shot of us sedately going downstream on our wonderful boat but the reality got very different. The Army helicopter that had originally dumped us in the jungle was due to collect us at about 5pm, but at about 4.30, it suddenly got desperately cold, and misty fog closed

Me as Captain Babble with Kathryn as Robinson Crusoe, Guildford, 1982 – the year we got married.

Relaxing with one of our Pekes, Jamie, in the drawing room at The Old Rectory, Bilton, Rugby 1991.

The Old Rectory 1987 / 92, our first house outside London.

The house we brought back to life, the former rectory in Cogenhoe, Northants.

The west wing of Abbots Lodge, Sibton.

With my lovely old newfoundland, Kent, in the garden at Sibton. He died in 2008.

In Green Park with the two
finalists and winner of the
Guide Dog of the Year, 2008.
(Left to Right) Jon Hastie and
Yaron, Me, Katie Meakin and
Theo (the overall winner) and
Lucy Jaques and Ashby.

Presented to HM the Queen at the BBC TV Centre in 2002.

Relaxing with a Guide Dog at the Gala Day in 2006.

With celebrity chef Paul Bloxham on the set of my chat show Destination Lunch in 2006.

Kathryn and I
in the garden of
Abbots Lodge in
2006.

With noakesy in the garden of
his house on Mallorca
in 2005, when filming
for Britain's Worst Celebrity
Driver - him I might add,
not me!

With Kay Laurence, and Annie Clayton as judges on the set of The Underdog Show in 2007.

Presenting an award at Crufts 2008 to Margaret Nawrockyi, the founder of the charity Dog Theft Action, to whom I am an advisor.

Photo by Nick Mays.

With my wonderful pack of Standard Wire-haired Dachshunds in my garden in Suffolk.

The back garden of our house in rural Suffolk.

And a view of the house from across the moat.

A nice portrait in my kitchen, taken by Nigel Ferris.

Preparing to present an award "we made earlier" to Ant and Dec at the NTA's in 2008 - ably supported by John and Val.

Autumn in Suffolk with four of our lovely dogs (from Left) Hattie, Dottie, Woody and Teddy.

in on the river. By this time, in preparation for departure, we had struck camp, and there was nothing left of it – the Gurkhas don't leave any evidence of their presence – and with visibility down to only a few yards or so, it looked as though we were going to have to do a real survival night. It would be dark by 5.30pm, so there was trouble ahead. Round about 5pm we heard the helicopter high above us, it was there for a little while and then we heard it move off. There was no radio contact and we began to feel seriously isolated. The soldiers had already regaled us with tales of people waking up in the jungle to find a snake eating their arm, and other such horror stories – so a night in the open wasn't sounding too much fun. But then we were reprieved. The fog was thick at about 12 feet above the ground, and we suddenly could hear the echo of the chopper's blades, and were delighted seconds later to see it emerging from the fog. The pilot had flown it brilliantly along the river, just above the water, and in it came to land. Seven people were never so pleased to see their transport arrive!

My last summer trip with *Blue Peter* was to Brazil in 1977. I'd always wanted to see Rio and here at last I got the opportunity. It didn't disappoint. This wonderfully exciting city with the most exotic of names was just what I both expected and hoped. In our films we did all of the touristy things you would expect – exploring the fabulous beaches of Copacabana and Ipanema; we rode in the cable cars up to the top of Sugar Loaf Mountain, and went to the enormous statue of Christ which stands at Corcovado above the city. We played some beach volleyball, and soccer, and watched the girls from Ipanema go walking. I was in heaven. But all good things have to come to an end, and we had to fly south to the Rio Grande. I wouldn't have missed it for the world. On the way we went to look at Iguaçu Falls; these waterfalls rival Niagara in both beauty and in size. They are spread over an enormous acreage, and there are lots of subsidiary falls as well as the six or seven major ones. We were thrilled to fly in a helicopter right into the oxbow of one of the major falls, and for me it was one of the most breathtaking experiences I have ever had. The falls are right at the border of Brazil, Uruguay and Argentina, and just so we could get our passports stamped in Uruguay we crossed the border. I have never experienced border towns like this – apart from the very few vehicles, I doubt that they have changed much since the days when the bandits roamed free!

The Rio Grande was a revelation – and I spent three days filming with the Gauchos. Now my riding experiences have never been the most glorious things I've ever done. Apart from getting the accolade of being called El Beatle in Mexico, my experiences have been poor. But, dressed in leather chaps and with a black sombrero big enough to cover the TV Centre, I set about herding the cattle on the range. My first attempt at getting on the horse proved to be an embarrassment as it ducked its head, and I went straight over its neck and onto the ground. Unfortunately it was recorded on film! Next time was better, and I was up and away, and I have to say, I rode quite well. The cowboys were great, and seemed to be enjoying the experience of filming with me. At the end of the day me and the crew, were invited to join them for their usual campfire meal of "chirascu"; fresh beef cooked on a skewer over open wood flames. The meat is tough, because it hasn't been hung at all, but it has a lovely flavour, and washed down with some local beer, we had quite a party.

The pleasures weren't over, because the next day I flew back to Sao Paulo to board a small light aircraft and we flew two hours into the interior to go to a coffee plantation. Coffee is one of the few things I would hate to have to do without, and there's an awful lot of coffee in Brazil. I learned a few things too – the principle thing being that coffee is not a bean, but a berry. Mind you, as long as it tastes good, I don't really care one way or the other. I looked at the plants in varying stages of development; the film was rounded off with a tasting. Actually, that took place back in Rio, at the institute that I think controls the quality of the coffee. The tasting was very interesting – equally as important as wine tasting – and you have to taste each brew with a slurp. Very rude. I like to think I have a good palate for most things and the various coffees were quite distinct in their individual flavour.

Unfortunately that brought me to the end of the trip, and I was sad to come home. John continued with his part of the trip to Menaus and on the great Amazon River. It was the first time that we had not really operated as a team, but more as individuals, and that had also been the case with the whole year previous on the programme. I didn't film very much, and John had been a bit preoccupied with his concurrent series of *Go with Noakes*. Lesley and I had also been involved in a *Blue Peter Special Assignment* series on Twin Towns. One way or another, there seemed to be a change in the air.

After I got home to the UK, I went on holiday with the family, and on my return, I thought, "I've had enough of this. It's time to move on." It was a big decision – I'd had a regular income for 10 years, and you don't throw that away too lightly. And in any case there were still only three TV channels so it wasn't as if there were a lot of different opportunities out there. In the end I telephoned Edward Barnes, who by this time was head of children's programmes for the BBC, and asked if I could have a chat with him.

A few days later I sat in his office at Television Centre and said I had been thinking it was time for a change and that I wanted to leave the show and he replied that, strangely enough, he and Biddy had been thinking the same thing, but weren't sure what that change should be. He thought for a while, and then asked if I would be happy to stay with the programme until Easter – it was now September. I didn't need much persuading with that, and I agreed.

Petra died in September 1977 and I had to announce it on the programme – that was a really sad time. She had been with Edith Menezes whilst I was in Brazil, and she had not been very well. It was the second programme of the new series and the cards and tributes to that little dog were legion. I doubt I'll be remembered with as much affection. But Petra had given me a real interest in dogs and she is one of the reasons that I have become associated with dogs and dog programmes in the most recent 30 years of my life.

I didn't make many films in that last half year but was still occasionally filming with Graham Dangerfield, and there was one film with Billy Smart's Circus at their winter quarters in Windsor. It was a trapeze film, and I was to be the catcher for Lesley as the swinger. We weren't terribly high but it was enough to frighten Lesley. I watched the young Smart boy as he demonstrated how I had to swing out to get into the catching position at exactly the right moment to catch the swinger who would be coming towards me. There was a safety net, but for Lesley it was nearly too much. It made quite a nice film, and I did catch her, but I wouldn't have wanted to do that for a living. And I discovered how weak my stomach muscles were compared with what they needed to be to execute the job properly.

I can't leave *Blue Peter* without a mention of the show's royal connections. Shortly after I had joined, Valerie was involved in one of the great TV coups of the time, when Edward Barnes organised and filmed the *Blue Peter* Royal Safari. Valerie accompanied Princess Anne, now the Princess Royal on a visit to Kenya, and I know it was one of the absolute highlights of Valerie's career. The princess seemed to be very relaxed in front of the camera, and had a very good rapport with Val. The film was invaluable for the Royals as it boosted the princess' image at a time when she and Prince Charles had seemed a bit aloof. It also spawned one of the great pieces of London graffiti a year or so later, when her engagement to Captain Mark Phillips was announced. It appeared on a bridge near to Shepherd's Bush in West London, and was reputed to have been penned by the poet Heathcote Williams. It just said, "Princess Anne is already married – to Valerie Singleton".

The spin-off from that safari did mean that we had several visits over the next few years to the studios by children of the Royals, including Prince

Edward, and the children of the Duchess of Kent, and we were privileged to be able to entertain them. And when we held our "Rags" appeal to support the charity Riding for the Disabled, Princess Anne, who was patron of the charity made two or three films with us in support. In fact, the princess was responsible for one of the biggest laughs we had in the 10 years I was on the show. Because she was present, the office hierarchy had to turn up at the filming location, including our boss, Biddy. For one sequence, the princess and Valerie were riding ponies towards the camera, with the cameraman and crew walking backwards. Biddy and the rest were all behind the camera and also walking backwards. Biddy never saw the horse trough until she hit it and went straight over on her back and into the icy water. On the soundtrack you can clearly hear the princess saying, "Oh, she's fallen in the trawf," before dissolving into laughter. Thanks for that Ma'am. That bit of film was never transmitted!

One sad memory remains. In all the time I worked on the show, I was never allowed to believe I was part of the team, and I think that went for John, Lesley and Val as well. I was part of the in-vision team, at the sharp end, but none of us were ever allowed or invited to be a part of the production team. Biddy's rule was such that we were almost deliberately excluded from the office set up. If we turned up in the office, which I soon learned not to do, we were not made welcome at all – we felt like intruders. I can remember asking Edward on one occasion in about 1974, if I could write and produce some of my own items on the show. To say he was dismissive would be the understatement of the year. "I've never employed anyone on that basis and I don't intend to," he said to me. This was the man who would employ John Craven on exactly that basis soon afterwards and Noel Edmonds likewise. It was as if we were taken totally for granted, and it made me smart. Isn't it a shame that producers treat their performers in such an offhand way – life could be so pleasurable if only they could let it. In my next life I will be a producer, but I will be a nice one, with an understanding that performers are not machines, and have probably more to offer than is often allowed.

I suppose some of my disquiet went back to the contract that my then agent had secured for me. It was a poor deal, but at every point when we renegotiated (there was no negotiation) it was a case of take it or leave it. Again, this was Biddy emphasising her power and contempt for us. The job was too good to turn down, but it remained unsatisfactory. What I found quite distressing ultimately was that my agent, (whom I eventually left, having been her first client and having sent many presenters to her) prepared nothing for my future – work came in but not through her efforts – and when she took on clients with more immediate earning power than I, she neglected me. And to cap it all, when Biddy ceased to be the editor of *Blue Peter*, and needed an agent for her speaking engagements and whatever else, it was my agent she went to, and was taken on the books. Loyalty? Never heard the word.

All too soon, the best job in television came to an end. My last appearance on the show was the 23rd March 1978, and it was a tearful moment indeed for me, and I think for Lesley and John too. Watching a compilation of my "best bits" I really got a lump in my throat and wondered if I had done the right thing. But it was time for a change, Petra had gone, and I suppose a little of my enthusiasm for the programme had gone with her. I was ready for the next part of my life.

And funnily enough it had already begun. Because I had handled the majority of the dog items on *Blue Peter*, and because I had, in 1976, devised a special segment involving children for the coverage of *Crufts Dog Show*, I was asked to introduce in 1978, the first demonstration in the UK of Agility at *Crufts* for the BBC. This would lead to a 31 year involvement with BBC events at the show.

Chapter Fifteen

I lose my mum; New opportunities in TV; Kickstart;

Noakes and I have a fantastic pantomime success;

I meet my last affaire; Darts hit the Bullseye;

Dog Agility takes centre stage

A lot had happened to my private life whilst all that stuff was going on. The children had grown into teenagers and went to secondary school. There were all the usual ups and downs associated with that. Lisa had been a really good violinist, but at secondary school she just dropped it and Matthew had played the piano a bit (a good friend at that time, Alan Lynton who had been in the Palladium chorus with me, had given me a piano). At that time, pianos were worth nothing, and if you could find the transport, usually you could have the piano for zilch. Matthew and his wife, Clare, still have the piano, a Swiss iron framed upright that my grandson Sam now plays rather well.

But rather more dramatically than that, my lovely mother died from cancer five days before Christmas in 1975. She hadn't seemed particularly ill, but had complained of bad indigestion. She had taken things like Rennies for months, but when she finally went to the doctor, the diagnosis was immediate. Sadly for all of us, the cancer had spread outside the stomach and she went steadily downhill. I was still presenting two shows a week, and immediately after transmission I would drive to the hospital near to Heathrow Airport and sit and read to her. For a short time, she came home to my dad and sister in Horton, but she needed constant care, and as Christmas drew closer she just gave up. It was a dreadful time for us all, and particularly for my dad. But mercifully her illness did not last long, nor was it as painful for her as might have been expected. Unfortunately she died whilst I was driving from the Television Centre to the hospital, but we had said our goodbyes on every occasion I left her in the previous seven days. She was a lovely woman, and my only regret for her is that she didn't live long enough to retire and enjoy some restful times. She worked all her life, and in the end one thought, what for? I still shed a tear when I think of her.

My social life in the mid 70's had revolved around some good friends. Rick Jones, a lovely Canadian who used to be one of the presenters of *Play School* on the BBC eventually gave up that show, as he felt he "couldn't walk around a studio with his feet in shoe boxes any longer". He's also in the hall of fame for being the presenter of *Fingerbobs*. He was an excellent songwriter, mostly the music and occasionally the lyrics. He and some other mutual friends formed a band that regularly played the London pub circuit, and pre-punk I would suggest they were the best band in town. Called Meal Ticket, they were filling every pub they played for four or five years. I loved what they played – an English version of the West Coast bands I admired like the Eagles and earlier, The Band. The main lyric writer was another mate, Dave Pierce, an actor and giant of a man, with the driest sense of humour and a fantastic way with words. These were people I really admired, and I must have watched them at least once a week for several years. It was also an excuse for a good drink with mates. They made three records with the Chrysalis label, and then the punk scene was upon us, and they ceased to be the flavour of the month. But the music scene in London in the 70's was really exciting, with bands like the Clash playing gigs at London University. I couldn't persuade Biddy to have Meal Ticket on the show; all we ever had were Slade and Showaddywaddy – the latter being a band from Leicestershire, which was on her doorstep, as it were.

I went on holiday to New York in 1976, and when I came back, the result of a terrible drought meant that subsidence caused the bay front of my house to almost fall off. The house gradually became uninhabitable, and we had to move out for many months whilst it was underpinned and rebuilt. The only place we could find large enough was a ground floor flat in South Kensington, Cadogan Square, for which our insurance company was happy to pay. I must say that I liked living in South Kensington again – only a stone's throw away from where we had been in Cornwall Gardens – and we were there for at least five months.

My wife, Gilly, had become an established dramatist by this time, having gone on a creative writing course, held by a commissioning editor of radio drama at the BBC. Her talent shone through, and she began to get her work performed. She wrote for a number of TV series, from *Rooms* to *Angels*, and eventually was one of the original writers on *Eastenders*. And at the end of the 70's she had a *Play for Today* on BBC1. But we were no longer the cohesive unit we had been, the cracks were appearing in the relationship, and it was inevitable that we would not be together much longer. The children were 16 by this time, and past the age that our break-up would affect them too severely, or so we thought.

I was away from home much more than previously as the work I was offered upon leaving *Blue Peter* all took place up in Manchester. Edward Barnes was extremely helpful and generous to me on my departure. He offered me a children's sports programme called *Stopwatch*, and a holiday programme for children called *We're Going Places*. In addition to that I was asked to present two series' of *Special Assignment* films that took me from the Tweed in Scotland to the Singapore River. So I was actually very busy indeed.

Stopwatch was a real challenge for me. I'd always loved my sport, and the opportunity to present a programme dedicated to that was a dream come true. I went up to Manchester to meet the producer, Hazel Lewthwaite (yes, yet another female producer for me) and her assistant Mike Adley. Mike was a regular on the production team for *Grandstand*, and was moving up to Manchester because the sport output there was growing. I also took the opportunity to meet up with the former *Blue Peter* director, David Brown, who would be producing *We're Going Places*.

Stopwatch launched in the autumn of 1978, but not until after I'd made a very sticky pilot. For the first time, I was offered autocue, and I rejected it at first. But when I started the recording for the pilot, I went into what could only be described as sports presenter mode. I didn't do it as me, but as I'd heard others doing it. After about three or four minutes, Hazel stopped the recording and came onto the studio floor, and asked what I thought I was doing. I immediately realised what an idiot I was being – they wanted me, not a clone of someone else. I collected my thoughts together, took a deep breath and went for it again, and this time it worked. We had a viable and exciting programme. Over the next five years we made five series' of the show, and my co-presenters included Daley Thompson, and Nigel Starmer-Smith. I interviewed some great sportsmen and women; David Gower; Kevin Keegan, Kenny Dalglish; Graeme Souness, Emlyn Hughes, Steve Coppell, Trevor Brooking, Howard Clark, Hugh Porter and Susan Cheeseborough, to name just a few, and I was absolutely in my element. We even built The Chair (the jump at Aintree Racecourse) in the studio, and brought Red Rum to inspect it. It was a fabulous time, and the programme was very popular. I remember one series ending, where we all went for a programme meal and Nigel and I said we would pay for the drinks. All I can remember of that evening was that we ended up drinking a bottle of sambuca between us, and I was literally poured out of the restaurant door into a taxi, and I took two days to recover.

But I am getting a bit ahead of myself. When the show was about to launch, *Blue Peter* asked me to return to talk about it and my projected *Special*

Here's one I wrote earlier...

Assignment films. John had also left *Blue Peter* in July, and the two of us had been contracted by Paul Elliott, the impresario later to become known as the Pantomime King, to appear in *Cinderella* at the Yvonne Arnaud Theatre in Guildford. Lesley who was going to be interviewing me on the live programme was under strict instructions from Biddy Baxter that we were only to talk about my two programmes and nothing else. But Lesley is a mate, and after talking about the two shows, she said, bold as brass, "and what else are you doing Peter?" And I said that Johnny and I would be appearing in *Cinderella* at Christmas in Guildford. There was nothing more than that, and she wished us good luck.

That evening, Paul Elliott got a call from the theatre asking what on earth had happened. The telephone hadn't stopped ringing and at 6pm they had a half-mile long queue right round the building. In the next three days the show was totally sold out for the whole run, and selling the standing room. I know Paul still tells the story, and I must say that it was yet another example of the power of television, and of *Blue Peter* in particular.

We had first done pantomime extracts in *Blue Peter* in 1973 or '74. The legendary comedian Arthur Askey joined us on the show and we did a couple of classic routines, with him as Baron Hardup and me and John as the Ugly Sisters. I still think I was prettier than John, but he disagrees! I have to say I was really looking forward to performing in the full show. Each year since 1972 or so, we had been privileged to take part in the *All Star Record Breakers* Christmas Specials with the late and very wonderful Roy Castle. It was an opportunity for all the children's show presenters to let our hair down and perform as we were not normally allowed to do. These shows involved us singing, dancing (well, a bit), acting, performing sketches, and playing roles in specially adapted musicals. But I hadn't acted properly since 1967, and John since 1965, so we were bound to be nervous when the pantomime came round.

Peter Purves

It turned out to be great fun. Paul Elliott directed us, and we were somewhat alarmed at the schedule. We began rehearsing on a Monday morning, and we sort of blocked the show. I was given a few ropey jokes to tell on my first entrance as Baron Hardup and John was given a bit of guidance on how to introduce himself as Buttons. Beyond that we had to fend for ourselves. To be honest we really weren't too sure what we were doing. We did have an opportunity to do a "slosh scene" but we'd never done one before and had to learn it. The one thing John and I had was a rapport, and an understanding of what the other was thinking and going to do next. We worked very hard and found that we were supposed to perform the show by the Wednesday afternoon of the first week's rehearsal, without our scripts. The whole cast was a little non-plussed at that. We just got on and did it. On the Thursday we ran the whole show, and again in the afternoon, the same on the Friday, and after rehearsing on the Saturday morning we adjourned, to meet again on the next Monday in Guildford.

To cut a long story short, it was a sensationally successful show. We had full houses each night, and we really began to enjoy it. The first rehearsal week had been hard, but by the start of the second week, I was able to take in the rest of the cast and begin to enjoy their company. Bonnie Langford was Cinderella – she was still only 14, and the script was altered at the end so that she only got engaged to Prince Charming! The Ugly Sisters were two excellent character actors, David Morton and Michael Sharvell Martin, who were extremely witty and great company, and became good friends for several years. Jacquie-Ann Carr was Prince Charming, but I was particularly interested in a strawberry blonde Dandini called Kathy Evans. She looked fantastic in her thigh high boots, and she had one opportunity to shine in a song with the chorus girls, called *Dance in the Old-fashioned Way*. She sang it wonderfully, and her dancing was brilliant. I stood in the wings to watch and never missed a single performance. This was obviously a show that would run and run!

Here's one I wrote earlier...

Before the season ended in January 1979, John and I had been invited to do the show again the following year in a venue to be decided, and as we'd had such a good time we agreed at once for double the money we had been paid in Guildford. And a few months later Kathy was engaged to play Prince Charming, so I have a lot for which to thank Paul Elliott.

In between times, *Stopwatch* was going strong, and another series fell into my lap that became the third cult show in which I have been lucky enough to be involved. *Kickstart* had aired for the first time the previous year, with Dave Lee Travis as presenter. The producer, John G Smith, was keen for a change for the second series and he approached me. For my part, I had only ridden a motorbike a few times previously, but I had great fun in 1974 taking part in the Royal Signals trials course over a long weekend at Catterick Camp. Again, I fell off quite a lot, and at one point on the course, having struggled through depths of deep mud and streams, I came to a small rock waterfall. The aim was to ride up it, and the soldiers managed it with varying degrees of skill. I rode hard at it and ended up spread-eagled on the bank, with the bike still running. The Signals officer in charge was heard to mutter, "Well, I've never seen that done before!" But in the end I completed the course, and was proud in the *Blue Peter* studio a couple of weeks later, to ride into the studio with the team, and to be presented with my own White Helmet, that I still have. And on a couple of occasions I was able to take part in White Helmet team demonstrations at large outdoor events. They were a great bunch of guys, and the present day team still perform regularly at events up and down the country. Thanks to that experience, I was asked to present the show. Naturally I was delighted to be asked, and began a relationship that was to last for 13 series' in total – that included the later *Junior Kickstart*.

It was a super programme to work on – I presented the opening link, and then went into the commentary box to do "live" commentaries on site. The format was simple – obstacles were set up over a stretch of countryside on Lord

Peter Purves

Hesketh's Estate, Easton Neston, in Northamptonshire. The riders had to negotiate the course in one direction for part one, and in reverse direction for part two, and the fastest aggregate time including penalties for faults, was the winner. It was show jumping on motorbikes! I always had an expert with me; first it was former World Trials Champion Mick Andrews who was a great guy. I haven't seen him for years, but he and his wife Gill still exchange Christmas cards with us. He was always keen for me to get on a bike and attempt some of the obstacles, and I fell off a lot; but that was fun. The first three or four series' had some of the world's top trials riders, but with limited sponsorship, the promoter, Nick Britain, eventually found it hard to make any profit. After six series' the professional event was abandoned, and *Junior Kickstart*, which had run for a couple of years in tandem, became the sole survivor of the genre.

The juniors were the future of the sport. The senior event had become a more difficult challenge each year, particularly with the arrival in series five of Jean Pierre Goy, a Frenchman who was a specialist in a fast developing sport on the continent, Arena trials. He demonstrated what were, in essence, circus tricks on a trials bike. Within moments, all of the riders were doing them, and the skills level moved up a few notches. My expert co-commentator was a former British Trials Champion, John Lampkin, and latterly an American, Jack Stites from Florida took his place. John's nephew Dougie would become one of the stars of our junior event, though he never actually won it. His main rival was a lad from the Isle of Man, Steve Colley, who, twice, pipped him to the title. By the late 90's, with both shows long dead, Dougie was to become World Trials Champion on at least five occasions, with Steve regularly the runner-up!

On one programme, the hardest obstacle was a pole over what looked like a World War bomb crater! One of the young riders has gone into the archives for falling off it. The video clip has been shown on TV many times, not with any sadistic intent, but because of what happened afterwards. I was commentating, and expressing concern that he wasn't hurt – had he been more mature, it could have done him a lot of damage, but what followed was hysterical. The St John's Ambulance people were always on site for the event and the two chaps on duty went rushing down into the crater, and for no apparent reason, proceeded to throw themselves on the floor. It was impossible not to laugh and although the poor lad was still in pain – mostly his pride was hurt – the antics in the pit defied belief. Amazingly, in 13 series', no rider was ever badly hurt, and the obstacles ranged from simple bunny-hops (that caught out the majority of the riders for some extraordinary reason) to a giant JCB with the arms extended that the riders had to negotiate, as it happened, in the rain!

I had also been in the right place at the right time yet again. I was spending a lot of time in Manchester presenting *We're Going Places* and *Stopwatch*, and that meant spending a little time in the BBC club. I had always played a little darts, since when my folks had owned the pub in Derbyshire, so I often played in the club. There were a few good players there, and I would usually win. Sid Waddell, who was to become the voice of televised darts, was often there too, but as a watcher – he never played a good game, but he could and can talk a good one. Tony Green, on the other hand was professional standard, and I struggled against him at first. It was round that time that I hit my first maximum 180, and amazingly after the first it became quite commonplace. I managed a 12-dart finish on one occasion, too, so I wasn't bad at all. Word obviously got round that I could play and enjoyed the game, and Nick Hunter, head of sport for BBC in the north, approached me to ask if I would be interested in hosting the televised British Championships, and I leapt at the opportunity. That in turn led to my presenting the World Championships after David Coleman stepped down in 1979, and my continuing in that role for the next six years. In that time I played with all the great professionals of the time, Eric Bristow, John Lowe, Jocky Wilson, and Bobby George. And on occasion I would manage to win the odd game – but I could never beat Eric. We also created a weekend knockout competition for the top British players called *Bullseye*, (long before the Jim Bowen show of the same name) which we recorded at Pontin's. There was also a series of Home International matches that we covered for 3 years, when the darts balloon was at its fullest. It was also when my stomach became its fullest – one tended to drink a lot of beer when playing and I put on quite a lot of weight. It was odd that I played OK until I had drunk three pints, and then for the next three pints I really played at my best. By seven pints I couldn't even stand up, let alone throw an arrow. And even when I wasn't in Manchester, I spent a lot of evenings in pubs in London, Young's and Fullers pubs mostly, and my friends in Meal Ticket were often my playing partners. Eventually it had to stop and the drinking had to be cut back too. I have hardly thrown a dart since the mid 80's! It had been fun while it lasted.

Agility had become the fastest growing sport in the dog world. After I introduced it at *Crufts* in my first show there in 1978 it had snowballed, and quite soon the equipment was being made professionally and standardised so that everyone knew what they would get in terms of obstacles. Safety was paramount, and it was soon realised that with some of the larger obstacles there needed to be contact points that would slow the dogs down. The three main obstacles requiring the contact points were the "A"-frame; the dog-walk (a narrow plank raised at about five feet from the ground with a narrow ramp at each end); and the seesaw. In the case of the seesaw it meant that the dogs had to make the seesaw tip before getting off and the rules remain the same up to today. I have made a lot of friends in the Agility world, including Dave and Mary Ray – Dave being an organiser of some of the biggest Agility events in the country, and Mary who was one of the first very successful competitors. Actually I'd first met her at *Crufts* when she won her first Obedience Championship, and I was asked to interview her. She won't mind my saying this but it was one of the worst interviews in history, and was never transmitted. I couldn't get anything out of her at all – once the cameras rolled she just clammed up. If I did it today, I doubt if I'd be able to shut her up.

I've always loved the activity events, even the Obedience that can, to the uninitiated be a bit like watching grass grow, but when you are either involved, or really understand what is going on it can be fascinating. With the activity events coming on stream, the amount of Obedience we could show diminished. The stalwart of Obedience had been the wonderful late Muriel Pierce. She had won the Obedience Championship with her dog Meg six times, which was an unbeatable record. She and I would watch the event from a corner of the ring – until recently it was still called Mu's Place. It was funny to watch with her as she criticised certain aspects of the event that had changed. She was very strict about the dog not "leaning on" the handler, and she was an excellent pundit for us, as was Sandy Wadhams who took over when the show went to Birmingham.

The next big innovation came with a new sport we introduced for the first time a couple of years before the show moved to the NEC in Birmingham; Flyball. There is still a lot of contention about what real Flyball is. Originally it was for a couple of teams running head to head, four dogs in each team with a Flyball box and a ball loader. The dogs would be lined up at the start line and the first on each team sent along a short course where they jump four low hurdles. When they reach the Flyball box, they step on a lever or plate, which threw a ball into the air. The dog would attempt to catch the ball and then return over the four hurdles, and the next dog would go. The fastest team to accurately complete the course would win.

So when this was first seen it was sensational; very noisy and it really got the crowd going. Teams formed up and down the country, and a great series of competitions were born. Then some clever person decided that they would come up with a better box. With this box, when pressure was put on the pedal or lever or plate, the ball was presented at the front of the box, and the dog just takes it. This was very much faster, but it wasn't Flyball. The ball didn't fly. I am glad to say that *Crufts* keeps the old Flyball box, but hardly any other competition does. The teams perpetually seem to strive for faster times, and if the ball doesn't fly, who cares. Well I do, and I think the TV audience does. It certainly makes it a spectacle, and there is always that small element of uncertainty as to whether the dog will catch the flying ball. It is great stuff, but one of the hardest events on which to commentate.

There has been yet another addition to the action events that has also grown very fast into a major competitive sport. It was born out of obedience training, but is much more entertaining. It is called Heelwork to Music, or doggy dancing. My friend Mary Ray was the first to bring this to my notice, and it mushroomed rapidly. Events started becoming more formal and sets of rules began to be laid down, and Freestyle became separated from the HTM giving two distinct types of competition. I found it quite fascinating and I was approached by one group and asked to become the president of the HTM Association. I was flattered and accepted, and I thought it would be fun, particularly as the organisers were trying at that time to get the Kennel Club to lay down the rules of competition, and for *Crufts* to include it as a competitive event. Sadly a gigantic schism appeared between rival factions, and it all got terribly political and I stepped down after less than a month in the position. I had never even attended a meeting, but I knew I didn't want to be involved. Eventually the arguments were resolved and the event became a recognised competition. Before that it had been demonstrated by Mary Ray in the main ring at *Crufts* just prior to the judging of Best in Show and it has become a traditional curtain-raiser to that supreme moment in the dog showing world in the UK.

Actually, that does make it quite amusing to me – to some of the more traditional dog show enthusiasts, HTM and Freestyle is a bit of an anathema.

Here's one I wrote earlier...

I've heard it described as "a circus act" and worse. But the fact remains, that when you see the best people performing, it is a wonderful sight to see. There are some great performers with whom I have become friends over recent years, Richard Curtis, Kath Hardman, Donelda Guy, Karen Sykes, and Lesley Neville have all provided a lot of great entertainment for people at shows up and down the country, and they really demonstrate what fun you can have with your dog. And let's face it, that's what owning a dog is all about. Spend time with it, train it, love it, and you will have a friend for life. It isn't all about having the finest pedigree line, though that is a part of it, but it is about having a healthy happy animal that is fit for life and fit for function and the activity events are one of the best ways of achieving that end. More about *Crufts* later.

Chapter Sixteen

More pantomimes; Directing beckons;

Snow makes life difficult; A flood forces a move;

LWT makes me an offer; I make a big mistake

I must go back now to 1979. It had been a busy year with the launch of the two new series' and the Special Assignments, the first of my involvement with darts, and the pantomime season was fast approaching. The *Cinderella* we had enjoyed so much in Guildford was to be reproduced in Wilmslow, but it wasn't the same success we'd had before. Talk about chalk and cheese. The venue was the Rex Cinema and to say the facilities were poor was an understatement; there were virtually no dressing rooms for a start. John and I had to share a small cupboard together with Shep, his dog. The rest of the cast were in equally unsuitable accommodation, and the whole place felt unprofessional. Also, the set didn't fit the theatre at all. When they first fitted up the ballroom scene, half of the giant staircase was out in the street! The stage depth meant that the backcloths gave us very little acting room, and the sound system was appalling. But we did the show, and for the first two and a half weeks we played to capacity houses – good news for me, and for John, as we were on a percentage. But as soon as we got into the New Year and the schools went back the matinees were almost empty, and the evenings weren't much better. It was a relief when the show finished.

Kathy Evans had played Prince Charming this time, and our relationship had grown very strong indeed. My marriage to Gilly was now on the rocks as was Kathy's to her husband, and we were of great comfort to each other at a difficult time. It was a sad moment when we parted company, and she went back to London and I went to Jolly's Club in Stoke-on-Trent to present the Darts World Championship – my second year at the event. I don't remember much of the darts that year, because most important was the fact that on February 4th 1980, Kathy telephoned me to say that she wanted to come up to join me – she was leaving her husband. I was absolutely elated, and was able to meet her at the station and bring her to the hotel before going to Jolly's for the evening session. This was the beginning of a new life. I have to say that the hotel and the darts championships were hardly what I had in mind for a romantic tryst, but as it happens we cemented a close bond that has lasted over almost 30 years and is still going strong.

After the darts championships we soon had to find a flat of our own. It wasn't the best flat in the world – above a grocer's shop near some traffic lights on the Northcote Road in Battersea – but it was ours. It wasn't really big enough to swing a cat – not that we had one. Actually, Kate had a small Pekingese called Georgie who was really beautiful, even though she wasn't that fond of me. But she was very easy to look after, and I enjoyed having a dog again.

Kate would often travel with me up to Manchester and elsewhere. I think she quite enjoyed things like *Kickstart* and she made friends with Mick and Gill Andrews, and was great company for me. She struggled with her career, and I kept on trying to boost her confidence. She had trained at the Royal Ballet School, and at Arts Educational in the city. She had worked as a soubrette in a summer show, and had spent a couple of years with The Second Generation, where her singing had been recognised. She had also formed a close harmony singing group called Jingles that was a runner-up in *New Faces* on TV. But it wasn't easy for her to get work as a solo artiste.

But there was always pantomime and Paul Elliott engaged me, John and

Peter Purves

Kate to perform *Jack and the Beanstalk* in Bath, for the Christmas season of 1980-81. John would play Simple Simon, I played the wicked Baron, and Kate played Jack. Lesley Judd also joined us as the princess. It was a lovely season, but it didn't start well. Kate and I had taken a really nice flat in the building adjacent to the Theatre Royal. It was on the first floor, and as we would be there for Christmas, we had taken Christmas presents for each other, and for my dad who would join us, and for Kate's mum, nan and grandfather. We unloaded the car, put everything in the bedrooms and went to the theatre for a welcome and tour. When we got back to the flat a couple of hours later, the burglar was just going out through the bathroom window, onto a flat roof and away. He must have been disturbed before he got going, because, amazingly, he took nothing but the £10 in coins that we had got for the electric meter, and a small tape recorder. The presents were untouched. We got another safety lock fitted and that was that.

The show was very well received, and of all the theatres we have worked, I think Bath is one of my favourites. It has since been fully refurbished, but even before that it was a joy to perform there. Kate had to suffer the indignity of ending Act One singing astride a lovely white horse that pooed at the climax of the song. What timing. But there was always going to be a problem with my timing. The Darts World Championships had been brought forward to January, and the eight days clashed with the end of the pantomime. Paul Elliott agreed to replace me with the director, Brian Hewitt-Jones for those eight days, and I could then return for the last week of the run, and in the event, it worked very well. It is always difficult for the management when the name at the top of the bill doesn't appear. I am sure a lot of people were disappointed by my absence, but with a great show, and John and Lesley on stage, I doubt if anyone felt short-changed. There was another star from the 50's in the show – Ben Warriss, the suave half of the comedy duo Jewell and Warriss, who were the 50's equivalent of Morecambe and Wise. Ben played the King – only a smallish role, but always made his mark – in more ways than one! He was the ultimate chain-smoker and always had a fag on the go, even in the wings of the theatre where smoking was strictly forbidden. His costume was a tabard sort of thing, so he looked rather like the king in a deck of cards. I watched him puffing away silently in the wings, as he heard his cue to enter stage, whereupon his hand holding the cigarette was just pushed into the pocket of his tunic, and on he went. On one occasion the inevitable happened and his costume started to smoke whilst he was still on stage. He only just got off into the wings in time for someone to throw a glass of water into his pocket before he went up in flames! There was a sad rider to that story in that Jimmy Jewell, his former partner, with whom he had worked for over 40 years wrote his autobiography that never mentioned Ben once!

The show was a huge success, and we broke box office records, so the following year we were all re-engaged to perform the same show in Torquay at the Princess Theatre. All of these pantomimes are produced in a very short time frame. Although a lot of the work is done in advance, such as choosing the songs, the script (yes, there really is one) being adapted for the specific artistes engaged, and the costumes and sets and properties already sorted, the actors meet for the first time on a Monday, and in some cases, 10 days later the show opens. Very tight indeed. Bath was one of those theatres that opened its pantomime on a Wednesday night, and that schedule was crippling for all concerned. Torquay was to have a Thursday matinee opening giving just a fraction more breathing space.

But as we gathered for our first rehearsal we waited for our director, Brian Hewitt-Jones to arrive. We had all been in the rehearsal room since 10.00am, the dancers had gone to work with the choreographer in our second rehearsal room, and we were twiddling our thumbs. So by 11.00am I said, "Come on folks let's start putting this together". And we did. We broke for lunch at 1pm, and the company manager made phone calls to find where Brian was, without any success. So in the afternoon we carried on, and I directed the show not only on the Monday, but on the Tuesday and on the Wednesday too. In fact on the Wednesday afternoon I got the dancers to come and join us, and we put all the musical numbers together, and added the dancers' extra work.

On the Thursday morning as we all gathered in the rehearsal room, in came Brian, apologising for his not having been with us as he had another show to direct, and started to tell us what to do. I just said to him, "Brian, sit down, shut up and watch". And we performed the show for him. Bearing in mind we had all (apart from the dancers) done the show the previous year, we gave a pretty damn good performance, which he watched with his mouth open. The remaining two days were spent tidying it up, and running the show several times, so that we all set off at the weekend for Torquay with high hopes.

During the year, Gilly and I had sold the house in Morella Road, and I was left with just enough for the deposit on a small house in Hampton, Middlesex that we would now have to close up for the five and a half weeks we would be away. Our next-door neighbour agreed to keep an eye on it for us. In Torquay we had rented a nice flat on a hill overlooking the bay and we began to enjoy ourselves – it was almost like a holiday if it hadn't been for the 12 shows a week! Actually, Paul Elliott asked us to do a morning show every Saturday as well, and John and I said NO! End of story. I sat in on the production team as they lit the show, so I got a feel for what the director did during the technical few days. I was determined that my foray into directing would not be the last. In fact it was just the first of the 31 major commercial pantomimes that I have directed to date.

The weather was to play a big part in that season. Once again I was going to have to leave the show for eight days to present the darts. I would have to leave on a Friday after the evening show, and drive up to Stoke-on-Trent. Brian Hewitt-Jones was to replace me again, and would turn up in time to see the show so that he could seamlessly drop into my part on the Saturday matinee. But the best-laid plans have a tendency to go pear-shaped at the drop of a hat, or in this case at the fall of some snow. Brian hadn't arrived before the evening show, and we just carried on. During the first act there was a dreadful snowstorm, and the police came to the theatre and advised that everyone should leave at once or there was a likelihood they wouldn't get home. After much grumbling the announcement was made, the audience were offered tickets for a show later in the run and at the interval we closed. It was a dreadful snowfall, and Brian had still not arrived. I had the problem of driving up to Stoke, knowing that the blizzard conditions could be difficult.

Anyway, I set off at 9pm, and found the conditions really bad. There were few cars on the road, and by the time I got up to Exeter, there was a virtual whiteout but I persevered. I was driving a fairly new Citroen CX that had a variable ride suspension – you could actually raise the car's body if necessary for crossing rough ground and so on. I took advantage of the technology and just kept my foot steady on the accelerator and proceeded up the M5 towards the north. A few brave travellers were still moving, but gradually it reduced to just the odd vehicle every mile. I stopped for fuel at the first service area, and was told the road ahead was closed. But there were no notices out, and it was before the idea of the matrix information had been implemented, so I crossed my fingers and kept going.

To cut a very long story short, it took me three hours to get as far as Bristol where there was a notice saying that the M5 further north was impassable. Again, and probably quite stupidly I decided my car was going so well I would just keep going at a steady speed. I did get caught a couple of times in deep ruts that took me off the road, but I managed to regain what should have been the roadway, and continued up towards Birmingham. Once I got there, the roads were a little better, and the M6 was comparatively clear. By the time I reached Stoke, the snow had stopped and there was no more than an inch or so lying on the ground. The journey had taken me seven hours, but I'd made it OK, and I telephoned Kate to let her know I was there safe and sound. On the Saturday afternoon I presented the first of 36 programmes from the World Championships. And after it, I telephoned again to see how Brian had been in my part. Horror of horrors, he hadn't arrived at all – he was stuck in Bath in heavy snow. The show had gone ahead, with Ben Warriss playing my part, and the company manager taking over as the King. Ben was at least six inches shorter than I, and my cloak swamped him. Kate said it was the funniest performance of the run – Ben had to carry a script, and he kept on losing it in the folds of the cloak. But he was an old school comic and he believed "the show must go on" – and it did. He had to play the part again in the evening, as Brian had still not turned up but by then it had ceased to be my problem.

As it happened, like Wilmslow the previous year, after the first two and a half weeks, the children went back to school, and the audiences became quite small – certainly for the matinees – and my non-appearance wasn't too much of a problem. Brian did arrive for the following Monday, and everything went smoothly from there on in. The darts again were a huge success – this was the time when John Lowe, Eric Bristow and Jocky Wilson were the three principal contenders, and the television audiences were growing by the minute. I even did a *Stopwatch* special from the British Championships later in the year. Just as snooker had taken off, darts was following. As previously it is hard to remember actual details from those events, because the social life was one of very heavy drinking and late-nights. These guys played darts for fun as well as for a living, and there were several unofficial tournaments in which I was often Jocky's doubles partner.

After eight days, it was all over, and I could head back to Torquay for the last week of the run. On my arrival back we got a telephone call from our neighbour in Hampton to tell us that our house had a burst pipe in the roof, and was flooded. Great! We could do nothing. He had gone into the house

Here's one I wrote earlier...

and turned off the water, which was the one thing we hadn't turned off when leaving the house. So after being away for six weeks we eventually returned to a freezing cold, wet house, and one that needed a lot putting right. We were insured, and the insurance company just got on with mending things. We needed new carpets, the walls were damaged and the entire ground floor had to be stripped out and redecorated. We lost some furniture as well, but gradually everything was repaired and we had a very nice looking house again.

We decided to sell it. Not only because of the flood, but because at the back of the house there was a pine-strippers yard, and the sound of the pressure hoses drove us mad. We hadn't been aware of that when we bought the house, and as everything was now pristine we knew we should be able to get the top price for it. And we did. But before then, as both our divorces had come through, we decided to get married – which we did at Richmond Registry Office on February 5th 1982. Our honeymoon was in Paris, where else, and it was a delightfully romantic experience.

It wasn't the first. We had gone to the near continent shortly after getting together. We took our car, a big Citroen at the time, on the ferry to the Hook of Holland and drove to Amsterdam, where we spent a couple of delightful days putting our twin beds together, only for the room cleaners to separate them every day. It kept us fit because we were getting seriously overfed on "ricestaffel" and other wonderful foods, before driving south to Belgium, our ultimate destination being Paris. On the way we stopped at a wonderful old castle in Belgium that had a moat and extraordinary silver treasures in cabinets, hardly guarded at all, in the middle of nowhere. There were no more than another three couples there all the time we were there. A lovely looking restaurant, where we decided to have lunch, adjoined it. Kate was unlucky in that she chose the frog's legs, and they were off. It wasn't a question of us not knowing what they should taste like, but they were seriously off, and inedible. That was a huge disappointment because we had always believed that Belgian cuisine was as good as, or even better than French. Some years later she also got ill when we went to Bruges, but luckily that only kicked in after we had dined in one of the most exquisite restaurants with three Michelin stars in the world, Di Karmeliet, which restored any belief we needed in Belgian cuisine.

We eventually arrived in Paris and had a few days in a delightful garret from whose window we could just see the Cathedral of Notre Dame, and from where we explored that most gorgeous of European cities. We walked a lot, talked a lot and got to know each other really well. Paris remains a favourite for us both.

That same year, I went to Singapore and took Kate with me. I was filming for the *Blue Peter Special Assignment* series on famous rivers, and the three mile long Singapore River was deemed a suitable one. Actually I found it all fascinating, but the climate was killing. I hate heavy humidity, and unfortunately when you go to a location to film, you don't get sufficient time to acclimatise properly. I suffer awfully from prickly heat, when your body sweats, but doesn't let the moisture escape, and it causes small and incredibly itchy blisters to form. I believe the reaction to the itching is called St Vitus' Dance, and I, who have three left feet when it comes to dancing, performed it with extreme skill. Kate thought it was hysterically funny, and I have to agree with her, but it is genuine suffering, and I had a bad few days. She was lucky, in that when we were filming the more mundane stuff, she had the run of the hotel and the pool but she did come to several of the more exotic locations, and we had a wonderful time. Actually, I never have been in receipt of "freebies". Whenever I filmed with *Blue Peter* we travelled tourist class, and never once got an upgrade but on this trip, I telephoned the organisers, the Singapore Tourist Board, to say I was going to be bringing my wife with me, and they gave me Kate's accommodation for nothing. The same with Singapore Airlines, so we had a wonderful trip together for no cost. And we had an incredibly nice social time, because the director, Sarah Hellings, and her then partner the cameraman, Paul Wheeler, were good fun to be with.

One night Kate and I went to the restaurant in the sky – it rotates overlooking the city like the old BT tower in London used to do – and had Peking duck. Now we'd been told this was an experience. First they bring the duck, which has been cooked. Then they take off the skin and cut a few slivers that they wrap in pancakes with Hoi Sin sauce and onions, just like the crispy duck you get in most Chinese restaurants nowadays. Then the duck is taken away, and we expected to get a soup made from it, and another two exotic dishes. They never came. That was it. We were totally conned, and I felt such a fool. I have never had such a poor meal in any restaurant anywhere in the world, that was the pits. Actually it wasn't the worst, because the following day or so, we went out and found a Thai restaurant. We ordered quite adventurously, but one dish arrived that we hadn't expected. It looked like a large, slightly discoloured gherkin. We asked what it was, and we were told, in broken Malay/Chinese/English that it was Eck! Or at least that was the best we could make of it. I believe that it was the 100 year old egg, or something like it. Anyway, I don't think I've ever tasted anything so disgusting in my life. It was such a shame, because everything else we ate was quite lovely.

Apart from that, the trip was a delight, and we have eternally thanked the Singapore Tourist Board for making it so pleasant, and so cheap and the breakfasts in our five star hotel were the best I have ever eaten. The saddest element of the trip was that Kate is absolutely terrified of flying. She had been to Canada, and Germany and Spain, and now to Singapore, but she had to steel herself to it each time. Over the years I have tried to make it easier for her, without much success. I remember us going to Madeira on the old Dan Air from Gatwick. I'd managed to secure us the front row in the cabin, facing the bulkhead on which were the stewardesses seats. The take-off was a tense affair, with Kate's fingers digging into my hand and wrist, but once we were airborne all seemed well. I asked the stewardess if we could visit the cockpit –

this was before the modern world took a grip and destroyed a way of life – and the captain indicated he would be happy to see us. I'd been on the flight deck many times before, and absolutely loved it. The pilots were happy to have a bit of company, and, I think, to show off a bit. Kate loved the experience, and the fear just drained away. As we approached the island, we were asked to go back to our seats, which we did, and even the noises as flaps were deployed, and ultimately the undercarriage lowered, didn't seem to bother her. I felt we'd cracked it. Just then the two stewardesses flew down the aisle and threw themselves into the two seats facing us, belted themselves in and one turned to the other and said, "God I hate this landing, it's the worst one we do." Back to square one!!

At the same time Alan Boyd at LWT offered me a new TV series. It was a show called *Babble*, a really clever word game that would employ the talents of some great comedians such as Graham Garden, Tim Brooke-Taylor, John Junkin, Barry Cryer, Willie Rushton and the like. I was the host and had the job of explaining the rules and trying to get some sense out of both the panellists and the guests. LWT was at that time one of the leaders in TV entertainment and Alan Boyd had been most innovative. At the same time, Russ Abbott was the funniest person on TV, and Michael Aspel and Gloria Hunniford each had new shows in the same stable. Michael's show was called *Child's Play*, and Alan had not been sure whether to let me present that one, and give *Babble* to Michael. In the end, he cast us rather against type, and I got *Babble*. I absolutely loved it, and it was also the best payday I had ever had in my career. So Kate and I looked for a house somewhat better than where we had been. We found it on the edge of Twickenham Green, opposite the cricket pavilion. It was a lovely small Victorian cottage, officially it had three bedrooms, but there was only one that I would really call a double. The ground floor was in a pretty bad state, with damp and peeling plasterwork. We opted to strip it all out, and with Kate acting as the project manager we ended up with a delightful property, for which we hadn't increased our mortgage, but which was going to be worth at least twice what we'd got for our old house. It was good business, but it was bought not as an investment but for us to live in.

Babble ran for three series' on Channel 4, but the incoming controller of 4 didn't like it, and so it was dropped. We did 39 episodes in all, and everyone who appeared on it had a really good time. We'd had all sorts of guest panellists, from Tim Rice to Giles Brandreth, from Melvin Bragg to Jack Tinker. For me it was a great time, and the set up at LWT reminded me of the best days at the BBC. Not surprising really as people like Alan Boyd had been at the BBC during its best times, and had worked on the great entertainment shows such as *The Generation Game* with Bruce Forsyth.

By 1983 I had completed the fifth very successful series of *Stopwatch*; *We're Going Places* had ended, and *Babble* would have just one series to go. The darts were still being very good for me, but I didn't know what the future would hold. I knew that producer Hazel Lewthwaite had put forward for another series of *Stopwatch* and one morning I received the worst phone call of my life. It was Hazel. She said, "Peter, hello. I've got some good news and some bad news. Which would you like first?" I hate questions like that, but asked for the good news. "We've got a new series of *Stopwatch*," she trilled. "The bad news is that you aren't doing it!"

I know that in our business one has to learn to cope with rejection, but that was a body blow. Apparently Edward Barnes had a young Irish presenter who had been on *John Craven's Newsround*, and he wanted a series for him. It was a fait accompli and that was that. It was disappointing because Hazel, and her husband Bob, had been very friendly towards me all the time I had worked there and Bob had been one of my darts mentors. Hazel went on to produce *A Question of Sport*, and eventually left the BBC and moved down south, and we lost touch. That is something that happens a lot when you are freelance. However, I do think that Edward might have warned me that it was happening.

That disappointment aside, it was a reasonably successful year for me, though Kate was still struggling but as ever, there was always pantomime. Paul Elliott invited me to direct *Robinson Crusoe* at the Yvonne Arnaud Theatre in Guildford, the site of our triumphant first panto, *Cinderella*. He asked me to play Captain Babble, John would play Idle Jack, and Kate would be Robinson. Political correctness would determine that this would be the last *Robinson Crusoe* for Paul or for any of the other large panto producers. We had great fun with it. Belinda Carroll played the Principal Girl, and there was a brilliant scene on the shore of the desert island, where John was sitting on a rock, wooing Belinda. He sang her a ballad, *Real Live Girl*, which is a sweet song. Behind him near a big boulder, there were three skulls on poles. After two verses, the skulls "sang" the chorus. There was uproar in the theatre. On the first night John was most upset – he thought they were laughing at his singing. Well, they might have been, but they weren't. It was a fabulous sight gag, and I used to go round front-of-house to watch it every night. It was a fun show, but it caused me quite a problem.

As usual I had to miss eight days of the show for the darts, and Paul was beginning to find it too difficult to replace me in the shows. I had a difficult decision to make, and in the end, thinking that my career might just edge back towards the theatre, I decided to tell Nick Hunter, that I wanted to stop presenting the darts. Mind you, I think I had seen the best days of them on the BBC – it was no longer as popular as it had been, so maybe I was getting out at the right time. The British Championship had been abandoned as an event, and *Bullseye* had been dropped. The three nations internationals were no longer being covered, and the only remaining event was the clashing World Championship. Nick wasn't happy, and for some reason he took it very much to heart, and we parted on poor terms. I honestly do not know why – it wasn't a sleight to him, it was an intended career move for me. But I had got it wrong!

Here's one I wrote earlier...

Quite inexplicably, Mr Elliott didn't employ me the following Christmas at all – neither as director nor as artiste, something he never explained to me. So from having at least two jobs that conflicted, I had managed to put myself completely out of work!

Chapter Seventeen

Kate's career takes off;

I become a businessman but not a very good one;

Chicanery in the city;

Major house moves;

Developments at Crufts; Our dogs;

Editing a magazine; The Underdog Show

Kate had always been terrified of auditions. I suggested to her that the only way to get over that would be to go to as many auditions as possible, whether she felt she had any chance or not. We saw an audition advertised in *The Stage* for the lead role in *Evita* at the Prince Edward Theatre, and I persuaded her to go for it. There was literally nothing to lose – she had never played a West End lead before, and apart from pantomime never appeared in a "book" musical. With much fear and trepidation she did go for it, and I remember watching her from the wings, knowing how frightened she was, and seeing her give a wonderful audition. To cut a long story short, she won the part to play Eva Peron as the alternate to the girl already in the role, and she took over the lead after nine months and played it until the show closed nine months after that. But more than that, the director Hal Prince asked her to lead the show when it moved to the Opera House in Manchester for a nine month season.

Not bad for a girl who hated auditions and it was a life-changing experience for Kate.

But when she started the job, she discovered that there was another Kathy Evans in Equity, and she had to revert to her full name, as that was the one she had used when first joining Equity – Kathryn Evans. By this time I was on speaking terms with Paul Elliott again, and I rang to tell him, not only of Kate's success, but also of the name change. In his usual bluff way he said, "Oh really? Well I suppose Kathryn sounds much better with Dame in front of it." And he has called her Dame Kathryn ever since!

Whilst her life was changing, so was mine. I still had *Junior Kickstart* and *Crufts* to present, and one or two other small TV jobs, but nothing that was going to pay the bills. Then I was contacted by a PR firm called Namemakers, who wondered if I would be interested in fronting a short campaign for a double glazing company. It was not for television but included four personal appearances and a localised press campaign. Naturally I agreed to do it, and on the first personal appearance I was collected from my house by the chief executive of Namemakers, John R Smith, who accompanied me to Southampton. We got on really well, and in the course of the car journey back, we agreed to meet up with his three co-directors with a view to exploring the possibilities of forming a video production company.

The outcome of the meeting was that I would be given facilities within the Namemakers office in New Oxford Street, to set up a company that would make corporate videos and would offer a consultancy in communications to various needy organisations. My closest colleague within the company was Alan Wickes, a lovely chap who had worked in both advertising and PR, both in this country and abroad, and he would handle most of the business side of things. Between us we would try to market the company, and hopefully we'd make some money. The two sleeping partners were John Lardge and John Smith, but their contribution in office space and support was immeasurable.

Peter Purves

Over the next few years we had quite a few successes and one or two failures, but we kept our heads above water. Alan and John had a number of business contacts that proved very valuable to us, but our set up wasn't right. We had no business development person, so that whilst we were working on a particular project, there was no one out getting the next one ready so we had highs and lows in equal measure. Having said that, our portfolio was quickly quite impressive, with several films completed for a number of blue chip companies like BT, Castrol, Levi's, Burmah Oil, and Midland Bank. I worked as presenter on one or two, director on others, producer on others, and writer on others which was both varied and really interesting. I enjoyed myself, and we made a living. The BT jobs, in particular were very successful, and came about at a time when mobile communications were beginning to happen. In fact we made a series of videos explaining how mobile communications would become integrated. Previously there had been BT mobile telephones, BT voicebank and BT mobile paging. Now they were all to be brought together under the umbrella of BT mobile communications.

When we made a film on the railways about pay phones on trains, the BT PR lady advised that it would be a good move on our part if we had our own mobile phones and they could do us a deal. So we bought three Telecom Pearl mobile telephones. These weighed about the same as a heavy brick, and weren't much more useful. The battery charge only lasted a couple of hours, and they weren't the most portable pieces of equipment. But they were at the cutting edge, and because we were working for BT on contract, we were able to buy three phones for only £1499 each, as opposed to £2000 each. More fool us – that was the last time we worked for BT as the mobile communications structure altered, all of our contacts moved and that was the end of our connection – and the majority of our profit on the job!

However when it worked well it was really good. We made one super film for Castrol to launch a new motor oil to the trade for high performance cars and we took a Lamborghini and the latest super-fast Jaguar onto the Mira test track, for a couple of days. We had our own little bit of *Top Gear* all to ourselves – and we also had a helicopter in the Peak District to get some truly stunning sequences of the cars beside the Ladybower Reservoir. But often the work was very much more basic and mundane.

I was able, on a couple of occasions to use good friends on some of the corporate work – Valerie Singleton presented a PR video for a merchant bank in the city, one in which we also got an endorsement of the bank from Robert Maxwell. Oops! I also got Lesley Judd to present one for a PR company. Valerie has always been very vocal in her praise of my directing skills, but I have to say, when watching some of the other directors I employed, I really did have a lot to learn. I think she liked me because I was nice to the artistes – not because I was a great director!

In one video for a major pension fund, we used Derek Martinus as director who had made such a cock-up in *Doctor Who*, but who was now more than competent, and I was pleased to have Chris Barry who directed me in my last *Doctor Who* serial, as director on a promotional video for some cancer treatment drugs. The variety in the work was splendid, but we just didn't do enough of it to make us really successful.

The company's name was originally The Planned Video Projects Company Limited. A bit of a mouthful and not what I would call memorable. In 1987 we were approached by a couple of financial wizards who wanted to create a multi-media one-stop-shop which would include a PR company, an advertising agency, a design consultancy and a video production wing. For this we had to provide a business plan with a three year forecast and Alan produced ours. I have to say I thought it was a lot of guesswork, and would also be very difficult to achieve. If we succeeded the rewards would be significant, and on that basis, my business partners decided we should accept the offer and allow us to be taken under the umbrella. I did not want to do the deal, but was outvoted 3 to 1.

Peter Purves

Kate was still in Manchester, having followed *Evita* with *Applause* in Wythenshawe. She suggested that we looked for a property out of London, and on the basis of the deal I had just struck I thought that was a good idea. I didn't have to live in London to do the work, and so we started looking in the countryside. BBC *Pebble Mill* had offered me a series that was a local spin-off of *Crimewatch* and so Hereford, Worcestershire and Warwickshire seemed like reasonable locations. Actually we were considering taking on a lot more than just a place in the country. Kate wanted us to find a place big enough for her mother, and her grandmother. My dad had died the previous year or he would have come to live with us as well. In the end we found a house on the southern outskirts of Rugby. It was a 6 bedroomed Victorian Rectory that had been built in 1854, in three quarters of an acre of landscaped garden, and it was magnificent. I can still remember the pleasure I felt when I first had gone through the door into the entrance hall with its beautiful straight staircase, and I looked at Kate and said, "I want it." So we upped the mortgage, and went for it. If the business went well, then the house would be paid for in three years time. It cost £201,000, and was the first house in the town to go over the £200,000 barrier. We'd had to go through a blind tendering as there were several people after it, and we won. We sold the Twickenham house for almost three times what we'd paid for it, and although I was sad to leave it, the new place was too good to miss. The prices in Rugby were just beginning to climb, so we were buying at exactly the right time.

My mother-in-law and grandmother-in-law came to stay, not without misgivings, I have to say, having watched my mother's experience of living with her mother-in-law. We had extended our doggie family as well, to three Pekingese, and as the house and garden was so large we went for a big dog too. We first bought Mishka, a beautiful Newfoundland bitch, who I absolutely adored and a little later we also bought Gulliver, her litter brother. These two were quite magnificent, but as different as chalk and cheese; Mishka was incredibly active and loved the water, Gulliver was lazy and hated the water. I would take them to Daventry Nature Park, and Mishka would be straight into the lake, whilst Gulliver would stand on the edge barking at her. In 1988, Steve Morris, who was one of the producers on *Crufts*, had devised a series called *Superdogs*, where we put teams of dogs and handlers from eight different regions through a number of difficult tests. It was a lovely show to work on, and I could take the big dogs with me.

One of the events was a race between a specialist racing dog in each team. After the heats we decided to put the two Newfies into a race along the same course, which we recorded and showed in the programme. They looked fantastic and even Gulliver worked up enough energy to give it a go. But not far from the end of the course was the lake, Mishka didn't stop running and continued straight into the water where she swam happily for half an hour resisting all my efforts to persuade her out. Gulliver spent the half hour barking from the bank.

They were wonderful guard dogs, and because they were so big, many people were quite wary of them, but their temperament was very gentle, and we chose the breed because they were so nice with other dogs. We didn't want a dog that would hate or terrorise the Pekes. They proved to be an excellent choice. A few years later I recall I watched from my office as a deliveryman approached our gate, behind which sat Jamie, one of the Pekes. He barked at the man who just laughed, particularly as the notice on the gate said "Beware of the Dog". He opened the gate and came in only to be confronted by two gigantic Newfoundlands who galloped round the corner from the back of the house with their tongues lolling as they ran. I don't think I've ever seen anyone move so fast – he almost leapt the gate!

You could have fitted our Twickenham house comfortably into the Old Rectory five or six times, so although we were happy to have made the move, we were rattling around in it like peas in a drum. But our contentment was not going to be all that long-lived. My TV work occupied only a few days at a time, so my principal work was now as joint managing director of the video company. I was commuting to London four days a week and I have to say it was pretty tiring. The trains weren't too bad, but from time to time it would be a nightmare. The worst time was immediately after the 1987 hurricane – you know, the one that wasn't supposed to be coming. I had a filming commitment for the newly merged media companies in Drury Lane that day. I knew we'd had some bad weather because I'd heard it overnight, and we lost one or two tiles from the roof. But in the daylight, the carnage was obvious to see. The main line from Rugby to Euston was not running any trains. The only way I could get to London was via Coventry and then on a train, if they were running, down to Marylebone. Amazingly I did make it, but I was two hours late to the location, where I discovered that only one other person had made it, and none of the subjects I was supposed to be filming. I was proud I'd made it, but that was the last time I would ever put myself out that much – no one else does. It just isn't worth it.

I guess that was the forerunner of a series of bad things that were to happen. The new board of directors of the company decided that our name was too much of a mouthful and asked us to change it to Purves Wickes. Which we did, and had all our letterheads and publicity material changed to reflect the change. John Smith and John Lardge stood down from our side of the business, leaving Alan and I as the joint MD's. We were still in the same office above the Umbrella Shop on New Oxford Street, but were advised we may have to find somewhere else in the near future. Work continued to dribble in, but not any more than we had managed on our own. The synergy between the several companies was not making itself evident, and there was a real animosity growing between the design company and us – originating, I have to say, from their side. Then on the 15th of December came the bombshell.

We received a letter from the CEO of the board telling us that we were being closed down on the 31ˢᵗ of December. Just that. No apology or thanks or anything. We were dead meat. Alan and I had each been paid a small sum when we joined as founder companies in the consortium. We decided that there was no way they would close us down, particularly as it now was named after us, and although it was almost the Christmas holiday we set about buying the company back. Our lawyers were as helpful as they could be, and miracle of miracles, they made it happen. On the 1ˢᵗ of January 1988 Alan and I became the sole owners of Purves Wickes with a huge overdraft and a tiny new office near to The Ambassadors Theatre. For the next 10 years we had to play "catch-up".

Reading between the lines, I suspect that the consortium had been set up to allow the new investors to go to the city and raise cash. Once that had been secured the individual parts of the company were of very little interest. I also understand that after about three years the consortium broke up with the whole tranche lost. The satisfaction gained by its demise didn't help us to pay our bills, however, and the hard work to pay off the debt began. We continued to make good quality videos for our clients, although our business skills didn't get much better, and we hardly ever went from one job to the next. It was usual that when one job finished we would set about trying to get the next. We never got ahead of the game.

Jumping well ahead from here, we finally paid off the company debt in 1996 – the bank still took our monthly money from us for another six months until we realised. We received no apology but we did get our overpayment money back plus the interest. In 1998 Alan and I finally decided to close the company down. We'd had some fun, and we'd done some good work, winning the occasional award, and we'd worked with some lovely people on the creative side. But in the end, we were both tired, and as we'd washed our faces, as it were, we got out of the rat race. Sadly Alan died three years ago, and is much missed.

Peter Purves

In the meantime, Kate had toured in *Hello Dolly* with Dora Bryan, and had appeared in *Anything Goes* in the West End, playing Erma, the gangsters' moll, and on more than 50 occasions, going on in the lead when Elaine Paige was off. Her career was beginning to take care of itself, and thanks to her work, the impact of the difficulties I was having with the video company wasn't too punishing. But it did mean that by 1992, when *Kickstart* had finally bit the dust – no sponsor could be found, and the promoter decided to call it a day – and my only TV at that time was *Crufts* for the BBC, we decided to sell up the Old Rectory, and find something a little cheaper. We'd been in Rugby for five years, and the house had nearly doubled in value, and cashing in on that seemed a good move. We had a large mortgage (at least it was large for 1992) and when we sold, we were able to buy our next house for cash. We'd looked good and hard, in many different areas of the country, but in the end we found a semi-derelict stone-built Tudor Rectory in Northamptonshire that the diocese of Peterborough was selling off.

It was a wonderful building, very pretty, with a massive Virginia creeper over the front, but it hadn't been lived in for three years, and had never been modernised in any way. There was rubble on the floor of what may have been a kitchen once; the pipe work was all lead, and there was a lead water tank in the roof; it was damp and decrepit throughout; and there had never been any central heating, but its potential was undeniable. It was offered for sale with a guide price, but closed bid offers were invited as there were several potential buyers. We made our best offer, and it was accepted, but when the survey showed up more dreadful faults than we'd estimated, we said we would have to pull out. Whereupon to our surprise the church asked what we'd be prepared to pay, and we dropped our price by £30,000, fully expecting them to reject it and to go with one of the other tenders. But no – they accepted and the Old Rectory in Cogenhoe was ours.

One of the abiding memories of that move from Rugby, was of Kate's nan, sitting on the bottom step of the back stairs with the new owners already in the house going through the house with cleaners and the rest, because we hadn't quite got out in time. Our removers had miscalculated the extent of the move, and we were late. She just said, "Well, I never expected to be thrown out of my own house."

The Old Rectory was completely uninhabitable, so we rented a small Georgian farmhouse nearby for four months, and set about restoring the house to its former glory. I was project manager and also became a general labourer for the four months we took. I had planned the timescale and engaged the builders, plumbers and electrician, but with one or two little glitches that meant I had to fire the electrician, we ran to time. Well almost. I was away in London on a video shoot, and my mother-in-law was going over to the house every so often to make sure the work was going ahead. One day she went there to find nothing much going on, and dropped into the conversation that did they think they would be ready for us to move in on November 15th. The three builders looked somewhat surprised and said, "You mean December 15th, don't you?" "No, November 15th," she stated quite clearly. Whereupon they all leapt to their feet and started running around like their feet were on fire. And they were ready by November 15th!

It had been a major piece of restoration – installing new boilers, doing all the plumbing and central heating; putting in one new bathroom and a shower room; opening up the hall and rebuilding one end of the house to create a new living room and kitchen for Kate's mum and nan; opening up a couple of chimneys; creating a library/office and completely redecorating the entire house. The end result was a lovely, lovely house, and it was ready for our friends to join us for a few days at Christmas. This was something we had initiated at Rugby. For the first Christmas there we had a full house and played silly games, did a murder mystery and ate wonderful food. That is something that has almost become traditional, and big old houses lend themselves to such celebrations. Some of our closest friends come every year, and we occasionally have others who make it just the odd once or twice. I think it is my favourite time of the year, even though the religious element is no longer a feature in my life.

As far as work was going, *Crufts* was becoming more and more important. It had moved to the NEC in Birmingham and I had been asked to become one of the principal presenters of the shows on TV. My co-presenter was Angela Rippon and we made quite a good fist of it together. It was interesting to watch her forge her way through the packed halls of the NEC – her news reporter's technique of using the elbows whenever needed was not something that came too easily to me. I really did have a very polite upbringing! For my part it was nice that I should be presenting the main parts of the show – since 1978 I'd had my own sort of section. As I said in an earlier chapter, I started with Agility and then went on to be the commentator and presenter of the Obedience Championships. For a couple of years this was a separate section of the show for the BBC, which expanded to take in the Team Agility Championship, and finally Flyball.

None of these shows were "live" – even the Best in Show was a delayed transmission. It was only after we got to the NEC that producer Steve Morris began to get a "live" show for the Best in Show judging, and even then it was only part live – the rest of the show had to be packaged up beforehand. But it was a start, and it pointed us in the right direction. In 1993, Angela left, and Steve engaged Jessica Holm to be my co-presenter and that was to continue for seven years. To this day we are the main commentators at the show for the BBC.

It has been an interesting experience for me – I love dogs as I am sure you have gathered, and my knowledge about them has increased over the years – you cannot fail to absorb an awful lot of general information when you have done a show like that for as long as I have. Kate has always said that when she met me I wouldn't have known a Chihuahua from a Great Dane. Not strictly true, but I certainly was no expert. Jessica Holm was a real asset to the presenting team – she bred dogs herself, Italian Spinones at first before the present love of her life, the Grand Basset Griffon Vendeen – a dog that is easier to look after than pronounce! She was knowledgeable at all levels, showing, breeding and training, and it is great to have worked with her for so long.

Steve always allowed original ideas into the show, and each year we tried to find new ways to introduce the programme. We were everything from the voices of a couple of dogs visiting the show, to being ourselves having a poke around the myriad trade stands. We did reports from the breed rings, and we were given the freedom to express our own likes and dislikes. Jessica always scorned my liking for Pekingese, but she isn't a small dog person. She did like my Newfoundlands.

Unfortunately things do have a habit of changing. *Crufts* itself was growing bigger and bigger, and the BBC coverage grew with it; from two programmes to three until it finally has got to the stage where we have six hours of "live" TV coverage direct from the show, including a wonderful two hour show on the final Sunday when the best pedigree dog or bitch is crowned Best in Show. But before we got to that stage, several things happened. First poor Steve Morris was made redundant, and the new producer was named as David Pickthall. I didn't have a problem with that as I'd worked with Dave several times before and he had briefly worked on *Blue Peter* whilst I was there but I was sorry to lose Steve who had been a real friend and supporter for many years, and I really liked him.

Dave wanted Philippa Forrester to front the show, and for Jessica and I to become occasional presenters and main commentators. Although we were a bit upset to lose the principal in-vision spot it actually made our work on the show very much easier. To be honest when we had done everything in the past we had spent the entire show rushing hither and thither without any respite. We had to do the commentaries as well as the in-vision links, and although we had the punditry of Mike Stockman to back us up, it was very hard work indeed. Now we only had to research and commentate on the group judging and the activity events. It was still a lot of work, but much less pressure. Mind you, I have always thrived under pressure.

But then the following year came a body blow. The head of the events department changed, and the new broom swept out a lot of what had gone before. Mike Ward, the new head of OB events, who had been a producer with me on *Blue Peter*, decided that Jessica and I were surplus to requirements and engaged Gaby Roslin to present the show. We were both truly upset by this move that came without warning, but yet again it was a fait accompli. 22 years after my first involvement I was dropped without a thank you.

What the great man failed to appreciate was that we, together with new co-commentators and pundits, Frank Kane and Wayne Cavanaugh, were the only ones who knew how it all worked. We had never had researchers, nor did anyone else give us information. We knew where we had to be at any one time, and with the advent of the live broadcasts we were able to do our work without any assistance at all. Nobody had to prepare scripts for us, and we lived or died by what we said on the show. Two weeks before *Crufts* Mike came to us cap in hand to ask us if we would still do the show. We both agreed to do it at four times the money we had been paid before. It was the first time I have held the upper hand in any work negotiations in my life, and it felt wonderful.

The happiest thing I can report about that whole time is that Mr Ward did not last long in the job. The other good thing was that Animal Planet had also come on board, to produce a programme for later transmission in the USA, and we were asked to contribute, not only commentary but also some punditry and links for their show too. The production company, Painless Productions from Los Angeles were a joy to work for but they had an odd

Here's one I wrote earlier...

brief. Their programme was made in such a way that it suggested that four-day *Crufts*, like the *Westminster Show* in New York, took place on one day only. 22,500 dogs judged to a Best in Show in one day – yeah right! But that was what was required and we went along with it. The first presenter of the US show was Ronnie Reagan – the former president's son – who turned out to be a really nice guy. We got to be with him a few times, but sadly not sociably. His work-load was really tough, and his jet-lag seemed to get the better of him. What surprised me was the lack of security around him; he was able to be just an ordinary guy. The following year, a former Miss America, Leanza Cornett was the presenter and she was with us until the Animal Planet involvement died in 2006. She told me the story of how she had been presenting a sports programme in the USA and found out she was being replaced as the host – by her husband. And I thought the business was tough on this side of the pond!

During all those years on the show Kate and I had kept a number of dogs. When Georgie, her first Peke died, we had already bought another, Billie. Freddie came along shortly afterwards. Jamie was added to make a trio, and as I've said earlier, the Newfoundlands Mishka and Gulliver completed the quintet. Freddie died before we moved to Cogenhoe and Billie and Jamie both died there. They had good lives, were greatly loved, and both nearly made 13 years old. The most unfortunate loss was Mishka. Newfoundlands normally live to between eight and 12 years. Mishka had been on medication for a heart problem since she was three, and she started to have a bit of a breathing problem. I took her to the vets and they changed her medication, and she really seemed to be responding. She had her breakfast, went outside into the garden and seemed back to normal. She came back into the kitchen and lay down by my feet as I made a telephone call, then she groaned and was gone. She was only six, and I wept buckets. Gulliver certainly missed her, and so we decided we would get another Newfie to keep him company. We already had two more Pekingese, a gorgeous sandy coloured bitch called Holly, and a tiny little black one we called Tillie. As I write, they are both 11 years old. Our replacement Newfie was the son of the 1996 *Crufts* Reserve Best in Show. He was a year old when we bought him, and he was called Karazan Superman, Kent for short (after Clark Kent). He was a fine dog, and would have probably been quite a winner if I'd wanted to show him, but when he was still quite young, certainly less than a year old, he slipped on a muddy bank, and tore the cruciate ligament in one of his back legs. Once that was repaired he had a permanent slight limp, which meant I couldn't really show him at all. Not that I minded that, because I never really had the time, nor do I now, to get into the showing world. However I am currently on the periphery having been elected to be a member of the Kennel Club in 2006.

Gulliver made well over 13 years old, and Kent, who died when I started to write this book a few months ago, was well past 12, so they had a really good innings and I miss them both. Funnily enough, although Gulliver had occasionally paddled, Kent never even put his feet in the water. I used to take him for walks on Sizewell Beach in Suffolk and he always kept back from the edge, and never swam once. For such a dog, born with webbed feet, it was bizarre that he disliked water so much.

But Newfoundlands take a lot of maintenance and we determined to find a breed that required less. Our friends, Ashleigh and Geoffrey Sendin, who are regular visitors for Christmas, had bought a Wire-Haired Dachshund bitch, and as they were going for a holiday to Jordan, asked if we would look after Maddie for a fortnight. We were happy to do that, and we absolutely loved her. She had the nicest temperament of any dog I have known, and that includes the Newfies. We said that if Maddie were ever to have puppies we would have one. She did have a litter the following year, and we bought Hattie. There was no pedigree attached to her, because Maddie was an unregistered animal, but she was the most adorable puppy, and after a few months we thought we'd get her a companion. This time we bought a handsome pedigree puppy from a respected breeder near Guildford. He was called Lankelly Woody Valentine, named after a racehorse apparently. His breeder, Pamela Poulter, whose affix is Lankelly, named all her puppies after racehorses. Woody was and is the dream dog with an almost impossibly fine temperament. He is such a happy chap, and for the first year his tail never stopped wagging, in fact it rarely stops now, and he's three years old. It was inevitable that Hattie and he would mate, and breeding their litter was one of the most beautiful experiences of Kate's and my life.

Hattie produced seven puppies, all born naturally, and they all survived. Hattie was a great mother, very attentive to them all, but there was one puppy that probably wouldn't have made it had we not made sure it got milk at every feed. She was the smallest, and had been caught up in the sac when she was born, so she always seemed to struggle. But she did survive, and now she is a right little madam. We called her Dottie, and we kept both her and her lookalike brother, Teddy. Three others went to nice homes in Devon, Dorset, and King's Lynn, and we found homes for the other two locally. All the owners keep in touch so we know how the puppies are. But in spite of the experience being so fulfilling, we won't breed another litter because it is heartbreaking to let the puppies go. When you've spent up to three months nurturing them you don't want to see them leave. I guess both Kate and I are very sentimental that way, but that's the way it is.

Whilst I am on the subject of dogs, I should mention I became a magazine editor in 1997. Publisher David Hall, who specialises in angling magazines, approached me. He had taken over a small dog magazine and as I was local, he asked if he could produce a feature on me. I agreed, we met up and the article was published. In the course of that meeting I intimated that I wouldn't mind writing the odd article myself and out of that, *Peter Purves' Mad About Dogs* was born. I would like to say that it was a huge success and is still going strong but, as any dog magazine publisher will tell you, they do take a lot of selling. It was a good magazine, and I had considerable involvement. I wasn't the day-to-day editor, more of an editor at large, but I certainly contributed three major articles and the editorial each month. However, the spade-work was done by my deputy Jane Goddard, and she was responsible for it looking so good.

One of my favourite features was called Peter's Friends, where I interviewed celebrity dog owners. In the course of the year I interviewed stars like Paul O'Grady (still Lily Savage in those days), Jean Boht, Liza Goddard, Dora Bryan, Rosemarie Ford and Gerry Anderson (the *Thunderbirds* creator). I also researched and wrote a feature called Breeder of the Month where I interviewed some of the most successful breeders of pedigree dogs in the country. It was great fun while it lasted, but in the end, after 12 issues, David pulled the plug. He hadn't been totally honest with me about the circulation and it proved not to be viable. It was a disappointing time, but the bottom line was that with sales of only 5000 copies a month no one was getting rich.

In spite of that, David and I became good friends during that relationship, and remain so. We used to play quite a lot of golf together, but my golf time has been severely restricted with the ownership of so many dogs. One just doesn't have the time. One way or another I have continued to write about dogs, and for a couple of years I wrote my own column, Purves Unleashed in *Our Dogs* newspaper. Consequently I have a lot of good friends in the dog world. I regularly meet up with Vince Hogan, the managing director of *Our Dogs* who always tries to entice me back, and I may just pen the odd article for him in the months to come. I do know a lot about dogs, but I would never claim to be an expert, at least not in the same way as Frank Kane or Jessica. They do fascinate me, and I find my current pets so funny; they provide me with hours of entertainment and pleasure, and I am lucky enough to have the time to indulge myself with them.

I had tried for years to sell a dog programme idea to the BBC but without any success. Steve Morris had tried to get *Superdogs* reinstated but there were no takers. Out of the blue in 2006, I was approached by Splash Media to see if I would be interested in being either a judge or the commentator in their new reality show, *The Underdog Show*. After meeting with the producers I accepted the role as a judge, and recommended my colleague Jessica Holm as the commentator. The shows, both an adult and a junior version went ahead and I thought it was a great idea. Celebrities would take a rescue dog from the Dogs Trust and train it to a reasonable level of obedience. Each programme would set a more difficult task for the dogs to perform, and on each show one celebrity would be voted off.

Julian Clary made a good job of hosting, and the audiences seemed to like it but although three of us judged the performances, the audience vote determined which celebrity would be voted off. I am amazed at the perversity of the audience vote. It is the same with shows like *Strictly Come Dancing*, where the viewers are determined to keep some under performing star in the show at the expense of someone who is better. And so it was with *The Underdog Show*. In the end it didn't matter because Selina Scott, who was exceptional with her Wolfhound /GSD cross, won the show but Huey Morgan, the American rock star from Fun Loving Criminals, who was totally inept throughout, survived right the way through to the semi-final, no matter how hard we tried to have him voted off. On his final appearance on the show I scored him just one out of 10, and at last the vote went against him. I think he wanted to do some damage to me for being so brutal with the score, but I was being honest. The celebs, with the exception of Huey, had really tried hard, but Clive Anderson, who was really good with his dog, was voted off in a head to head with Huey. There's nowt so strange as folk! I thoroughly enjoyed the show, but the BBC did not re-commission it, and that was the end of it as far as I was concerned.

The best thing about the show was the increased profile it gave to rescue dogs. For a nation of supposed "dog-lovers" there are a huge number of dogs in rescue at any one time. Every single breed registered in the UK has its own rescue organisation, and charitable trusts like the Mayhew and the Blue Cross look after huge numbers of non-pedigree rescues. I have always maintained an interest in a number of dog charities, and have in the past done work for the Dogs Trust. I am a vice-patron of Dogs for the Disabled, a wonderful charity that provides assistance dogs for seriously disabled wheelchair users and am also president of The Canine Supporters Charity that holds a major fund-raising event called the Contest of Champions a month after *Crufts*, which then distributes the money raised to a number of different charities each year. And as you would expect, my involvement with the Guide Dogs for the Blind Association continues.

All of these events and my regular TV appearances on dog-related shows have meant that I also attend a number of big outdoor shows, and they are something I really enjoy. It all started when I was asked to host and commentate at the Brentwood Show. Roy Dyer and his wife Carol were the organisers, and they run the Essex Dog Display Team. When Roy devised the All About Dogs Show to replace the town show I was once again asked to attend, and have been doing so for several years now. This sort of show is wonderful for whole families, whether they have a dog or not. I feel privileged to be able to talk about so many remarkable dogs and demonstrations. These shows have proliferated so that now I also attend the Wag and Bone Show, and The Cold Wet Nose Show, as well as the Kennel Club event in London, Discover Dogs. In fact for the first time, I presented *Discover Dogs 2008* for TV on Horse and Country TV, a new channel on the Sky platform. Frank Kane also joined me, and we produced three one hour programmes from the show. I had first come across Horse and Country TV when they asked me to present and commentate for them at the Game Fair at Blenheim earlier in the year. It turned out that the director, Nigel Mercer, had been a film editor and worked on *Blue Peter* when I was on the show, and that his PA, Jake, had also been my PA when I ran Purves Wickes. Have I said before that it is a very small world?

Chapter Eighteen

More pantomimes; West End success and failure;

A major accident; Another house change;

A different theatrical experience

I make no apology for breaking the chronology of my life, and if you need to know when certain events took place, there is a full chronology of my career in an appendix at the end of the book. In the previous chapter I jumped almost to the present day, but it's time to go back now to look at some other aspects of my work. I have already mentioned the start of my career in pantomimes, and the way it almost came to a halt. The year after I missed out, Paul Elliott contacted me again and I was back in the fold, both as a performer and director, and I have directed at least one major show each year since. One show I directed was *Cinderella* at the Beck Theatre in Hayes, starring Dennis Waterman, Rula Lenska and me. Dennis was Buttons, Rula was Dandini and I was Baron Hardup (again). It was quite fun, but hard work. The theatre wasn't the easiest in which to work, with small wing space and storage so it was a bit of a struggle to make it magical. We also had the strange casting of a young female harpist as Cinderella.

We managed to get the harp into the act so that Cinders, instead of singing a wistful song before the Fairy Godmother arrives, sat by the fireplace and played the harp. And why not? At the end of the show, as was traditional, Buttons would bring some children onto the stage for a bit of a chat. There was no love lost between him and Cinders, and on one performance, a sweet little girl was talking to him. The conversation went:

Dennis: "Can you sing?"

Girl: "No."

Dennis: "Can you dance?"

Girl: "No."

Dennis: "Can you act?"

Girl: "No."

Dennis: "Do you want to play Cinderella?"

And the entire cast and backstage staff collapsed in heaps! It wasn't very kind but it was very funny.

I directed Cannon and Ball when they were at the height of their popularity, both in Hull and Darlington. In fact the Hull show, *Dick Whittington* in 1989 was a fantastic success, breaking all of the theatre's box office records, and in terms of bums on seats has never been beaten. I am now directing in Hull again (2008-09) with The Grumbleweeds and Vicki Michelle (from '*Allo '*Allo*) as the Wicked Queen in *Snow White*.

Back in 1982, I think it was, I was filming for some corporate job in Blackpool at the height of the summer season. Cannon and Ball were appearing on the North Pier in a show that was extended by five weeks and every single performance was a sell-out. Also on the bill was Lenny Henry, whom I'd met a couple of times when he was a little lad in *The Fosters* with my friend Norman Beaton on ITV back in the 70's. Stutz Bear Cats were the music act. Kate was with me, and Chris Hennen who had been with her in the singing group Jingles, was now running the Bear Cats. Kate asked if we could possibly see the show, and I said I'd do what I could. It was a Saturday, and I was off to film, and I asked the hall porter at our hotel, The Clifton, opposite the entrance to the pier, if he would try to get us tickets. When I got back to the hotel at about 3pm he said that it was all sold out and there was no chance.

The North Pier has a ticket kiosk on the promenade by the entrance, and

I went over to it. There was a board outside saying quite clearly that all tickets were sold for both performances, and queuing for returns for the second show began at 8pm. Nothing ventured I went up to the kiosk and tapped on the glass window. A rather severe elderly lady opened the window and glared at me. I apologised for asking, but I said that I was only in town for the one day, and I knew that there would be some "house seats". These are the seats that the management keep back in case a visiting manager or producer turned up. It was a long shot, but if they weren't being used could I please buy them.

She looked at me, without any obvious recognition, sighed and went behind the ceiling high central barrier which was where books of tickets were stacked. She disappeared behind it. After a moment, she looked round the end, and a second or two later another head looked round as well. Then they both disappeared. I was beginning to feel quite vulnerable out there on the promenade when the first lady came back and slid a small envelope towards me, and with a twinkle in her eye, she said, "And don't let anyone see you sitting in them seats!"

I have to say it was an amazing show, with the boys being the funniest live act I had seen since Jewell and Warriss 30 years earlier. And there was the bonus of saying hi to Chris and Lenny.

After *Cinderella* with Dennis and Rula, I decided I wouldn't perform in the shows any more and would concentrate on directing. The list of stars I have worked with in pantomime exceeds the number of big names I met when I was on *Blue Peter*. One show I remember fondly was another *Cinderella*, this time in Bath, when an elderly Rolf Harris played Buttons with Sylvester McCoy as the Baron. We also had former England and Bath rugby star Gareth Chilcott as the Broker's Man. Although it was very successful at the box office it was an odd show. Somehow I had to accommodate Jake the Peg, and Two Little Boys, and for some inexplicable reason, Sylvester juggling sausages. I remind him of it every time I meet him at the occasional *Doctor Who* gathering. What

Peter Purves

I remember best are the rehearsals. They were held at the former swimming baths in Fulham Broadway in London. We had two of the Danceworks studios upstairs. On the ground floor was a small and not very inviting coffee shop for the dancers and actors. The wall that faced you as you entered was large and completely bare. On the third morning, Rolf arrived with his estate car, parked close to the building and took out lots of cans of paint, cloths and brushes and put an original mural on the wall. When I last looked a few years ago it was still there. It was a generous act of his, and I found him delightful to work with. I also enjoyed working with Sly, but the two of them didn't hit it off. At the first rehearsal, Rolf was quietly marking up what he said, and where he moved, when he was confronted by Sylvester who was giving it 150% right from the start. To be honest, I think the intensity of performance from Sly actually frightened him. I managed to tone him down a bit and to pacify Rolf.

One of the things I like about pantomime is that it is probably the first live theatre that most children see, and for that reason I do want it to be excellent. I have no time for people who say "Oh it's only panto." For me, those people are a waste of time, and money. If the show is poor then the kids won't want to come again and that means also that as the audience gets more sophisticated and used to seeing magical effects on film and TV, then the theatre has to find some way of making magic in a live environment. I love that, and I like to think that the transformations I get in my shows are magical and exciting.

The Cinderella transformations are the ones I like best – it is amazing what you can do with lights and cloths. I can remember one that I created in one of the more difficult venues, The Hexagon in Reading. The stars were Bobby Davro and Linda Robson. Linda was heavily pregnant, and had originally been engaged to play Cinderella, but we had to recast her as the Fairy Godmother. At the last moment I was able to cast my friend Ashleigh Sendin to play Cinders. On the opening night I sat in the audience next to her partner (now husband) Geoff. When we reached the transformation,

Here's one I wrote earlier…

Cinderella never left the stage, and at the moment of magic she ducked down in her rags into the dry ice and chiffon cloths, and with a flash she stood there in her ball gown. Geoff just turned to me and said, "How did you do that?" For me that was the exact effect I wanted because if he hadn't spotted his girlfriend's double, nobody could!

One of the most disappointing shows was in Bournemouth. As far as I was concerned it was the best *Dick Whittington* I could have done. It starred magician Paul Daniels, one of the most generous men I have ever met, and his wife Debbie. It was a magical show in every way, with three good routines from Paul that had everyone guessing. The show had a good script, was well acted, and Paul was excellent as the storyteller and Alderman Fitzwarren. The music was tight, and the dancers looked lovely. Yet in spite of a stunning first night and excellent local reviews, it was a total flop. I really felt for Paul, and am angered when I hear people who have never met him slag him off. We all went for a company meal and the deal was that we would all pay for ourselves, yet when we went to pay, Paul who had already left, had paid the bill for us all. At Christmas he did everything he could to help one of the two comics get home to Liverpool to spend the day with his children. They were a double act, and could only afford for one of them to go home. Without going into detail, Paul fixed it. He's a lovely man, and a true professional.

For four of the last six years I have worked with the country's most successful double act, the Chuckle Brothers. Each year they have been in a different show; *Aladdin* first, then *Cinderella*, *Dick Whittington* and *Jack and the Beanstalk*. And they have all been excellent. It is quite funny to listen to the audience – I often eavesdrop – the children are always fans and the parents seem to come along grudgingly, but by the interval they are completely won over. I must say that it is a very good "live" act. I have seen most of their performances many times now, and I still find them funny. They are a truly traditional old-fashioned northern comedy act, in the style of those I grew up with in Blackpool, and I am a sucker for it. Frank Randle, Nat Jackley, Ken Platt and the rest – the Chuckles are up there with the best. Serious belly laughs, combined with absolute stupidity are right up my street.

Pantomimes also did another favour for the Purves' – my son, Matthew got his equity card via Paul Elliott, when he got his first theatre job as assistant stage manager for *Cinderella* in Stevenage. Just as an update he worked in the theatre for a year or two before joining the staff of the BBC following an introduction by Julia Smith, producer and original deviser, with Tony Holland, of *Eastenders*. There was a closer connection in that his mum was one of the original writers on the series, and he was pleased to take advantage of any contacts he could. He is now a first assistant director in TV drama, but no longer on the staff at the BBC, a victim of the John Birt era of cuts. He is married to Clare who also was made redundant from the BBC at the same time (great employer) and they are both now freelance. My grandson, Sam, will be nearly 11 when this book is published.

Being married to a dancer, I've always had a soft spot for the dancers in pantomimes. They are not very well paid, and they often have a pretty difficult time, but they really do help to make the shows work. They provide extra bodies on stage when you need a crowd of villagers, and they have to dance really well. I have worked with a lot of excellent choreographers, and some of them give the dancers really demanding work. And bearing in mind the time-scale to get the show on, they do very well indeed. However, almost without exception the reviews rarely mention them. It's a lot of hard work with very little recognition or reward.

Through the 90's, Kate had a number of good jobs too – including touring in *Aspects of Love*, Andrew Lloyd Webber's most romantic score. She played Rose, the lead, and when the show came back into London for a short season at the Prince of Wales Theatre, the late Jack Tinker gave her a review to die for in the *Daily Mail*. As is Kate's luck, it didn't lead to anything much but she kept at it in a truly stoic fashion. She also played the lead in *On The Twentieth Century*, a wonderful musical farce about show business, to universal praise. It was performed at the tiny Bridewell Theatre, just off Fleet Street, and I did my best at that time to transfer it to a small West End theatre. I was armed with a CD of the live show's soundtrack, and an armful of the best reviews anyone could ever wish for, but raising the money was just impossible. Or so I found. Because the show takes place on a train, I approached Richard Branson, as I thought there would be a good marketing opportunity for Virgin Trains, and that he might enjoy the experience. But it was stony ground and came to nothing. In the end, the story ceased to be hot, and we had to concede defeat. I had hoped that maybe another West End impresario might pick it up, but again the interest just wasn't there.

I've really felt for Kate over the years, because to my mind she is the consummate professional. She always gives 100% and backs it up with a great acting talent and the most wonderful voice. A lot of people do recognise it, but for some reason she never became the star her ability warranted. As I write she is about to start rehearsals to play the lead in *Sunset Boulevard* at the Comedy Theatre in the West End. This is the much awaited transfer of the show from the tiny Watermill Theatre in Newbury. If I had to list my 20 best films of all time, then Billy Wilder's *Sunset Boulevard* with Gloria Swanson and William Holden would certainly figure large. Kate plays the part like a silent film star and I think she is magnificent in the role. Again it is an Andrew Lloyd Webber score, and has two of the most stunning songs for her, with Don Black's wonderful lyrics. It is a small chamber piece compared with the original somewhat overblown West End production, and utilises actor musicians in all of the other roles. Maybe, by the time this book is published, Kate will have had the recognition I've always felt she deserves.

Once again, I am in danger of getting everything out of order. I need to go back into the 90's when I'd just closed down Purves Wickes. I was not doing a great deal of TV, just the occasional show, but I was presenting some big outdoor events like the Royal Bath and West of England Show at Shepton Mallett, and the Royal Show at Stoneleigh in Warwickshire. In each case I ran the Country Pursuits arena and I can honestly say they were two events I enjoyed immensely. I had also been engaged to present a similar arena at the Swansea Show and all of these shows were re-booked for 1999 and for several years had been working occasionally at Elstree for the BBC as a trainer for TV presenters. This was something I thoroughly enjoyed, and I suppose it was a way of giving something back to the industry that had been generally quite kind to me. I had just finished *Crufts* in March 1999 when I suffered a dramatic fall.

The old rectory had four gables across the front and the huge Virginia creeper had crept up onto parts of the roof. I had a few days free, and I determined to tidy everything up. In the morning I had cleaned out the cellar, filling a small skip in the process, and after lunch I started on the roof. I used a long extending ladder, and began clearing the creeper, whilst Kate footed the ladder for me. Everything went well, and after a couple of hours, I was almost finished. I had one more section to clear, and I suggested to Kate that she got us a couple of gin and tonics and I would finish off outside. It was an accident waiting to happen. I put the ladder up, and climbed to the last bit of the roof. At the top of the ladder I was about to step onto the gulley, when the ladder slipped away from the wall, and down I came. I actually stayed on the ladder as it slid down, and my mind slowed everything up. I can remember thinking that it was probably going to hurt a bit, but that I needed to try to take the sting out of it by rolling as I landed – like the techniques John and I had been shown when filming with the Army years earlier. I had fallen 20 feet and the landing was quite hard but I did roll away from it, and that may well have saved my back, and possibly my life. I'm told that a 20 foot fall is a killing height, and as I was landing on tarmac, which doesn't give much, I could have been hurt far worse than I was.

In the event, I broke both my heels. Apparently this is quite a common builders and window-cleaners injury. The fact that I broke both heels made it very serious. I had tried to get up after the fall, but the pain was excruciating, and I had to give up and wait. Kate and her mother had come rushing out to see what had happened, and to make things even more comfortable, it started to rain. The local ambulance service was brilliant, arriving in less than 15 minutes, and the crew looked after me very well. I can remember asking the ambulance man if I would be kept in hospital overnight, and he almost laughed. "Oh Yes," he said, "I think you'll find they'll keep you in".

And they did. I was in Northampton General for 16 days. The first eight days being spent with my feet in ice-cold water-boots, trying to get the swelling down so my surgeon, Bill Ribbans could operate. He gave me such encouragement, so I never felt I would have a problem walking, and when the op was finally performed he said I'd be fine, though I could expect my ankles to go arthritic. Bill had been the surgeon who mended Michael Schumacher after his crash at Silverstone two years earlier, and for which he was never even thanked! I can't really thank Bill enough, and eventually I was able to walk again. I had to spend three months in a wheelchair, and then go through some intensive physiotherapy first. In fact I got a real shock when I first tried to stand up, and even with two crutches I couldn't do it. It had never occurred to me that I wouldn't be able to carry on exactly as before. How stupid.

Of course, all my work ground to a halt. There had been a number of things in the pipeline that flew out of the window, and life was very difficult for a time. I was able to work at the Royal Show, and the Royal Bath and West, but I had to have a mobility tricycle to get around. I could walk a bit on my crutches, but to be honest it was December before I was properly able to get around without assistance. The previous year we had mortgaged the house to get some cash together, and without much work, and no opportunity to increase it, we had a bit of a dilemma. In the end the solution was simple.

We sold the house. We'd been in Cogenhoe for seven years, the house had doubled in value, including everything we'd lavished on it, and we decided to find something cheaper. What we found was something very much bigger. We'd sold the house, but hadn't anywhere to go to and we just hoped our buyer would hang on. In the end, having decided that we liked Suffolk, Kate was surfing the net and she found a lovely red-brick Georgian house near to Saxmundham. We telephoned the agents, and they said they hadn't printed the details yet, because it had just come onto the market that morning. We twisted their arms, and drove over to see it that same afternoon. This was on Thursday. We had bought the house on the Monday afternoon, and three and a half weeks later, we moved in.

The move to Suffolk was probably the best thing we'd ever done. No it wasn't all that convenient for getting to and from London, but as much of my work was not likely to be London based, that wasn't really a problem. Where it would prove to be awkward was if Kate was asked to be in the West End. We didn't have a base there, and to be honest we couldn't afford one either. But we soon found it really welcoming and we have made more friends here than any other place we have been. Whilst we had a couple of good friends in Cogenhoe, and no close friends in Rugby, apart from David Hall, we have a big circle of great friends close by, one or two in the business, but mostly not. There are former advertising execs, antique dealers and restorers, lawyers, writers, property developers, artists and retired folks.

A couple of months after we moved into the new house, I saw an advertisement in the local press for applicants who would like to be on the board of the Wolsey Theatre in Ipswich. The theatre had been closed for 18 months and the local council, the county council and the arts council wanted to get it open again. What a way to be involved with the theatre locally, I thought, and made my application. I was successful, and the board set about creating a business plan for the theatre that would be viable for a long future. Eventually, we were able to produce a plan that satisfied the funding partners, and we set about finding an artistic director.

That was something I rather fancied for myself, and I applied for the job. As it turned out, there were several far better qualified applicants than I, and the board eventually appointed a joint chief executive and artistic director, Sarah Holmes and Peter Rowe. And I have to confess that I would not have been as accomplished as they have been. A little over a year after the board was formed, the theatre reopened as The New Wolsey Theatre, and it is both a producing and a receiving house, and goes from strength to strength. One of its major successes is an annual pantomime, very different from those I direct, in that Peter Rowe uses a team of actor-musicians to play all the roles. They are superb Rock and Roll shows, and it is amazing that you can see Cinderella playing a scene in the foreground, and two minutes later she is on the drums. These shows run for quite a long season, and are virtually sold out each year. This success helps fund some of the less commercial works on offer. I was proud to serve on the board, and eventually became chairman. During my chairmanship, we were able to persuade the local council to give us a new roof, which now keeps the audience totally dry – a big improvement on the Heath-Robinson guttering that existed before. After six years, I stood down, as I was required to do, and I'm pleased to see that the current board is equally as excited and energised by what the theatre is doing.

In 2005 I had a successful, albeit short-lived show on a satellite channel. The channel was dedicated to property abroad and all of the programmes except mine were geared to promote property sales. My show was an hour long, and was called *Destination Lunch*. In each programme a chef would cook a three-course meal appropriate to a particular destination, say Spain, or Cyprus or Turkey. I would have a star guest who may have an interest in that place, and another guest who was an expert in the particular country. And to round it off we'd have a wine expert who would choose wine that would match the meal. It was a lovely show – a little bit rushed as these things often are; we made three shows a day. It did mean that I couldn't fully enjoy the food cooked by Paul Bloxham, or the wine on offer, but it was great fun to do. However, it was one of those jobs that was never properly contracted. When my agent was first approached the deal was supposed to be for a year. In the event, when the job was offered it was only for three months, and in fact no contract was ever given. After three months, the show schedule was cut down and my workload reduced alarmingly, and after another two months, just into 2006, I was offered three days in three months, which I turned down. I suspect the show disappeared because they weren't "hard-sell" enough for the channel sponsor. I was disappointed, because I had so many wonderful guests on the show that I interviewed, and many of them were old friends I hadn't seen for a few years, or people I had worked with in the past. Bearing in mind that I am now quite long in the tooth in TV, I should never have believed what I was told. I always assume I am being told the truth, but I really should know better. Having said that, I really enjoyed working with my production team, even though the bosses were not to my taste. The channel had its pound of flesh, and it is still showing some of the programmes two years after they were made, without paying for the privilege, of course.

And as a rider to all of this, I manage to teach at the London Academy of Radio Film and Television in Euston. I teach a three-day foundation course in Television Presenting each month. In an ideal world I only have three or four students and it gives me a great chance to do a lot of one-to-one tutorials. I enjoy the work, and as I said when I was at the BBC training centre at Elstree in the 90's, it is a way of giving something back. I won't say I have trained a great many successes – there are a lot of people who think that TV presenting is an easy job, but they are surprised when I tell them it is no sinecure. It is a hard professional career, and no one does you any favours. You can succeed if you are both able and lucky. But make no mistake, both elements are needed, and unless you give it 100% and are absolutely committed to being successful, you have very little chance. Two girls I trained this year will have successful careers, I am sure, but them apart, it will be a hard slog for the rest. The world is full of wannabes!

Chapter Nineteen

So at the end of 2008 where am I? I have no intention of stopping work because I actually love it. I don't like the politics, and I have had quite enough of that over the years, but I rarely look back. Writing this book has been quite an experience for me, I know I have missed out an awful lot, and I know that my memory may not always be 100% accurate, but I have tried within these pages to illustrate a little of who I am, and what has pleased me and excited me over the years. I was involved in TV when it was quite young, and the thrill of working regularly at the BBC was just indescribable. I wish it were still the same. But many of the people who are now running television didn't grow up in it – they have no feeling for the traditions that made the BBC such a great organisation. I cannot believe that the concrete doughnut is to be sold, and probably pulled down. This was the most iconic TV building in the world, and at its height all eight major studios would be in full production every day. You would rub shoulders with all of the TV names of the day every time you walked into the building. I was recently at the TV Centre, and two shows were in the studios, neither of them BBC productions. So sad, I think.

Kate and I have moved house again, I hope this will be for the last time, but maybe it won't be. We have both come from families who never stayed in one place for long, and I guess it is in our make-up. It's another complete change in style, but not in location. We have only moved 10 minutes away from where we were, to a 17th Century timber-framed farmhouse with a few acres of land. Our Dachshunds have a large garden in which to run and play, and we are surrounded by lovely Suffolk countryside. It is extraordinarily peaceful, and there are probably less than half a dozen vehicles passing along our lane every hour, and that is mostly farm traffic. I do still go up to London to work, and the back end of 2008 has been very busy indeed particularly with the extraordinary celebrations surrounding the 50th Anniversary of *Blue Peter*.

Here's one I wrote earlier...

It is remarkable that this small children's hobbies programme can have grown into such an established and iconic show.

John Noakes, Valerie Singleton, Lesley Judd and I figured for more than a quarter of the time the show has been on air, and we were each honoured to be invited to Buckingham Palace to take tea with Her Majesty the Queen at the end of October, 2008. It was the second time I have been in a line-up to meet her, and it was a lovely experience. Think of the thrill for the three youngsters who were with us, and who were presented with Gold *Blue Peter* Badges by none other than the queen. Fantastic!

I regard myself as a very lucky man – I have enjoyed every second of my working life – I have found it fulfilling, thrilling and rewarding in so many ways; frustrating even at times. If I could do it all again, I doubt I would change very much. For the most part, when work has been offered I have said "Yes", and have made so few decisions that have had any real bearing on my career. I never planned a career, but just followed wherever it took me. I have made friends both in and out of the business, and no doubt the occasional enemy. I continue to work in TV, occasionally being asked to comment in compilation shows of various kinds, and I have made short programmes for DVD release on *Doctor Who*, and one original new *Doctor Who* story as a radio play on CD, called *Mother Russia*. Work continues to be varied and fun.

Sadly, as I finish writing, the news has come through that the BBC will be suspending its coverage of *Crufts Dog Show* in March 2009, and that means that a 31 year involvement with the show has come to a premature end. There has been a lot of fallout following a BBC documentary called *Pedigree Dogs Exposed*, which suggested, or rather implied, that most Pedigree dogs suffered from illness and disease because of in-breeding. Unfortunately, there is a minority who breed badly, but the programme didn't acknowledge that the Kennel Club is and remains very concerned about the health of all dogs, and has a number of schemes in place to improve the health and conformation of all breeds. This has produced a locking of horns between the Kennel Club and the BBC that has been resolved by the BBC withdrawing from the 2009 event. I find it very sad. But one door closes, and I am sure another will open. The cup is still at least half full.

My and Kate's life is made more pleasant by our close friends, and it just wouldn't be the same without Mike, Annie, Sean, Gerald, Cyd and Sid, Ashleigh and Geoff, Jon and Jonathan, Clive and Doris, Michael and Oswaldo, Michael and Jonathan, Wendy, and the legion of other close acquaintances we have made through them, far too many to list here, but they can all rest assured they are not ignored. And of course, there is also my son Matthew, his wife, Clare, and my grandson, Sam. Unfortunately my adopted daughter, Lisa, is now somewhat estranged, and we haven't really spoken in many years.

I hope my life may go on providing me with rewarding experiences and exciting prospects. I always look forward rather than backward, and tomorrow is always more important than yesterday. Kate and I seem to grow stronger by the day, and our future is still unknown. My mother and father came from large families and the opportunities for continuing the line were considerable but it didn't work out that way. I was an only child who came from humble stock, and I am proud of my achievements – I am not rich with money, but as a man I am enriched and fulfilled. I have been, and I hope I continue to be a lucky man.

Here's one I wrote earlier...

Chronology

Major Credits

Television, Radio & Events

** Denotes ongoing

2008	**Paul O'Grady Show** Guest
2008	**Your Dog/Your Cat Awards** Host/Presenter
2008	**Cooks Daily Challenge** Guest/Judge ITV1
2008**	**Discover Dogs** Presenter Horse & Country TV
2008	**Doctor Who DVD** Guest Presenter
2008	**Blue Peter 50th Anniversary Show** BBC
2008	**Generation Sex** Guest C5
2008	**Blue Peter Interactive Quiz** Presenter CBBC
2008**	**CLA Game Fair** Presenter Horse & Country TV
2008	**Liverpool Fire Service Alternative Olympics** Commentator
2008	**The Cold Wet Nose Show** Main Arena Commentator
2008	**Waste Management films** (x2) Voice over AVP
2008**	**Tails of Achievement** Host and Presenter James Wellbeloved
2008**	**The Wag and Bone Show** Main Arena Commentator
2008**	**Guide Dog of the Year** Host and Presenter
2008**	**Guide Dogs Gala Day** Main Arena Commentator and MC
2008	**Celebrity Weakest Link** Contestant BBC2
2008**	**Notcutts All About Dogs** MC and Commentator (4 shows)
2008	**Crufts Dog Show** Principal Commentator and Presenter BBC2
2008	**The One Show** Guest Presenter BBC1
2007	**Now That's What I call Xmas TV** Guest ITV1

Peter Purves

2007	***Doctor Who*** Mother Russia, Big Finish Productions Narrator and Stephen Taylor
2007	***Harry Hill's TV Burp*** Guest ITV1
2007	***The Underdog Show*** (series) BBC2 Splash Productions
2007	***The Underdog Show on CBBC*** (series) Splash Productions
2007	***Zurich Insurance*** Presenter National project for schools
2007	***Crufts Dog Show*** Presenter Animal Planet USA Painless Prods
2007**	***Crufts Dog Show*** Principal Commentator and Presenter BBC2
2007**	***Guide Dog of the Year*** Host and Presenter
2007**	***Notcutts All About Dogs*** MC and Commentator (2 shows)
2007**	***Tails of Achievement*** Host and Presenter James Wellbeloved
2006**	***The Wag and Bone Show*** Main Arena Commentator
2006	***Destination Lunch*** Host Overseas Property TV (90 programmes)
2006	***Retire Abroad*** Presenter Overseas Property TV (20 programmes)
2006**	***Discover Dogs*** Arena Commentator (3 years)
2006**	***All About Dogs*** Main Arena Commentator (6 years)
2006**	***Royal Show, Stoneleigh*** Official Commentator (13 years)
2006**	***Tails of Achievement*** Host and Presenter James Wellbeloved
2006**	***Guide Dogs Gala Day*** Main Arena Commentator and MC
2006**	***Notcutts All About Dogs*** MC and Commentator
2006**	***Crufts Dog Show*** Presenter Animal Planet USA Painless Prods
2006**	***Crufts Dog Show*** Principal Presenter and Commentator BBC2
2005	***TV's favourite Xmas moments*** UK Gold
2005	***Television's favourite animals*** C4
2005	***Britain's Worst Celebrity Driver*** Navigator C5
2005	***Breakfast of Champions*** pilot Mentorn for C4
2005**	***Crufts Dog Show*** Presenter Animal Planet USA Painless Prods
2005**	***Crufts Dog Show*** Principal Presenter and Commentator BBC2
2005	***Vitalin Pick of the Litter***

Here's one I wrote earlier...

2005**	**Guide Dogs Gala Day** Main Arena Commentator and MC
2005**	**The Wag and Bone Show** Main Arena Commentator
2005**	**All About Dogs** Main Arena Commentator (5 years)
2005**	**Discover Dogs** Arena Commentator (2 years)
2005**	**The Royal Show, Stoneleigh** Official Commentator (12 years)
2005	**Royal Bath and West Show** Official Commentator (8 years)
2005	**Predictions for 2000 –The Tomorrow People** Presenter BBC Radio Documentary
2004	**Crufts Dog Show** Presenter Animal Planet USA Painless Prods
2004**	**Crufts Dog Show** Principal Presenter and Commentator
2004**	**Seven Seas Pick of the Litter**
2004	**Harry Hill**
2004	**Project Mayhem** pilot C5
2003	**The Way We Travelled** BBC
2003	**Dom Joly** Guest BBC
2003	**Crufts Dog Show** Presenter Animal Planet USA Painless Prods
2003**	**Crufts Dog Show** Principal Presenter and Commentator
2003**	**Seven Seas Pick of the Litter**
2003	**Britain in a Box** Guest BBC Radio 4
2003	**Rise** Guest C4
2003	**Pet Rescue** Guest Presenter BBC
2002-03	**Goodfellows Pizza** Network Commercial
2002	**Blue Peter Documentary** BBC
2002	**Teen Trials** series for Granada Television
2002	**Crufts Dog Show** Presenter Animal Planet USA Painless Prods
2002	**Crufts Dog Show** Principal Presenter
2001	**The Channel Challenge** Presenter BBC Radio 4
2001	**The Priory** Guest C4
2001	**Burgess Dog Food** Host NEC

Peter Purves

2001	**Doctor Who 'Daleks Masterplan** Voiced BBC
2001	**The Noonday Witch** Narrator North Downs Music Group
2001	**Stupid Punts** Vox Pops Challenge BBC Television
2001	**Recommended Daily Allowance** BBC Choice
2001	**Crufts Dog Show** Presenter Animal Planet USA Painless Prods
2001	**Crufts Dog Show** Principle Presenter BBC2
2001	**Vetzyme Puppy Presentation**
2001	**Peter and the Wolf** Narrator City of London Sinfonia
2001	**The Office** Featured part BBC1
2001	**Fame Show** Guest Anglia Television
2001	**Doctor Who 'Celestial Toys** Voiced BBC
2001	**Banzai** Guest E4 Digital
2001	**I Love a 70s Christmas** Presenter BBC1
2000	**Cornhill Direct Insurance** TV Commercial
2000**	**Crufts Dog Show** Principal Presenter BBC2
2000	**Esther** Guest BBC2
2000	**Blue Peter** Guest BBC1
1999-2000	**BBC International 2000** English Language Commentator
1999	**The Club** Consultant BBC1
1999	**Breed All About It** Discovery Channel (13 programmes)
1999	**The Royal Show, Stoneleigh** Official Commentator
1999	**Royal Bath and West Show** Official Commentator
1999	**The Swansea Show** Official Commentator
1999	**The Jack Docherty Show** C5
1999**	**Cornhill Direct Insurance** TV commercials @ 2
1999**	**Crufts** Principle Presenter BBC2 (5 programmes)
1999	**Crufts** 3 @ Specials Discovery Channel USA
1999	**Backstage** Guest Presenter BBC Choice
1998	**Backstage** Guest BBC Choice

Here's one I wrote earlier...

1998	**Blue Peter 40th Anniversary** BBC2 Theme Night
1998	**Blue Peter Documentary** BBC2
1998	**Pet's Go Public** Host C5 (65 programmes)
1998	**The Royal Show, Stoneleigh** Official Commentator
1998	**Royal Bath and West Show** Official Commentator
1998	**The Swansea Show** Official Commentator
1998**	**Crufts** Principle Presenter BBC2 (5 programmes)
1998	**Collector's Corner** C4
1998**	**Breed All About it** Discovery Channel (13 programmes)
1998**	**Cornhill Direct Insurance** TV commercials @ 2
1997	**The Royal Show, Stoneleigh** Official Commentator
1997	**Through the Keyhole** BBC1
1997	**18.30 Club** BBC Radio 5
1997	**Record Breakers** Guest Presenter BBC1
1997	**Looking Forward to the Past** BBC Radio 4
1997	**Light Lunch** C4
1997	**Five's Company** C5
1997	**The Brentwood Show** Official Commentator
1997**	**Crufts** Principle Presenter BBC2 (5 programmes)
1997	**Live and Kicking** BBC1
1997	**Noel's House Party** BBC1
1997	**Noel's Telly Years** BBC1
1997	**Pull the Other One** Action Time for Carlton Select
1996**	**Peter Purves Meets...** BBC Radio Northampton (series)
1996	**TV60** Featured Artist BBC1
1996**	**Brentwood Show** Official Commentator
1996**	**The Royal Show, Stoneleigh** Official Commentator
1996	**Tellystak** Zenith for UK Gold (5 programmes)
1996**	**Cornhill Direct Insurance** TV Commercials @ 3

Peter Purves

1996	*The Time, The Place* ITV
1996	*Children's BBC* Guest BBC1
1996	*Through the Keyhole* Yorkshire TV Mentorn/Sky
1996	*Hot Gossip* Anglia TV
1995-96	*The Saturday Show* BBC Radio Northampton
1995-96	*The Sunday Show* BBC Radio Northampton
1994	*Film Review* Mentorn for ITV Guest Reviewer
1994	*The Day Today* Anglia Television Guest
1994	*The Myth Makers* Reeltime Pictures
1993	*This Morning* Granada Television
1993	*Happy Families* Guest Presenter Mentorn for BBC
1993	*TV Heroes* Featured subject BBC1
1992	*National Power* TV Commercial Wembley
1992	*Dr Who Special* B SKY B
1990	*Inside Story* Presenter BBC2 B'ham
1990	*Crimewatch Debates* Anchorman BBC2 B'ham @ 3
1989-93	*Superdogs* Presenter 3 @ series BBC1
1989	*Ten Glorious Years* Noel Gay TV for BBC1
1988	*Eastenders* BBC1 (3 episodes)
1987-91	*Crimewatch Midlands* Anchorman B'ham (5 series) BBC2
1985	*Food/Drink Correspondent* Video Doctor
1984	*Motoring Correspondent* Video Doctor
1984	*Woolworth Xmas* TV Commercial
1984	*Work Out* Presenter HTV (6 programmes)
1983-90	Numerous guest appearances LWT, C4, TVS, BBC
1982-86	*Babble* Host LWT for C4 3 series @ 13
1982-86	*Bullseye* Presenter BBC Sport 5 series
1982-83	*The Acting Game* Host BBC1 NW 2 series
1982-84	*Makers* Presenter HTV 3 series (6 programmes)

Here's one I wrote earlier...

1982	*Here Today* Guest Presenter HTV (3 programmes)
1981-87	*BBC Darts* Presenter BBC1 & BBC2 (195 programmes)
1981-82	*As It Happens* BBC Radio 4 (12 programmes)
1981	*King Size Bed* Plays BBC Radio 4
1979-91	*Kickstart/Junior Kickstart* Presenter 13 years
1978	*Blue Peter Special Assignment* BBC1 Rivers @ 3
1978	*Stopwatch* Presenter BBC1 5 series @ 8
1978-81	*We're Going Places* Presenter BBC1 3 series @ 8
1978	*Blue Peter Special Assignment* Twin Towns @ 3
1978	*Blue Peter Special Assignment* Presenter BBC1 @ 3
1976-96	*Crufts Dog Show* BBC2 (5 programmes per year)
1976-78	*Driver of the Year* Presenter BBC1 3 series @ 4
1976	*Sunday Live* Presenter BBC1 OB events @ 3
1971-80	*Record Breakers Xmas Special* BBC1 (10 programmes)
1967-78	*Blue Peter* Presenter BBC1 (860 programmes)
1966-67	*Colour Training courses* Various BBC Drama
1965-66	*Doctor Who* (Steven) BBC1 44 episodes
1965	*Doctor Who* (Morton Dill) BBC1
1965	*The Girl in the Black Bikini* Leading Role BBC1 serial
1965	*The Villains* Leading Role Granada Television
1964	*The Girl in the Picture* Lead Armchair Theatre (ABC)
1963	*Luther* Supporting Role Play for Today BBC1
1963-5	Various supporting roles:- *Z-Cars, Gideon's Way, The Saint, Court Martial, Dixon of Dock Green, World of Wooster,* etc.

Peter Purves

Theatre Credits

2008/9	**Snow White** New Theatre, Hull Director (Vicki Michelle/The Grumbleweeds)
2007/8	**Snow White** Orchard Theatre, Dartford Director (Wendi Peters)
2005/6	**Jack & the Beanstalk** Theatre Royal, Plymouth Director (The Chuckle Brothers)
2004/5	**Dick Whittington** Opera House, Manchester Director (The Chuckle Brothers)
2003/4	**Cinderella** Southend on Sea Director (The Chuckle Brothers)
2002/3	**Aladdin** Stoke on Trent Director (The Chuckle Brothers)
2001/2	**Dick Whittington** Southend on Sea Director (Hale and Pace)
2000/1	**Cinderella** Llandudno Director
1999/2000	**Jack and the Beanstalk** Southend on Sea Director (John Inman)
1998/9	**Jack and the Beanstalk** Sheffield Director (David Benson-Phillips)
1996/7	**Dick Whittington** Bournemouth Director (Paul Daniels)
1995/6	**Cinderella** Reading Director (Bobby Davro, Linda Robson)
1994/5	**Dick Whittington** Southend Director (Bobby Davro, Ross Kemp)
1993/4	**Dick Whittington** Croydon Director (Cheryl Baker, Roger Kitter)

Here's one I wrote earlier...

1992/3	**Cinderella** Bath Director
	(Rolf Harris, Sylvester McCoy)
1992/3	**Babes in the Wood** Darlington Director
	(Cannon and Ball)
1990/1	**Aladdin** Bath Director
	(Tom O'Connor)
1990/1	**Dick Whittington** Hull Director
	(Cannon and Ball)
1988/9	**Cinderella** Aberdeen Director
	(Bill Owen)
1987/8	**Jack and the Beanstalk** Wimbledon Director
	(Anita Harris, Harry Worth)
1985/6	**Cinderella** Hayes Director/Baron
	(Dennis Waterman, Rula Lenska)
1984/5	**Aladdin** Hayes Director
	(Colin Baker)
1983/4	**Aladdin** Torquay Director
	(Matthew Kelly, Sarah Kennedy)
1983/4	**Jack and the Beanstalk** Guildford Director
	(Kathryn Evans, Basil Brush, Macdonald Hobley)
1982/3	**Robinson Crusoe** Guildford Director/Cpt Babble
	(John Noakes, Kathryn Evans,)
1981/2	**Jack and the Beanstalk** Torquay Director/Baron
	(John Noakes, Kathryn Evans, Ben Warris, Lesley Judd)
1980/1	**Jack and the Beanstalk** Bath Baron
	(John Noakes, Kathryn Evans, Ben Warris, Lesley Judd)
1979/80	**Cinderella** Wilmslow Baron
	(John Noakes, Kathryn Evans, Bonnie Langford)
1978/9	**Cinderella** Guildford Baron

Peter Purves

	(John Noakes, Kathryn Evans, Bonnie Langford)
1964	Tour Wimbledon, Westcliff
1963/4	Chorus, London Palladium
1963	Tour, Wimbledon, Bath, Coventry, Westcliff, Hull
1961/3	Younger Leading Man, Repertory (2 Years)
	Renaissance Theatre Company, Barrow
1957/58	Three plays in Rep. Barrow

Hobbies

Sports All sports especially golf. Regularly plays in charity events.

Cars Especially classics. Has owned 1938 Austin 16, 1938 Wolseley 16, 1938 Morris 10, 1955 Ford Popular, 1960 Mini Minor, 1951 Bentley Mark VI (one of his favourites), 1963 Ford Anglia, 1967 Citroen DS21 (another favourite), 1969 Bond Equipe 2-litre Sports, 1972 Ford Zodiac, 1975 & 1978 Citroen 2CV, 1978 Citroen CX, 1982 Citroen CX, 1982 Rover 3500, 1984 Daimler Sovereign (certainly a favourite), 1985 Jaguar Sovereign (the best of all), 1988 Volvo 740 estate, 1992 Volvo 240 estate (the estates for the dogs!!), 1998 Volvo 940 Turbo, 2005 Volvo V70 estate, 2008 Volvo Saloon S80

Dogs Have kept many: Rusty (Cocker Spaniel); Petra (Xbreed)

Pekingese: Georgie, Billie, Freddie, Jamie, Holly and Tillie

Newfoundlands: Mishka, Gulliver and Kent

Standard Wire-Haired Dachshunds: Hattie, Woody, Dottie and Teddy

Here's one I wrote earlier...

Peter Purves